S0-BIV-642

3 0301 00031113 0

Twenty-three

Modern British Poets

Modern British Poets

**edited by
John Matthias**

**introduction by
Peter Jay**

**THE
SWALLOW PRESS**
CHICAGO   **INC.**

LIBRARY
College of St. Francis
JOLIET, ILL.

Copyright © 1971 by John Matthias
All Rights Reserved
Printed in the United States of America

Published by
The Swallow Press Incorporated
1139 South Wabash Avenue
Chicago, Illinois 60605

ISBN   0-8040-0507-9
ISBN   0-8040-0508-7 paper
LIBRARY OF CONGRESS CATALOG No. 71-150757

Note: Requests for permission to reprint
any of the poems in this book should
be directed to the poets or their
publishers as indicated above.

821.908
M443

The poetry   The poets

DAVID JONES was born of Anglo-Welsh parentage in 1895. As a volunteer in the Royal Welsh Fusiliers, he fought in France in the First World War. In his forties he journeyed as a convalescent to Palestine but has lived mostly in London. He has published two book-length poems, *In Parenthesis* and *The Anathemata,* and a collection of essays, *Epoch and Artist.* In 1967 Agenda magazine published his work in progress, including "The Wall," "The Dream of Private Clitus," "The Tutelar of the Place," "The Hunt," and "The Sleeping Lord." David Jones' most recent publication is *The Tribune's Visitation,* another fragment from the work in progress. He is also a painter and engraver.

HUGH MacDIARMID was born in Langholme in 1892. He is a Scottish Nationalist and a Communist. Among his many books, including works of fiction, autobiography, criticism, translation, and editions of Scottish poets, are *Sangschaw, Penny Wheep, A Drunk Man Looks at the Thistle, To Circumjack Cencrastus, Stony Limits and Other Poems, First Hymn to Lenin and Other Poems, Second Hymn to Lenin and Other Poems, In Memoriam James Joyce, The Collected Poems of Hugh MacDiarmid, A Lap of Honour,*

58720

GEORGE MacBETH was born in Scotland in 1932 and educated at Oxford. As a talks producer for the B.B.C. his enthusiasm for innovative work has provided and continues to provide a forum and an audience for new poetry in Britain. He has published six collections of poems: *The Broken Places, A Doomsday Book, The Colour of Blood, The Night of Stones, A War Quartet,* and *The Burning Cone.* He has also edited three anthologies for Penguin, the remarkable *Penguin Book of Sick Verse* among them.

GAEL TURNBULL was born in Edinburgh in 1928. He is a physician doing general practice and anaesthetics in Worcestershire. He has published two volumes of poems, *A Trampoline* and *Scantlings.*

ROY FISHER was born in 1931 and lives in Birmingham where he works as a jazz pianist. Fisher has published *City, The Memorial Fountain, Ten Interiors & Various Figures, The Collected Poems 1968,* and an experimental prose volume called *The Ship's Orchestra.*

IAN HAMILTON FINLAY was born in 1925. He has made poems, stories, and plays, as well as poem/prints and poems in various materials such as glass, wood, and stone. Among some twenty-five books and pamphlets, many printed by his own Wild Hawthorn Press, are *The Dancers Inherit the Party, Glasgow Beasts, Cythera, Ocean Stripe Series 5,* and *Rhymes for Lemons.* Mr. Finlay is presently assembling a Selected Poems. He lives in Lanarkshire, in Scotland.

CHRISTOPHER LOGUE was born in 1926 and lives in London. In the early Sixties he received a grant from the Bollingen Foundation to translate part of Homer's *Illiad*. *Patrocleia* and *Pax,* both of which are drawn upon for this collection, were the resulting volumes. He has recently written and produced a series of poster-poems. His most recent book is *New Numbers.*

MATTHEW MEAD was born in 1924 in Buckinghamshire. From 1942 to 1947 he served in the British Army and at present lives in Germany. With Ruth Mead he has translated Johannes Bobrowski's *Shadow Land,* Hans Winfried Sabais' *Generation,* and some of the poems in Nelly Sachs' *O The Chimneys.* He also has edited the magazine *Satis.* His poems have been collected in two volumes, *Identities and Other Poems* and *The Administration of Things.* He appears as well in the *Penguin Modern Poets* series.

D. M. THOMAS was born in 1935 and spent most of his early life in Redruth, Cornwall. He was educated at New College, Oxford, and now lectures in English at the Hereford College of Education. He is best known for his poems that have evolved from myths suggested by science-fiction stories, but is here represented chiefly by concretist or quasiconcretist work. He has published a selection of his poems called *Two Voices* and is represented in *Penguin Modern Poets 11* as well as in a number of anthologies including *British Poetry Since the War, The New S.F.,* and *Inside Outer Space.*

ANSELM HOLLO was born in 1934 in Helsinki, Finland. For the last ten years he has lived mostly in London. A translator of Yevtushenko, Voznesensky, Brecht, Paavo Haavikko, and other Finnish, French, German, and Russian poets, Hollo has published fourteen volumes of his own work including *& it is a song, Faces and Forms, The Coherences, Ferry Moments,* and *Maya.*

Anselm Hollo is currently teaching in the Writing Program at the University of Iowa.

KEN SMITH was born in 1938 in Yorkshire. He studied at Leeds University and has taught both in England and America. In 1964 he won the Eric Gregory Award for a group of poems forming the basis of *The Pity*. Ken Smith has recently completed a second collection which will be called *Work, Distances/Poems*. He co-edits *Stand* magazine with Jon Silkin.

PETER WHIGHAM was born in 1925 and is self-educated. He has worked as a gardener, schoolmaster, actor, reporter, script writer, and broadcaster for the BBC. He left England in the early sixties to live in Italy where he finished his Catullus translations and at present teaches at the University of California, Berkeley. Peter Whigham has published, among other volumes, *Catullus, The Blue Winged Bee,* and *Astapovo* or *What We Are to Do.*

LEE HARWOOD was born in Leicester in 1939. From 1958-61 he studied at the University of London and subsequently worked as a stone mason, librarian, packer, book shop assistant, forester, and bus-conductor. He edited and published a series of little magazines during the 1960's and began his translations from the work of Tristan Tzara. Among other books, Lee Harwood has published *The Man With Blue Eyes, The White Room, The Beautiful Atlas,* and *Landscapes.* At present he lives in Brighton and is preparing his Tzara translations for publication.

JOHN DANIEL was born in Middlesex in 1935. He attended state school, Merchant Taylors' School, and, after two years National Service, Cambridge

and the University of Minnesota. He
has worked as a journalist on *The
Guardian* and taught in Colleges of
Further Education. John Daniel lives in
Barnet, Hertfordshire, where he finds,
and sometimes writes, poems. His work
has been anthologized in Faber's *Poetry
Introduction I,* read on the BBC, and
published in a number of journals.
"Auto Icon," first found by John
Matthias, was especially commissioned
for this anthology. John Daniel is at
present working on a novel.

JOHN MONTAGUE. Though Irish,
John Montague was born in America in
1929. He has lived mostly in Dublin and
Ulster, but also in France, Mexico, and
the United States. He has been a film
critic and a journalist and has published,
along with his poetry, a volume of short
fiction called *Death of a Chieftain*. At
present, John Montague lives in Paris
where he is working on an Ulster epic.
His most recent volumes of poems are
A Chosen Light and *Tides*.

HARRY GUEST was born in Penarth,
Glamorgan, in 1932. He studied at
Cambridge and the Sorbonne where he
wrote a thesis on Mallarmé. He now
lectures in English Literature at
Yokohama National University and
lives in Tokyo. Harry Guest's poems
have been collected in two volumes,
Arrangements and *The Cutting-Room*.
He also appears in the *Penguin Modern
Poets* series.

NATHANIEL TARN was born in
France in 1928. Educated at the
universities of Cambridge, Paris, Yale,
Chicago, and London, he is an
anthropologist with field experience in
Central America and the Far East. He
has been general editor of Cape Editions
in London and was a founding director
of Cape-Goliard Press. He has lectured
both in England and the United States.

Nathaniel Tarn has published five volumes of poetry: *Old Savage/Young City, Where Babylon Ends, The Beautiful Contradictions, October,* and *A Nowhere for Vallejo.* He has also done some translations from the Spanish, chiefly from the poetry of Pablo Neruda.

TOM RAWORTH was born in 1934 of Anglo-Irish parentage. He has been an insurance clerk, laborer, assistant transport manager, continental telephonist, and editor of the magazine *Outburst.* Tom Raworth has published four volumes of poems, *The Relation Ship, The Big Green Day, Lion Lion,* and, with John Esam and Anselm Hollo, *Haiku.* He is at present studying Latin-American Literature at the University of Essex.

GAVIN BANTOCK was born near Birmingham in 1939. He attended New College, Oxford from 1960-64 where he wrote his 7,000 line epic poem *Christ.* Since *Christ,* Gavin Bantock has written four long poems and is at present working on a fifth. His second book, *A New Thing Breathing,* was published in 1969. He teaches at Reitaku University in Japan.

Foreword

There *is* a contemporary British poetry which is modern; for a while that
seemed to be in doubt. Perhaps, in America at least, it's still in doubt. In
a preface to a fairly typical anthology of recent poetry in open forms, the
editors write: "We decided to keep it American because we knew
American and because, with a few exceptions . . . nothing much has
happened in English poetry since Lawrence laid down his pen and died."
The introduction to another—just as typical, just as parochial—has it:
"While most English poetry, whatever its imagery, sounds very much
like English poetry written fifty years ago, much American poetry sounds
like something new. . . ." The remarks are condescending and flippant: a
friend of mine likes to call this kind of talk "American Literary Jingoism"
—which it is. It's not enough to "know American." But the attitude is
widespread among American poets, editors, and teachers; worse, it's
often fed by the British themselves. I have assembled this anthology
because I admire a good number of British poets whose work is
insufficiently known in this country. Because the work of these poets is
insufficiently known British poetry is too often thought to be genteel,
reactionary, and anti-experimental. Too often "British" means *old* or
tired in America, "contemporary" rather than "modern," Philip Larkin
rather than Tom Raworth. In fact, the best British poets are refining and
extending the work of the modernist revolution in the same way their
American contemporaries are.

I had thought at first to include only the younger poets, but a growing
irritation over the neglect in this country of Jones, Bunting, and
MacDiarmid prompted me to begin the anthology with their poems and,
once I had decided to do that, to include as well the work of several fine
poets whose English reputations were made in the 1950's. There are not,

therefore, as many new poets represented as I had at first hoped. The book has aged a bit—but thereby it has acquired a longer memory. That, and a history; which is to say a form. In the first poem perplexed legionaries guard a Jerusalem wall. Dimly and darkly they looked forward—to us, our world. In the last poem that world is scourged. Between the two is the business of living, of living and of making: *anaphora, anamnesis, anathemata.*

But someone is bound to quarrel with my ordering of the material. After, say, George MacBeth—perhaps even after Bunting—the structure may seem arbitrary. "Hiroshima," if it was going to come at all, had to come last. Further, the conclusion of any book ought to be strong—and in this one, some 400 pages, that meant keeping Tarn and Raworth and Bantock grouped together at the end. The concrete sections required some distance between them. So did Harwood and Guest, for example; and Hollo and Raworth. Also people doing very heavy things: Hughes, Fisher, Mead, Smith, Tarn. The essential principle was variety and change of pace.

There are omissions which I regret (Volume Two would be easy), and some of these will be obvious ones. I intend no disrespect. While there was clearly no room for poets whose work contradicts the thrust and argument of the anthology and contributes, however good in kind it may be, to American misconceptions about British poetry, there should have been room for others whom I expect a number of readers will miss. Given the space, I made my decisions. I should also note that I have excluded certain poets whose poetry moves me very much when I hear it read aloud or set to music but which, naked on the page, unperformed, dies. I hope, like all of the poets here assembled, that the reader will read the poems in this book aloud. But I include nothing which cannot live on the page.

I admit, finally, as most anthologists ought, to some eccentricities of taste and some odd enthusiasms. I hope they will be contagious.

J. M.

Introduction

Introductions to anthologies are often most notable for the
discrepancy revealed between the editor's ideas about, and
aspirations for, poetry in general—and the poems themselves.
John Matthias has, with justification, waived the traditional
introductory essay, leaving me, as an English reader, to consider
the collection from the British standpoint. Certainly I share
his hope that this book, which I believe to be a good collection,
will undermine the notion that "nothing much has happened in
English poetry since Lawrence laid down his pen and died". (All
that has happened here, as in America, is that a few exceptional
poets have produced outstanding bodies of work, and a larger
number of good poets have written a large number of good poems.
What else is there? A lot of talk about new techniques, new
schools of poetry, influences and so on: some of which has
some bearing on some poems.)

I also hope that this anthology will serve as a starting-
point for much more exchange between the poets of Britain and
America, and their audiences. It seems natural today for
English readers to turn to American poetry—and not only to
poets of the international stature of Lowell and Berryman; but
few Americans will readily read British poetry. Why? Are
we too modest about our own poets? Too easily impressed by
the latest Transatlantic developments? Both, perhaps. Or
are we jealous of the immensity and variety of the American
experience, its terror and violence? Are Americans somehow

proud of the global influence of their way of life—and does
this give their poets exclusive rights to the raw material of
Important Poetry? Are the British languishing in a tired and
now provincial country, whose experience is somehow less
relevant, less readily the material for poets of international
stature? Or is it a question simply of individual talents,
and if so, are we short of talents which are likely to develop?
All these are questions which are prompted by the fact of
the publication of this anthology in America, in the present
climate.

This anthology should not be treated as any sort of map
of current judgments of the relative worth of British poets.
It doesn't offer you the historical perspective supposedly
given by printing two or three pages each by a hundred poets,
and doesn't pander to the tourist guidebook approach to poetry,
whereby readers are invited not so much to feel their way into
a poet's work—with a small handful of poems that is impossible—
but to get an idea of whether, and for advanced students, why,
x is better than *y,* without really having to read either of them.
There aren't any prepackaged opinions here for "placing" the
poets. The anthology does no more and no less than present to
the American audience a generous selection of the work of
twenty-three British poets at different stages of their writing
careers, whose work stems from the modernist tradition. It
doesn't cover every movement in a "representative" way—there
is no Philip Larkin here to represent the best of the witty,
suburban middle-class poetry of the fifties; there are no
pop-poets, no neo-beats, no neo-confessionalists. Yet to my
mind it does, while steering clear of received critical opinion
and remaining catholic in taste, bring out the variety of British
modernist poetry.

2

Ten years ago, an anthology which started with the three poets
whose work opens this book would have been inconceivable.
A. Alvarez's *The New Poetry* (1962) began with two American
poets—Lowell and Berryman—presumably to contrast their range
and power with the comparative limitations of the eighteen
British poets whose work followed. (Four of them—Hughes,

Middleton, Tomlinson and MacBeth—are in this collection.)
Modernism, it seemed, had dried up in Britain, and the typical
poets of the fifties had entered a safety-first period: their poems
were formal, detachedly observant, attempting to use wit and
irony to create verse of social reportage. This was a reaction
to the welter of imitation Dylan Thomas in the hectic post-war
period—the neo-romantic poets, alias "The New Apocalypse".
The name of the reaction was The Movement. This was the sort
of response The Movement's typical poetry evoked: "at times
I have felt appreciatively that she probably washes her hands
and puts on new white gloves before she starts to write" (Kenneth
Allott on Elizabeth Jennings). Kingsley Amis typifies the
anti-romantic, anti-aesthetic approach with lines like:

> Should poets bicycle-pump the human heart
> Or squash it flat?

and said, in 1955, that "nobody wants any more poems on the
grander themes for a few years". All this might have been
different had not young poets of exceptional promise such as
Sidney Keyes and Keith Douglas been killed in their twenties
in the last stages of the war. Bunting was unknown in England
at this time; David Jones published infrequently, and was
nobody's cup of tea; and MacDiarmid has always been treated
rather as a mad Scotsman by the English. With hindsight, Ted
Hughes and Charles Tomlinson were clearly the most individual
new voices of the late fifties; and Tomlinson was more appreciated
in America than in England at the time.

"Sometimes I wonder if England ever came to modern art
at all," wrote Donald Hall in 1965, introducing his revision
of *The Faber Book of Modern Verse.* "While Stravinsky and
Picasso and Henry Moore—to mention one Englishman at least—
were inventing forms and techniques, W. H. Auden was 'experimenting'
with sonnets and off-rhyme and Anglo-Saxon metres. Of course
I am unfair to Auden, but I do not think I am unfair to the
history of modern poetry in English. In the sense that Spain
and Latin America and France and Germany had modernist poets—
new forms, and new experiences of the spirit—perhaps England
and America are only beginning." Perhaps: or are we beginning
to pick up where poets of the earlier part of the century left

xvii

off? Lorca, Neruda, Mayakovsky and Aragon are poets not to
be imitated or easily transplanted. Yet no-one is blind to their
importance in the global context; nor to the contribution
translated foreign poetry has to make to our cultures. But
poetry is not a competitive sport; never mind if we have no-
one to match Neruda; let us read Neruda as best we can.

3

The modernist revolution in English-language poetry was a
combined Anglo-American phenomenon. Pound in particular was
active in England, when with H.D. and Richard Aldington he
formulated the poetic tenets of Imagism. Imagism was the first
of a series of developments which opened up new possibilities
for English and American poetry. The modernism of Pound and
Eliot differs from that of William Carlos Williams, their
contemporary who stayed in America, in one important respect:
Pound and Eliot saw their experiments as a rediscovery of for-
gotten traditions—both poets were acutely conscious of the
heritage and relevance of European literature. Williams, on the
other hand, was specifically trying to evolve a poetry in an
American idiom, free of historical-literary associations which
he considered irrelevant for American literature. For Williams,
The Waste Land was disastrously retrogressive—it returned
poetry to the classroom. Williams' idea of the American idiom
has been at the basis of later experiments by the Black Mountain
poets (the polymath Robert Duncan being, perhaps, the exception
to prove the rule); and, one need hardly add, it was a problem
which could not affect English poets in the same way. At any
rate, there have always been these two diverging strands of
modernist poetry—the Europeanising and the Americanising;
the one (to oversimplify rather brutally) "making new" the past,
the other responding to the texture of language and things
around it. Considered purely theoretically, the two would
seem to be mutually exclusive: but the practice of the two
methods, and the intellectual outlooks which formed them, were
based on differing temperaments and abilities; and there is
probably a bit of both outlooks in most of the best British
poets writing now. Both Bunting and MacDiarmid, for instance,
are almost polemically conscious of their identity with their

regions—MacDiarmid politically so, as a Scots nationalist,
Bunting more linguistically ("Southrons would maul the music
of many lines in Briggflatts").

In an interview (*Akros* magazine, April 1970), Duncan Glen
put this to MacDiarmid—"In a way Eliot, with his Tradition
and the Individual Talent, and Carlos Williams, with his belief
in the future of the American idiom—both of them are in you
in a way, aren't they? You have gone not only for a Scottish
idiom but also for reuniting Scotland with the European tradition,
although I don't know if you'd accept Eliot's belief in the
individual talent working within that tradition." MacDiarmid:
"No. I go much nearer Eliot, of course, than I do William Carlos
Williams, but my man is Pound, definitely. Eliot, after all,
showed a narrowing tendency . . . but Pound opened out all along
the line, took in more and more."

4

It is more than fifty years since the first period of experimental
ferment in poetry in the 1910s; revolutions and wars have
intervened, and we are nearer our somewhat less than brave
new world. Consider for a moment Britain's position in the world
at this point of time. Most of her colonies, bar a rock and
an island or two, were shed some time ago. With the growth of
America, Russia and the spectre of China, Britain has declined
as a force in international affairs. Sometimes the country
seems, even to the British, like some sort of cultural and
political museum. Unlike America, Britain has no such dilemmas
as the Vietnam war to tax its resources and divide its conscience;
nor such desperate social problems as the ghettoes and racial
conflicts arising from oppression of a tenth of its people.
Britain has not suffered the convulsions which have split
Eastern Europe, oppressed the people of Russia, and established
fascist regimes in Spain, Portugal and Greece. As a Hungarian
poet said to me recently—England is basically a happy country.
That is a comparative judgment, of course. I don't wish to
imply that Britain is a social paradise; only that our problems
are less obvious, and as yet on a much smaller scale.

Gradually, Britain is identifying with Europe; and whether
or not it enters the European Economic Community—which would

lead it into political unity, in time, with Western Europe—
the British feel more and more a part of Europe than of any
other political or cultural society; and we respond more and
more to European experience. European poetry, past and present,
is spiritually closer to us than it can be, perhaps, to most
American readers. Certainly the influence of Eastern European
poetry is a factor in Ted Hughes' most recent poems.

American readers may feel, subconsciously or overtly,
that the newness and largeness of the American experience is yet
more inescapable and vital than anything that is happening in
Britain: therefore that the subject-matter of American poetry
is necessarily more vital, and more productive of vital poetry.
I am sure that, whether or not the first part of this notion
is meaningful, its corollaries are fundamentally mistaken: though
I grant that the American situation, acting on exceptional
talents (I am thinking primarily of Robert Lowell), will
produce poetry of vital impact. Lowell would, I think, be the
last person to subscribe to the idea (what John Matthias calls
"American literary jingoism") that the problems facing American
poets in responding to their experience are more important than
anybody else's. (Thinking of Lowell, one ought to recall
how much European poetry has deepened his sense of the American
situation.) Vietnam is no guarantee of vital poetry. Nor, of
course, is the lack of British military involvement in Vietnam
any guarantee of anything to do with poetry: it simply means
that the British do not write so many poems, good or bad, about it.

What all such notions ignore is the active role of the
poet's creative imagination. Poets *make* poems, they aren't just
picked out of the surrounding air. Every poet has at his dis-
posal his mind, which is, at least potentially, unfettered by
temporal limitations. Thus a poet may (and in countries where
censorship prevails, is compelled to) treat essentially political,
contemporary material in an indirect way: either in allegorical
form, or by transferring the subject to a different historical
context. The difference between a good political poem and a bad
one is in their art, not their politics—other things being
equal. Neither good poems nor bad ones will build houses, give
freedom to the oppressed or prevent injustice.

John Matthias points in his Foreword to notions that "British

xx

poetry is too often thought to be genteel, reactionary, and anti-experimental." The poems are sufficient refutation, and I don't propose to go into arguments about the nature of 'experimental' poetry. In poetry, as in other arts, the label is currently applied at random to anything looking vaguely way-out, as if its connotations of daring and innovation are sufficient evidence of originality. Technical developments, re-instatements or adaptations of previous, perhaps forgotten techniques, extensions and rediscoveries of subject-matter—these are rather different from any notions of haphazard experimentalism. Just as there is no 'pure' stream of modernist poetry with a single source— no admirer of Pound, say, wants merely to imitate him—so there is no such thing as a purely experimental poetry; and as long as people continue not to live in a total mental vacuum, there never will be.

Hazarding a guess, I'd say that recent British poets have been less partisan in their attitudes to their art than most Americans. Less dogmatic, at any rate, than the Black Mountain poets, and more willing to entertain, and learn from, a diversity of 'schools' of poetry. If we can use the word 'experimental' to mean anything, it should be applied to poetic developments which are not superficially concerned with external, but internal techniques: structure and organization, texture of language, new forms of narrative. Matthew Mead and Christopher Middleton are worth mentioning in this context. Olson's dictum "form is never more than an extension of content" is true of these poets in their own ways; it is not true of most of what passes for experimental poetry, which merely imitates the external, superficial elements of experiment. All real poems are a marriage between their content and their form; the happier the marriage, the more successful the poem.

Take Ian Hamilton Finlay's work in non-literary forms: there is no theoretical reason why a poem should not be made in the form of a sculpture or an inscription. (We are historically accustomed to poetry being made in the form of song.) In fact, a number of modernist techniques in verse cannot helpfully be described in purely literary terms. For instance, though one can talk of Robert Creeley's poems as a literary development of the lyric epigram, it is as helpful to think of them as verbal miniature

sculptures. Basil Bunting stresses the musical analogy in talking
about his poems; Charles Tomlinson was a painter, and his poetry
reveals a painter's awareness of visual detail. Harry Guest recently
in a sequence of long poems called *Metamorphoses* in using a
near-cinematic form in his narrative. Nathaniel Tarn's anthropological
studies influence his method as well as his matter.

5

But Modernism is an indefinable term. It is easier now to say what
is not modernist than what is. Poets establish their own terms
of reference, and many excellent poets have found traditional
modes an adequate vehicle—Robert Graves and Richard Wilbur,
to give both English and American examples. I suppose Modernism
encompasses poetry which, in general, draws on, or extends, the
experiments of Pound and subsequent developments—not all of
which are either purely literary-technical, like free verse, or
American in origin. Surrealism, for instance. At any rate, you
will not find here any slavish imitation of the "Americanising"
strands of modernism; although poets like Tomlinson and Turnbull
have both lived in America and acquired some of their technique
from American poetry. Anselm Hollo, a Finn by origin, is super-
ficially American-looking in his verse, but his blend of the
surreal with projective technique shows a very personal, English
humour and outlook. Lee Harwood and Tom Raworth have much in
common with the New York poets, but their sensibilities are not
derivative. There has been so much cross-fertilisation in
contemporary poetry which was impossible a century ago: consider
the excellent Czech poet, Miroslav Holub, who is a scientist
himself, and whose powerful, politically conscious yet subtly
ironic poetry is based on empirical techniques new to Czech
verse which he developed from reading Carlos Williams.

I don't know whether American critics categorise their poets,
as the British do, into Decades. Auden and Spender are consigned
to the Thirties; Dylan Thomas is locked with the neo-romantics
in the forties; Larkin and The Movement belong to the fifties.
I hope journalists will have a problem with the sixties.
Certainly the three older poets who start this collection won't
fit anywhere; which may explain why they have tended to be
ignored. They are loners. Poetry doesn't develop chronologically,

year by year, decade by decade. There's really no such thing
as the history of poetry in that sense; there are only poems.
The history of poetry is a simultaneity of poems, the survival
of the fittest, across time and frontiers. Catullus, Sappho
and Villon are all very much alive. Others need men to bring
them to life, as Pound did the Troubadours. The modernist
movement in poetry is anti-parochial, exploratory of time
past, present and future; and international in outlook.

Ted Hughes' words have come to have meaning for everyone
interested in poetry in Britain:. "However rootedly national
in detail it may be, poetry is less and less the prisoner of its
own language. It is beginning to represent, as an ambassador,
something far greater than itself. Or perhaps it is only
now being heard for what, among others things, it is—a universal
language of understanding, coherent behind the many languages,
in which we can all hope to meet."

6

British poetry has, I feel, widened its horizons from the
insularity of ten years ago. Even then, poets like Ted Hughes,
Thom Gunn and Christopher Middleton stood out for their wider
outlook. A. Alvarez wrote in 1962, "My own feeling is that a
good deal of poetic talent exists in England at the moment. But
whether it will come to anything largely depends not on the
machinations of any literary racket but on the degree to which
the poets can remain immune to the disease so often found in
English culture: gentility." And immediately before that final
paragraph of his introduction to *The New Poetry,* he wrote:
"In the seriousness of what I have called the new depth poetry,
the openness to experience, the psychological insight and
integrity of D. H. Lawrence would, ideally, combine with the
technical skill and formal intelligence of T. S. Eliot. If
this were to happen, we would have contemporary work which,
like Coleridge's Imagination, would reconcile 'a more than usual
state of emotion with more than usual order'." Prescriptions
for poetry are unlikely to help anyone deliver the goods, but
surely he is, in principle, right. Nevertheless, I feel more
cynical than Alvarez about the literary racket, which denies any
public discussion in reviews to poets like Gavin Bantock, whose

poetry is precisely the kind which an intelligent society
ought not to be able to ignore, while promoting its own kind
with staggering lack of scruple.

The last ten years have brought the republication of Basil
Bunting's work of over thirty years, and his superb long poem
Briggflatts—the finest since Eliot's *Four Quartets*—after
years of almost total obscurity. MacDiarmid and Jones have
continued writing and publishing, and are beginning, thanks
largely to the efforts of the magazine *Agenda,* to attract the
wider attention they deserve. They are all poets with strong
roots and developed historical senses. The last ten years have
also brought exciting work from Ted Hughes; have produced
brilliant translations from the classics—Peter Whigham's
Catullus and Logue's episodes from *The Iliad*. Even science-
fiction has entered poetry, in the work of D. M. Thomas and
George MasBeth. Roy Fisher has made of urban poetry an art
with something of the atmosphere of L. S. Lowry's paintings.

The variety of this collection hardly needs remarking on:
it spans from the Roman-Celtic world of David Jones's poems
to the post-atomic; every shade of modern writing is represented
here, and if this collection gives the impression that there
is no prevailing orthodoxy in English poetry at present, that
would be a fair summary. Each poet must stake out his own
boundaries; "no verse is free for the man who wants to do a
good job"; poets have only their nerve, skill and imagination
to guide them, and these qualities are not lacking. Few poets
of any age combine all the qualities desirable in a poet, the
breadth of vision with the maximum of skill; but this anthology
gives one hope.

Peter Jay
London, August 1970

DAVID JONES

The Wall

We don't know the ins and outs
        how should we? how could we?
It's not for the likes of you and me to cogitate high policy or
to guess the inscrutable economy of the pontifex
        from the circuit of the agger
        from the traverse of the wall.
But you see a thing or two
        in our walk of life
        walking the compass of the vallum
walking for twenty years of nights
        round and round and back & fro
on the walls that contain the world.

You see a thing or two, you think a thing or two, in our walk
of life, walking for twenty years, by day, by night, doing the
rounds on the walls that maintain the world
        on the hard tread of the silex
        on the heavy tread of the mound
up in the traversed out-work, stepping it at the alert, down on
the *via quintana* stepping it double-quick by numbers to break
y'r tiro-heart . . .
        dug in wrong side the *limes*
or walled in back at depot?
                        it's evens, more or less
as far as jumping to it goes.

        But what about the Omphalos
there's the place for the proud walkers
        where the terminal gate
        arcs for the sections in column

stepping their extra fancy step
        behind the swag and spolia
o' the universal world

                   . . . out from The Camp
in through the dexter arch of double-wayed Carmenta
by where Aventine flanks The Circus
              (from Arx the birds deploy?)
to where the totem mother
          imported
          Ionian
          of bronze
brights Capitoline for ever
                (from the Faunine slope
of creviced Palatine does the grey wraith erect her throat to
welcome the lupine gens?)

Erect, crested with the open fist that turns the evil spell,
lifting the flat palm that disciplines the world, the signa lift
in disciplined acknowledgement, the eagles stand erect for Ilia
          O Roma
          O Ilia
          Io Triumphe, Io, Io . . .
          the shopkeepers presume to make
the lupine cry their own
              the magnates of the Boarium
leave their nice manipulations. You may call the day ferial,
rub shoulders with the plebs. All should turn out to see how
those appointed to die take the Roman medicine. They crane
their civvy necks half out their civvy suits to bait the maimed
king in his tinctured vesture, the dying *tegernos* of the wasted
landa well webbed in our marbled parlour, bitched and be-
wildered and far from his dappled patria far side the misted
Fretum
        You can think a thing or two
on *that* parade:

        Do the celestial forechoosings
        and the hard journeyings
come to this?

2

                    Did the empyreal fires
hallow the chosen womb
                    to tabernacle founders of
                    emporia?
Were the august conjoinings
                    was the troia'd wandering
                    achieved
did the sallow ducts of Luperca
                    nourish the lily white boys
was Electra chose
                    from the seven stars in the sky
did Ilia bear fruit to the Strider
                    was she found the handmaid of the Lar

did the augurs inaugurate, did the Clarissimi steady the
transverse rods, did they align the plummets carefully, did they
check the bearing attentively, was the templum dead true at
the median intersection

                    did the white unequal pair
labour the yoke, tread the holy circuit
                                        did they, so early
in the marls of Cispadana
                    show forth, foretoken
the rudiments of our order
                                        when the precursors
at the valley-sites made survey of the loam, plotted the trape-
zoids on the sodden piles, digged the sacred pits, before the
beginning . . .
                            did they square the hill-sites
for the hut-circles, did the hill-groups look to each other, were
the hostile strong-points one by one, made co-ordinate
                            did Quirinal with Viminal
call to the Quadrata
                            did the fence of Tullius
embrace the mixed kindreds
did the magic wall
                            (that keeps the walls)
describe the orbit
did that wall contain a world

                    from the beginning
did they project the rectilineal plane upwards
to the floor of heaven
had all
            within that reaching prism
                        one patria:
                rooted clod or drifted star
                dog or dryad or
                man born of woman
did the sacred equation square the mundane site
was truth with fact conjoined
                        did the earth-mother
blossom the stone lintels
                        did *urvus* become *urbs*
did the bright share
                        turn the dun clod
to the star plan
                        did they parcel out
per scamna et strigas
                        the *civitas* of God
that we should sprawl
                        from Septimontium
a megalopolis that wills death?

Does the pontifex, do our lifted trumpets, speak to the city and
the world to call the tribes to Saturnalia to set misrule in the
curule chair, to bind the rejected fillet on the King of the Bean?
                    It's hard to trapes these things
from the circuit of the agger
from the traverse of the wall
waiting for the middle watch to pass
                        wanting the guard-house fug
                        where the companions nod
                        where the sooted billikin
brews the night broth

                        so cold it is, so numb the intelligence,
so chancy the intuition, so alert the apprehension for us who
walk in darkness, in the shadow of the *onager,* in the shadow of

the labyrinth of the wall, of the world, of the robber walls of the world city, trapesing the macrocosmic night.

Or, trapesing the night within, walking the inner labyrinth where also the night is, under the tortoise of the skull, for every man walking?

Under the legionary's iron knob, under the tribune's field crest, under the very distinguished gilt *cassis* of the Legatus himself?

                 We don't know the ins and outs how can we? how shall we?

What did our mothers tell us? What did their mothers tell them? What the earth-mother told to them? But what did the queen of heaven tell *her?*

What was it happened by the fire-flame eating the griddle-cake . . . or by the white porch where our sister sang the Sabine dirge.

           . . . they used to say we marched for Dea Roma behind the wolf sign to eat up the world, they used to say we marched for the Strider, the common father of the Roman people, the father of all in our walk of life, by whose very name you're called . . .

          but now they say the Quirinal Mars turns out to be no god of war but of armed peace. Now they say we march for kind Irene, who crooks her rounded elbow for little Plutus, the gold-getter, and they say that sacred brat has a future . . .

             now all can face the dying god
             the dying Gaul
             without regret.

But you and me, comrade, the Darlings of Ares, who've helped a lot of Gauls and gods to die, we shall continue to march and to bear in our bodies the marks of the Marcher—by whatever name they call him . . .

             we shall continue to march
             round and round the cornucopia:
that's the new fatigue.

Two sections from *The Anathemata*

Angle-Land

Did he strike soundings off Vecta Insula?
        or was it already the gavelkind *ígland*?
Did he lie by
        in the East Road?
was it a kindly *numen* of the Sleeve that headed him clear of
South Sand Head?
Did he shelter in the Small Downs?
Keeping close in, did he feel his way
between the Flats and the Brake?
But, what was her draught, and, what was the ocean doing?
        Did he stand on toward the Gull?
did his second mate sound
        with more than care?
was it perforce or Fortuna's rudder, circumstance or superb
pilotage or clean oblation
        that sheered him from smother
(the unseen necropolis banking to starboard of her).
Or was it she
        Sea-born and Sea-star
whose own, easy and free
        the pious matlos are
or, was it a whim of Poseidon's
(master o' the cinque masters o' lodemanage)
whose own the Island's approaches are
        that kept her?
Was the Foreland?
        was the Elbow?
under fog.
        He might have been deeped in the Oaze!
Or
        by the brumous numen drawn on
or
        in preclear visibility
by the invisible wind laboured
it might have been Dogger or Well
        to bank her a mound

without a sheet to wrap her
without a shroud to her broken back.
        Past where they placed their *ingas*-names
where they speed the coulter deep
        in the open Engel fields
to this day.
          How many poles
of their broad Angle hidage
to the small scattered plots, to the lightly furrowed *erwau,*
that once did quilt Boudícca's róyal *gwely?*

Past where they urn'd their calcined dead from Schleswig
over the foam.
(Close the south-west wall of the chester, without the orbit,
if but a stone's throw: you don't want to raise an Icenian
Venta's Brettisc ghost.
He'll latin-runes tellan in his horror-coat standing:
IAM REDIT ROMA
        his lifted palm his VERBVM is.)

Past where the ancra-man, deeping his holy rule
in the fiendish marsh
        at the *Geisterstunde*
        on *Calangaeaf* night
heard the bogle-*baragouinage.*
        Crowland-*diawliaidd*
Waelisc-man lingo speaking?
        or Britto-Romani gone *diaboli?*
or Romanity gone *Waelisc?*

Is Marianus wild Meirion?
is Sylvánus
        Urbigéna's son?
has toga'd Rhufon
        (gone Actaéon)
come away to the Wake
        in the bittern's low aery?
along with his towny
        Patricius gone the *wilde Jäger?*

From the *fora*
                    to the forests.
Out from *gens Romulum*
            into the *Weal*-kin
dinas-man gone *aethwlad*
cives gone wold-men
                    . . . from Lindum to London
bridges broken down.

What was his *Hausname?*
                    he whose North Holstein urn
they sealed against the seep of the Yare?
If there are *Wealas* yet
                    in the Waltons
what's the cephalic index of the *môrforynion,* who knell
the bell, who thread the pearls that were Ned Mizzen's eyes,
at the five fathom line off the Naze?
                    On the past the low low lands of the Holland that
Welland winds to the Deepings north of the Soke
past where Woden's gang is *gens Julia* for Wuffingas new to
old Nene and up with the Lark
past the south hams and the north tons
past the weathered thorps and
                    the Thorpe
that bore, that bred
                    him whom Nike did bear
her tears at flood
and over the scatter of the forebrace bitts
                    down to the orlop
at twenty five minutes after one of the clock
in the afternoon, on a Monday
twelve days before the Calends of November
outside the Pillars
                    where they closed like a forest
                    . . . in 13 fathoms' water
unanchored in the worsening weather.
                    Far drawn on away
from the island's field-floor, upwards of a hundred fathoms
over where, beyond where, in the fifties, toward the sixties,

8

north latitude

                                        all our easting waters
are confluent with the fathering river and tributary to him:
where Tamesis, Great Ouse, Tyne from the Wall's end, de-
marking Tweed, Forth that winds the middle march, Tummel
and wide looping Tay (that laps the wading files when Birnam
boughs deploy toward Dunsinane—out toward the Goat
Flats).
Spey of the Symbol stones and Ness from the serpentine mere
all mingle Rhenus-flow
                        and are oned with him
in Cronos-*meer*.
I speak of before the whale-roads or the keel-paths were from
Orcades to the fiord-havens, or the greyed green wastes that
they strictly grid
quadrate and number on the sea-green *Quadratkarte*
                            one eight six one G
                            for the fratricides
of the latter-day, from east-shore of Iceland
bis Nerwegen
(O Balin O Balan!
                how blood you both
the *Brudersee*
                toward the last pháse
of our dear West.)

Redriff

Or
        did he make the estuary?
was the Cant smiling
        and the Knock smooth?
Did our Tidal Father bear him
                by Lower Hope to Half Reach?
Did he berth in the Greenland or was she moored
in the Pool?
Did he tie up across the water
                or did she toss at the Surrey shore?

Had he business at Dockhead?
Did he sign Tom Bowline on:
                    ord-in-ary-seaman
in place of the drownded Syro-Phoenician?
Did he bespeak
                    of Eb Bradshaw, Princes Stair:
listed replacement of sheaves to the running-blocks, new
dead-eyes to the standing shrouds, some spare hearts for the
stays, a heavy repair in the chains, some nice work up at
the hound
                                    . . . would he expedite.
It 'ld be well worth his while—for a tidy consideration
could she have preference—for she must weigh on time or
the dues 'ld ruin 'em—would he, for once, oil an elbow—
would he please to hustle the job—and not so over nice with
the finish.
Not for a gratis load of the sound teak in
Breaker's Yard

                    and that we could well do with.
Not for a dozen cords of Norweyan, red nor yaller, paid for,
carried and stacked.
Not for a choice of the best float of Oregon in the mast-pond.
Not for as many cubic fathoms of best Indies lignum vitae
as 'ld stock us till we re-sheave the blocks for master-
bargees plying the Styx.
Not for a pickin' of all the bonded stuffs passed over the
quays in a full working week between the Bridge and Battle-
bridge Stairs
                    and there's a tidy jorum
to pile a mint in sterling—to rig out Ann my wife like Suky
Tawdry.
Not at the price of half the freights, felled of the living wood,
a lent o' tides, brings to all the wharves, from here round to
the Royal Vi't'lin', when Proserpine unbinds the Baltic.
Not if he signed me fair a note of hand for all the gold on his
fleece.
Nor for this port's authorities
                    and I'm a citizen.

Not if the Trinity Brethren
                    and Clemens himself
stood caps in hand for a month of Sundays
                    and them I must needs respect.
Not if the Holy Ghost made ready to blow on his mainsail.
Nor for a boozed Murphy's bull in curial-cursive and leaded
from the scarlet pontiff o' the West.
And, as for next Thor's Day's night tide
                    tell the Wop, to-go-to
                              Canute
if he can find him
                    down at the Galley Wall
(though he's many times before *his* time).
But tell him:
                    we scamp no repairs here; no botched Riga
deal nor wood that's all American, softs nor hards, hewn or
sawn, heart n'r sap, cis- or trans- Gangem-land teak, or fair-
grained *ulmus* from sylvan wester lands or goodish East Mark
oak via Fiume in British bottoms
                    let alone
heart of island-grown
                    seasoned in m' neighbour's yard
leaves this bench.
But
      tell him
tell him from me
                    if he waits his turn an' damps down his Sicily
sulphur we'll spokeshave those deadeyes for him as smooth
as a *peach* of a cheek
                    we'll fay that hounding trim and proper—and of
the best spruce, to rhyme with her mainmast, we'll square
true and round to a nicety the double piercin's o' that cap—
and of keel-elm.
      If he leaves it to us
we'll fix him dandy.
But tell him—with respects from me
tell him—tell the old Jason:
                    As sure as I was articled, had I the job of mortisin'
the beams to which was lashed and roved the Fault in all of

us, I'ld take m' time and set that aspen transom square to
the Rootless Tree
            or dash m' buttons!
                            . . . he's got
till the Day o' Doom
to sail the bitter seas o' the world!

Three sections from *In Parenthesis*

I

You drop apprehensively—the sun gone out,
strange airs smite your body
and muck rains straight from heaven
and everlasting doors lift up for '02 Weavel.
    You cant see anything but sheen on drifting particles and
you move forward in your private bright cloud like
one assumed
who is borne up by an exterior volition.

You stumble on a bunch of six with Sergeant Quilter getting
them out again to the proper interval, and when the chemical
thick air dispels you see briefly and with great clearness what
kind of a show this is.

The gentle slopes are green to remind you
of South English places, only far wider and flatter spread and
grooved and harrowed criss-cross whitely and the disturbed
subsoil heaped up albescent.

Across upon this undulated board of verdure chequered
bright
when you look to left and right
small, drab, bundled pawns severally make effort
moved in tenuous line
and if you looked behind—the next wave came slowly, as suc-
cessive surfs creep in to dissipate on flat shore;
and to your front, stretched long laterally,
and receded deeply,
the dark wood.

12

And now the gradient runs more flatly toward the separate
scared saplings, where they make fringe for the interior thicket
and you take notice.
There between the thinning uprights
at the margin
straggle tangled oak and flayed sheeny beech-bole, and fragile
birch whose silver queenery is draggled and ungraced
and June shoots lopt
and fresh stalks bled
       runs the Jerry trench.
And cork-screw stapled trip-wire
to snare among the briars
and iron warp with bramble weft
with meadow-sweet and lady-smock
for a fair camouflage.

Mr. Jenkins half inclined his head to them—he walked just
barely in advance of his platoon and immediately to the left of
Private Ball.
He makes the conventional sign
and there is the deeply inward effort of spent men who would
make response for him,
and take it at the double.
He sinks on one knee
and now on the other,
his upper body tilts in rigid inclination
this way and back;
weighted lanyard runs out to full tether,
          swings like a pendulum
           and the clock run down.
Lurched over, jerked iron saucer over tilted brow,
clampt unkindly over lip and chin
nor no ventaille to this darkening
        and masked face lifts to grope the air
and so disconsolate;
enfeebled fingering at a paltry strap—
buckle holds,
holds him blind against the morning.
Then stretch still where weeds pattern the chalk predella
—where it rises to his wire—and Sergeant T. Quilter takes over.

II

Lift gently Dai, gentleness befits his gun-shot wound in the
lower bowel—go easy—easee at the slope—and mind him
—wait for this one and
slippy—an' twelve inch an' all—beating up for his counter-
attack and—that packet on the Aid-Post.

Lower you lower you—some old cows have malhanded
little bleeders for a mother's son.

Lower you lower you prize Maria Hunt, an' gammyfingered
upland Gamalin — down cantcher — low — hands away me
ducky—down on hands on hands down and flattened belly
and face pressed and curroodle mother earth
she's kind:
Pray her hide you in her deeps
she's only refuge against
this ferocious pursuer
terribly questing.
Maiden of the digged places
            let our cry come unto thee.
Mam, moder, mother of me
Mother of Christ under the tree
reduce our dimensional vulnerability to the minimum—
cover the spines of us
let us creep back dark-bellied where he can't see
don't let it.
There, there, it can't, won't hurt—nothing
shall harm my beautiful.

III

And to Private Ball it came as if a rigid beam of great weight
flailed about his calves, caught from behind by ballista-baulk
let fly or aft-beam slewed to clout gunnel-walker
below below below.

When golden vanities make about,
                you've got no legs to stand on.

He thought it disproportionate in its violence considering
the fragility of us.

14

The warm fluid percolates between his toes and his left boot fills, as when you tread in a puddle—he crawled away in the opposite direction.

It's difficult with the weight of the rifle.
Leave it—under the oak.
Leave it for a salvage-bloke
let it lie bruised for a monument
dispense the authenticated fragments to the faithful.
It's the thunder-besom for us
it's the bright bough borne
it's the tensioned yew for a Genoese jammed arbalest and a scarlet square for a mounted *mareschal,* it's that county-mob back to back. Majuba mountain and Mons Cherubim and spreaded mats for Sydney Street East, and come to Bisley for a Silver Dish. It's R.S.M. O'Grady says, it's the soldier's best friend if you care for the working parts and let us be 'aving those springs released smartly in Company billets on wet forenoons and clickerty-click and one up the spout and you men must really cultivate the habit of treating this weapon with the very greatest care and there should be a healthy rivalry among you—it should be a matter of very proper pride and
    Marry it man! Marry it!
Cherish her, she's your very own.
    Coax it man coax it—it's delicately and ingeniously made —it's an instrument of precision—it costs us tax-payers, money—I want you men to remember that.
    Fondle it like a granny—talk to it—consider it as you would a friend—and when you ground these arms she's not a rooky's gas-pipe for greenhorns to tarnish.
    You've known her hot and cold.
You would choose her from among many.
You know her by her bias, and by her exact error at 300, and by the deep scar at the small, by the fair flaw in the grain, above the lower sling-swivel—
but leave it under the oak.

Slung so, it swings its full weight. With you going blindly on all paws, it slews its whole length, to hang at your bowed neck like the Mariner's white oblation.

You drag past the four bright stones at the turn of Wood Support.

It is not to be broken on the brown stone under the gracious tree.
It is not to be hidden under your failing body.
Slung so, it troubles your painful crawling like a fugitive's irons.

The trees are very high in the wan signal-beam, for whose slow gyration their wounded boughs seem as malignant limbs, manoeuvring for advantage.
The trees of the wood beware each other
                          and under each a man sitting;
their seemly faces as carved in a sardonyx stone; as undiademed princes turn their gracious profiles in a hidden seal, so did these appear, under the changing light.

For that waning you would believe this flaxen head had for its broken pedestal these bent Silurian shoulders.
For the pale flares extinction you don't know if under his close lids, his eye-balls watch you. You would say by the turn of steel at his wide brow he is not of our men where he leans with his open fist in Dai's bosom against the White Stone.

Hung so about, you make between these your close escape.

The secret princes between the leaning trees have diadems given them.
Life the leveller hugs her impudent equality—she may proceed at once to less discriminating zones.

The Queen of the Woods has cut bright boughs of various flowering.
These knew her influential eyes. Her awarding hands can pluck for each their fragile prize.
She speaks to them according to precedence. She knows what's due to this elect society. She can choose twelve gentle-men. She knows who is most lord between the high

trees and on the open down.

Some she gives white berries
some she gives brown
Emil has a curious crown it's
made of golden saxifrage.
Fatty wears sweet-briar,
he will reign with her for a thousand years.
For Balder she reaches high to fetch his.
Ulrich smiles for his myrtle wand.

That swine Lillywhite has daisies to his chain—you'd hardly credit it.

She plaits torques of equal splendour for Mr. Jenkins and Billy Crower.

Hansel with Gronwy share dog-violets for a palm, where they lie in serious embrace beneath the twisted tripod.

Siôn gets St. John's Wort—that's fair enough.

Dai Great-coat, she can't find him anywhere—she calls both high and low, she had a very special one for him.

Among this July noblesse she is mindful of December wood —when the trees of the forest beat against each other because of him.

She carries to Aneirin-in-the-nullah a rowan sprig, for the glory of Guenedota. You couldn't hear what she said to him, because she was careful for the Disciplines of the Wars.

At the gate of the wood you try a last adjustment, but slung so, it's an impediment, it's of detriment to your hopes, you had best be rid of it—the sagging webbing and all and what's left of your two fifty — but it were wise to hold on to your mask.

You're clumsy in your feebleness, you implicate your tin-hat rim with the slack sling of it.

Let it lie for the dews to rust it, or ought you to decently cover the working parts.

Its dark barrel, where you leave it under the oak, reflects the solemn star that rises urgently from Cliff Trench.

It's a beautiful doll for us
it's the Last Reputable Arm.

But leave it—under the oak.

leave it for a Cook's tourist to the Devastated Areas and crawl
as far as you can and wait for the bearers.

Mrs. Willy Hartington has learned to draw sheets and so has
Miss Melpomené; and on the south lawns,
men walk in red white and blue
under the cedars
and by every green tree
and beside comfortable waters.
But why dont the bastards come—
Bearers!—stret-cher bear-errs!
or do they devide the spoils at the Aid-Post.

But how many men do you suppose could bear away a third
of us:
drag just a little further—he yet may counter-attack.

Lie still under the oak
next to the Jerry
and Sergeant Jerry Coke.

The feet of the reserves going up tread level with your fore-
head; and no word for you; they whisper one with another;
pass on, inward;
these latest succours:
green Kimmerii to bear up the war.

Oeth and Annoeth's hosts they were
who in that night grew
younger men
younger striplings.

The geste says this and the man who was on the field . . . and
who wrote the book . . . the man who does not know this
has not understood anything.

HUGH MacDIARMID

O wha's the bride?

O wha's the bride that cairries the bunch
O' thistles blinterin' white?
Her cuckold bridegroom little dreids
What he sall ken this nicht.

For closer than gudeman can come
And closer to'r than hersel',
Wha didna need her maidenheid
Has wrocht his purpose fell.

O wha's been here afore me, lass,
And hoo did he get in?
—*A man that deed or was I born*
This evil thing has din.

And left, as it were on a corpse,
Your maidenheid to me?
—*Nae lass, gudeman, sin' Time began*
'S hed ony mair to gi'e.

But I can gi'e ye kindness, lad,
And a pair o' willin' hands,
And you sall ha'e my breists like stars,
My limbs like willow wands.

And on my lips ye'll heed nae mair,
And in my hair forget,
The seed o' a' the men that in
My virgin womb ha'e met. . . .

19

Second hymn to Lenin

Ah, Lenin, you were richt. But I'm a poet
(And you c'ud mak allowances for that!)
Aimin' at mair than you aimed at
Tho' yours comes first, I know it.

An unexamined life is no' worth ha'in'.
Yet Burke was richt; owre muckle concern
Wi' Life's foundations is a sure
Sign o' decay; tho' Joyce in turn

Is richt, and the principal question
Aboot a work o' art is frae hoo deep
A life it springs—and syne hoo faur
Up frae't it has the poo'er to leap.

And hoo muckle it lifts up wi'it
Into the sunlicht like a saumon there,
Universal Spring! For Morand's richt—
It s'ud be like licht in the air—

Are my poems spoken in the factories and fields,
    In the streets o' the toon?
Gin they're no', then I'm failin' to dae
    What I ocht to ha' dune.

Gin I canna win through to the man in the street,
    The wife by the hearth,
A' the cleverness on earth'll no' mak' up
    For the damnable dearth.

"Haud on haud on; what poet's dune that?
    Is Shakespeare read,
Or Dante or Milton or Goethe or Burns?"
    —You heard what I said.

—A means o' world locomotion,
The maist perfected and aerial o' a'.

Lenin's name's gane owre the haill earth,
But the names o' the ithers?—Ha!

What hidie-hole o' the vineyard d'they scart
Wi' minds like the look on a hen's face,
Morand, Joyce, Burke, and the rest
That e'er wrote; me noo in like case?

Great poets hardly onybody kens o'?
Geniuses like a man talkin' t'm sel'?
Nonsense! They're nocht o' the sort
Their character's easy to tell.

They're nocht but romantic rebels
Strikin' dilletante poses;
Trotsky—Christ, no' wi' a croon o' thorns
But a wreath o' paper roses.

A' that's great is free and expansive.
What ha' they expanded tae?
They've affected nocht but a fringe
O' mankind in ony way.

Barbarian saviour o' civilization
Hoo weel ye kent (we're owre dull witted)
Naething is dune save as we ha'e
Means to en's transparently fitted.

Poetry like politics maun cut
The cackle and pursue real ends,
Unerringly as Lenin, and to that
Its nature better tends.

Wi' Lenin's vision equal poet's gift
And what unparalleled force was there!
Nocht in a' literature wi' that
Begins to compare.

Nae simple rhymes for silly folk
But the haill art, as Lenin gied

Nae Marx-without-tears to workin' men
But the fu' course insteed.

Organic constructional work,
Practicality, and work by degrees;
First things first; and poetry in turn
'll be built by these.

You saw it faur off when you thocht
O' mass-education yet.
Hoo lang till they rise to Pushkin?
And that's but a fit!

Oh, it's nonsense, nonsense, nonsense,
Nonsense at this time o' day
That breid-and-butter problems
S'ud be in ony man's way.

They s'ud be like the tails we tint
On leavin' the monkey stage;
A' maist folk fash aboot's alike
Primaeval to oor age.

We're grown-ups that haena yet
Put bairnly things aside
—A' that's material and moral—
And oor new state descried.

Sport, love, and parentage,
Trade, politics, and law
S'ud be nae mair to us than braith
We hardly ken we draw.

Freein' oor poo'ers for greater things,
And fegs there's plenty o' them,
Tho' wha's still trammelt in alow
Canna be tenty o' them—

In the meantime Montéhus' sangs—
But as you were ready to tine

The Russian Revolution to the German
Gin that ser'd better syne,

Or foresaw that Russia maun lead
The workers' cause, and then
Pass the lead elsewhere, and aiblins
Fa' faur backward again,

Sae here, twixt poetry and politics,
There's nae doot in the en'.
Poetry includes that and s'ud be
The greatest poo'er amang men.

—It's the greatest, *in posse* at least,
That men ha'e discovered yet
Tho' nae doot they're unconscious still
O' ithers faur greater than it.

You confined yoursel' to your work
—A step at a time;
But, as the loon is in the man,
That'll be ta'en up i' the rhyme,

Ta'en up like a pool in the sands
Aince the tide rows in,
When life opens its hert and sings
Withoot scrupe or sin.

Your knowledge in your ain sphere
Was exact and complete
But your sphere's elementary and sune by
As a poet maun see't.

For a poet maun see in a'thing,
Ev'n what looks trumpery or horrid,
A subject equal to ony
—A star for the forehead!

A poet has nae choice left
Betwixt Beaverbrook, say, and God.

Jimmy Thomas or you,
A cat, carnation, or clod.

He daurna turn awa' frae ocht
For a single act o' neglect
And straucht he may fa' frae grace
And be void o' effect.

Disinterestedness,
Oor profoundest word yet,
But how far yont even that
The sense o' onything's set!

The inward necessity yont
Ony laws o' cause
The intellect conceives
That a'thing has!

Freend, foe; past, present, future;
Success, failure; joy, fear;
Life, Death; and a'thing else,
For us, are equal here.

Male, female; quick or deid,
Let us fike nae mair;
The deep line o'cleavage
Disna lie there.

Black in the pit the miner is,
The shepherd reid on the hill,
And I'm wi' them baith until
The end of mankind, I wis.

Whatever their jobs a' men are ane
In life, and syne in daith
(Tho' it's sma' patience I can ha'e
Wi' life's ideas o' that by the way)
And he's nae poet but kens it, faith,
And ony job but the hardest's ta'en.

The sailor gangs owre the curve o' the sea,
The hoosewife's thrang in the wash-tub,
And whatna rhyme can I find but hub,
And what else can poetry be?

The core o' a' activity,
Changin't in accordance wi'
Its inward necessity
And mede o' integrity.

Unremittin', relentless,
Organized to the last degree,
Ah, Lenin, politics is bairns' play
To what this maun be!

From *In Memoriam James Joyce*

'The world is fast bound in the snares of Varuna'

The world is fast bound in the snares of Varuna
—'Cords consisting of serpents', according to Kulluka
(Pasaih sarpa-rajjughih). The winkings of men's eyes
Are all numbered by him; he wields the universe
As gamesters handle dice. These are the unexampled days
of false witness—a barbarous régime which gives power over life and death
To an oligarchy of brigands and adventurers,
Without security from vexation by irresponsible tyrants,
Without protection of the home against the aggression of criminal bands,
Without impartial justice, without dignity.
We are denied all the deepest needs of men who do not wish
To sink to the level of the beasts—condemned
To a life deprived of its salt.

Already, everywhere,
The speed-up, the 'church work,' the lead poisoning,

58720

LIBRARY
College of St. Francis
JOLIET, ILL.

The strain that drives men nuts.
The art of teaching fish by slow degrees
To live without water.
Men cheaper than safety
—Human relations have never sunk so low.
'The meaninglessness of the individual
Apart from his communal framework,'
The men in power who are worth no more
Than an equal number of cockroaches,
Unconcerned about values,
Indifferent to human quality
Or jealous and implacably hostile to it,
Full of the tyranny of coarse minds and degraded souls;
The abominable clap-trap and politicians' rhetoric,
The tawdry talk about the 'King' and 'the King's lieges'
And 'the Government' and 'the British people';
The concentration camps, the cat o' nine tails,
The law more lawless than any criminal,
The beatings-up by the police,
The countless thuggeries of Jacks-in-office,
The vile society woman, infernal parasites,
The endless sadism, Gorilla-rule,
The live men hanging in the plaza
With butcher's hooks through their jaws
—And everywhere the worship of 'efficiency,'

Of whatever 'works' no matter to what ends,
The general feeling that if a thing
'Runs like a machine' it is all right
—That there can be no higher praise;
Mechanical authoritarianism,
A Lord Lloyd thinking 'the whole method of conference
Adverse to efficient government'
—Those (as Leonard Woolf has said)
Who question the authority of the machine,
Who claim the right to do what they want
And to be governed by themselves,
Condemned as rebels and extremists
Against whose claims to freedom of soul
It is the primary duty of all loyal citizens

26

To vindicate the machinery of law and order
—Against the claims of
Aminu Kano in Nigeria,
Cheddi Jagan in 'British' Guiana,
Liam Kelly and the Fianna Uladh in Northern Ireland.

But if, as could be, ninety per cent
Of human drudgery were abolished tomorrow
And the great masses of mankind given
Ample incomes and freed for 'higher things'
They could no more live than fish out of water,
They could not sustain life on that level
—On any level worthy of Man at all.

The ancestors of oysters and barnacles had heads.
Snakes have lost their limbs
And ostriches and penguins their power of flight.
Man may just as easily lose his intelligence.
Most of our people already have.

It is unlikely that man will develop into anything higher.
Unless he desires to and is prepared to pay the cost.
Otherwise we shall go the way of the dodo and the kiwi.
Already that process seems far advanced.
Genius is becoming rarer,
Our bodies a little weaker in each generation,
Culture is slowly declining,
Mankind is returning to barbarism
And will finally become extinct.

Esplumeoir

'It was an amazing discovery, like the inside of your head
being painlessly scraped out. There was an amazing clarity,
like the brilliant moon falling into it and filling it neatly.'

'The utter stillness o' the timeless world,'
The haill creation has vanished forever
Wi nae mair noise or disturbance than a movie fade-out.

Naething to see—you sudna ha'e far to gang
For an analogy frae your Earth experience tho'.
Sin' at winter's edge when a'thing's gane sere
Toomed o' a' Simmer's routh and bare as a bane gey near
Bacteriologists say the soil's teemin' mair thrang
Wi' life than at any ither time, wi' nocht to show.

'Aloof as a politician
The first year efter election,'
You grumble, 'There's naething to see.'

It's a' expressionless as tho' it micht be
Enamelled wi' an airbrush yon tawnish grey
Nae colour sae common on motors—was't only yesterday?—
Yet bright as when the stars were glowin'
Wi' sic a steady radiance that the lift
Seemed fu' to owreflowin'. I wadna hae't in a gift.
It mak's me feel upon my word
Like a fly on the edge of a phonograph record.'
(A phrase divertin'ly *vergeistigt* here!)

Eternity is like an auld green parrot
I kent aince. Its conversational range was sma'
Yet when it tilted its heid and cocked
A beady eye at you, you got the feelin'
That, gin it but chose, it could tell you a thing or twa;
That, as the French pit it,
Il connut le dessous des cartes.

Or like cricket's deceptive impression o' slowness
Tho' the split second decisions sae often required
Ha'e to be made quicker than in ony ither game;
Or as a day that was ga'en to be
Oppressively het wi' thunder later
Used to egg-on a'thing to live
Brimmin'ly afore the cataclysm.
Till a'thing that ran or flew or crawled
Abune or alow was filled pang-fu' wi' life
Like yon cicada shrillin' piercin'ly

Ettlin' to stert up the haill chorus.
He'd been undergrund an 'oor ago
And micht be doon a bird's throat by nicht.
That he was alive richt then was reason eneuch
For singin' wi' a' his micht.

Eternity's like that—a'thing keyed up
To the heichest pitch as if
A cataclysm's comin'—only it's no'!

Or pit it like this—Eternity
Is twa doors in frae the corner a'where,
A sma', demure, white buildin'
Wi' shutters and a canopy.
The canopy is royal blue
And it says *Eternity*
In discreet soap-glass letters

On ilka side. Under the canopy
You walk up and the front door
Is a' mirror wi' a cool strip
O' fluorescent licht on top.

You push the pearl button
And listen to the delicate chimes
And adjust your tie in the mirror
And fix your hat—but the guy
Ahint the bullet-proof mirror
Sees a' that tae,
Only you canna see him.

The guy ahint the mirror
Is Tutti-Frutti-Forgle,
A muckle nigger wi' fuzzy-white hair
Wha kens his business.
Aince past Tutti you check your hat
In a quiet soft-lit anteroom.
And the haill place is yours.

Diamond Body

In a cave of the sea

What after all do we know of this terrible 'matter'
Save as a name for the unknown and hypothetical cause
Of states of our own consciousness? There are not two worlds,
A world of nature, and a world of human consciousness,
Standing over against one another, but one world of nature
Whereof human consciousness is an evolution,
I reminded myself again as I caught that sudden breathless glimps
Under my microscope, of unexpected beauty and dynamic living
In the world of life on a sliver of kelp
Quite as much as the harpooning of a forty-two foot whale shark.

Because, I reminded myself, any assemblage of things
Is for the sake of another, and because of
The existence of active exertion
For the sake of abstraction,
In like manner, as Gaudapada says,
As a bed, which is an assemblage
Of bedding, props, cotton, coverlet, and pillows
Is for another's use, not for its own
And its several component parts
Render no mutual service,
Thence it is concluded that there is a man
Who sleeps upon the bed
And for whose sake it was made
So this world, which is an assemblage
Of the five elements is for another's use,
And there is another for whose enjoyment
This enjoyable body of mine,
Consisting of intellect and all the rest,
Has been produced.

And all I see and delight in now
Has been produced for him—
The sand-burrowing sea urchins with shells
Delicate as those of hen's eggs,
Burrowing by movements of long backwardly-directed spines;

And the burrowing star-fish which settle into the sand
By rows of pointed 'tube feet',
Operated by hydraulic pressure,
On the under-side of each of the five arms;
And the smooth-bodied sand eels and the shrimps
And sea-weeds attached by broad hold-fasts
—Not roots!—to the rocks or boulders,
Brown masses a host of small animals
Grow on or shelter amongst, protected here
From the buffeting of the sea when the tide is in
Or kept moist under the damp weight of weed
When the tide is out. And high up the shore
The limpets wandering about
Grazing on fine encrusting weeds,
And the acorn barnacles, the dog-whelks
Grey-shelled unless they have mussels to feed on
When the change of diet puts brown bands on the shells;

And, in a rock pool, 'crumb of bread' sponge,
Hydroids red, green, purple, or richly patterned
Like the dahlia anemone, yellow sea-lemon, and now and again
A rapidly moving snail shell which shows me
It is inhabited by a hermit crab
Much more active than its original occupant.
Countless millions of creatures each essential
To that other, and precisely fashioned
In every detail to meet his requirements.
Millions upon millions of them
Hardly discernible here
In the brilliant light in which sea and sky
Can hardly be distinguished from each other
—And I know there are billions more
Too small for a man to see
Even though human life were long enough
To see them all, a process that can hardly
Be even begun.
Our minds already sense that the fabric of nature's laws
Conceals something that lies behind it,
A greater-unity.—We are beginning more and more
To see behind them something they conceal

31

For the most part cunningly
With their outward appearances,
By hoodwinking man with a façade
Quite different from what it actually covers.
I am convinced that behind this too
There is another and many more.
Today we are breaking up the chaste
Ever-deceptive phenomena of Nature
And reassembling them according to our will.
We look through matter, and the day is not far distant
When we shall be able to cleave
Through her oscillating mass as if it were air.
Matter is something which man still
At most tolerates, but does not recognise.
Here in the brilliant light, where the mandala is almost complete,
The circumference of a blinding diamond broken
Only by a few points and dashes of darkness yet,
The shapes and figures created by the fire of the spirit
Are only empty forms and colours. It is not necessary to confuse
The dull glow of such figures with the pure white light
Of the divine body of truth, nor to project
The light of the highest consciousness into concretized figures,
But to have the consciousness withdrawn, as if
To some sphere beyond the world where it is
At once empty and not empty,
The centre of gravity of the whole personality
Transferred from the conscious centre of the ego
To a sort of hypothetical point
Between the conscious and the unconscious,
The complete abolition of the original
Undifferentiated state of subject and object;
Thus through the certainty that *something lives through me
Rather than I myself live*
A man bridges the gap between instinct and spirit,
And takes hold upon life, attacks life,
In a more profound sense than before.
In the reconciliation of the differentiated
And the inferior function, the 'great Tao
—The meaning of the world' is discovered.

Crossing the island I see the tail of my coat
Wave back and forth and know
It is the waves of the sea on my beach.
And now I am in the cave. A moment ago
I saw the broad leather-brown belts of the tangleweed,
And the minute forms that fix themselves
In soft carmine lace-stencils upon the shingle,
The notched wrack gemmed with lime-white bead-shells
Showing like pearls on a dark braid,
And minute life in a million forms.
And I saw the tide come crawling
Through the rocky labyrinths of approach
With flux and reflux—making inch upon inch
In an almost imperceptible progress.
But now I know it is the earth
And not the water that is unstable,
For at every rise and fall of the pellucid tide
It seems as though it were the shingle

And the waving forest of sea-growth
That moves—and not the water!
And, after all, there is no illusion,
But seeming deception prefigures truth,
For it is a matter of physiographical knowledge
That in the long passages of time
The water remains—and the land ebbs and flows.

I have achieved the diamond body.

BASIL BUNTING

Vestiges

I

Salt grass silent of hooves, the lake stinks,
we take a few small fish from the streams,
our children are scabby, chivvied by flies,
we cannot read the tombs in the eastern prairie,
          who slew the Franks, who
          swam the Yellow River.

The lice have left Temuchin's tent. His ghost
cries under north wind, having spent
strength in life: life lost, lacks means of death,
voice-tost; the horde indistinguishable;
worn name weak in fool's jaws.

We built no temples. Our cities' woven hair
mildewed and frayed. Records of Islam and Chin,
battles, swift riders, ambush,
tale of the slain, and the name Jengiz.

Wild geese of Yen, peacocks of the Windy Shore.
Tall Chutsai sat under the phoenix tree.
—That Baghdad banker contracts to
double the revenue, him collecting.
Four times might be exacted, but
such taxation impoverishes the people.

No litigation. The laws were simple.

II

Jengiz to Chang Chun: China
is fat, but I am lean

eating soldier's food,
lacking learning.
In seven years
I brought most of the world under one law.
The Lords of Cathay
hesitate and fall.
Amidst these disorders
I distrust my talents.
To cross a river
boats and rudders,
to keep the empire in order
poets and sages,
but I have not found nine for a cabinet,
not three.
I have fasted and washed. Come.

Chang: I am old
not wise nor virtuous,
nor likely to be much use.
My appearance is parched, my body weak.
I set out at once.

And to Liu Chung Lu, Jengiz:
Get an escort and a good cart,
and the girls can be sent on
separately if he insists.

What the chairman told Tom

Poetry? It's a hobby.
I run model trains.
Mr Shaw there breeds pigeons.

It's not work. You don't sweat.
Nobody pays for it.
You *could* advertise soap.

Art, that's opera; or repertory—
The Desert Song.
Nancy was in the chorus.

But to ask for twelve pounds a week—
married, aren't you?—
you've got a nerve.

How could I look a bus conductor
in the face
if I paid you twelve pounds?

Who says it's poetry, anyhow?
My ten year old
can do it *and* rhyme.

I get three thousand and expenses,
a car, vouchers,
but I'm an accountant.

They do what I tell them,
my company.
What do *you* do?

Nasty little words, nasty long words,
it's unhealthy.
I want to wash when I meet a poet.

They're Reds, addicts,
all delinquents.
What you write is rot.

Mr Hines says so, and he's a schoolteacher,
he ought to know.
Go and find *work*.

from *Briggflatts*

I

Brag, sweet tenor bull,
descant on Rawthey's madrigal,
each pebble its part
for the fells' late spring.
Dance tiptoe, bull,
black against may.
Ridiculous and lovely
chase hurdling shadows
morning into noon.
May on the bull's hide
and through the dale
furrows fill with may,
paving the slowworm's way.

A mason times his mallet
to a lark's twitter,
listening while the marble rests,
lays his rule
at a letter's edge,
fingertips checking,
till the stone spells a name
naming none,
a man abolished.
Painful lark, labouring to rise!
The solemn mallet says:
In the grave's slot
he lies. We rot.

Decay thrusts the blade,
wheat stands in excrement
trembling. Rawthey trembles.
Tongue stumbles, ears err
for fear of spring.
Rub the stone with sand,
wet sandstone rending

roughness away. Fingers
ache on the rubbing stone.
The mason says: Rocks
happen by chance.
No one here bolts the door,
love is so sore.

Her pulse their pace,
palm countering palm,
till a trench is filled,
stone white as cheese
jeers at the dale.
Knotty wood, hard to rive,
smoulders to ash;
smell of October apples.
The road again,
at a trot.
Wetter, warmed, they watch
the mason meditate
on name and date.

Rain rinses the road,
the bull streams and laments.
Sour rye porridge from the hob
with cream and black tea,
meat, crust and crumb.
Her parents in bed
the children dry their clothes.
He has untied the tape
of her striped flannel drawers
before the range. Naked
on the pricked rag mat
his fingers comb
thatch of his manhood's home.

Gentle generous voices weave
over bare night
words to confirm and delight
till bird dawn.
Rainwater from the butt

she fetches and flannel
to wash him inch by inch,
kissing the pebbles.
Shining slowworm part of the marvel.
The mason stirs:
Words!
Pens are too light.
Take a chisel to write.

Stone smooth as skin,
cold as the dead they load
on a low lorry by night.
The moon sits on the fell
but it will rain.
Under sacks on the stone
two children lie,
hear the horse stale,
the mason whistle,
harness mutter to shaft,
felloe to axle squeak,
rut thud the rim,
crushed grit.

Stocking to stocking, jersey to jersey,
head to a hard arm,
they kiss under the rain,
bruised by their marble bed.
In Garsdale, dawn;
at Hawes, tea from the can.
Rain stops, sacks
steam in the sun, they sit up.
Copper-wire moustache,
sea-reflecting eyes
and Baltic plainsong speech
declare: By such rocks
men killed Bloodaxe.

Fierce blood throbs in his tongue,
lean words.
Skulls cropped for steel caps

huddle round Stainmore.
Their becks ring on limestone,
whisper to peat.
The clogged cart pushes the horse downhill.
In such soft air
they trudge and sing,
laying the tune frankly on the air.
All sounds fall still,
fellside bleat,
hide-and-seek peewit.

Every birth a crime,
every sentence life.
Wiped of mould and mites
would the ball run true?
No hope of going back.
Hounds falter and stray,
shame deflects the pen.
Love murdered neither bleeds nor stifles
but jogs the draftsman's elbow.
What can he, changed, tell
her, changed, perhaps dead?
Delight dwindles. Blame
stays the same.

Brief words are hard to find,
shapes to carve and discard:
Bloodaxe, king of York,
king of Dublin, king of Orkney.
Take no notice of tears;
letter the stone to stand
over love laid aside lest
insufferable happiness impede
flight to Stainmore,
to trace
lark, mallet,
becks, flocks
and axe knocks.

Dung will not soil the slowworm's
mosaic. Breathless lark
drops to nest in sodden trash;
Rawthey truculent, dingy.
Drudge at the mallet, the may is down,
fog on fells. Guilty of spring
and spring's ending
amputated years ache after
the bull is beef, love a convenience.
It is easier to die than to remember.
Name and date
split in soft slate
a few months obliterate.

Coda

A strong song tows
us, long earsick.
Blind, we follow
rain slant, spray flick
to fields we do not know.

Night, float us.
Offshore wind, shout,
ask the sea
what's lost, what's left,
what horn sunk,
what crown adrift.
Where we are who knows
of kings who sup
while day fails? Who,
swinging his axe
to fell kings, guesses
where we go?

Chomei at Toyama

(Kamo-no-Chomei, born at Kamo 1154, *died at Toyama on
Mount Hino,* 24*th June* 1216)

Swirl sleeping in the waterfall!
On motionless pools scum appearing
                    disappearing!

Eaves formal on the zenith,
lofty city Kyoto,
wealthy, without antiquities!

Housebreakers clamber about,
builders raising floor upon floor
at the corner sites, replacing
gardens by bungalows.

In the town where I was known
the young men stare at me.
A few faces I know remain.

Whence comes man at his birth? or where
does death lead him? Whom do you mourn?
Whose steps wake your delight?
Dewy hibiscus dries: though dew
outlast the petals.

I have been noting events forty years.
On the twentyseventh May eleven hundred
and seventyseven, eight p.m., fire broke out
at the corner of Tomi and Higuchi streets.
In a night
palace, ministries, university, parliament
were destroyed. As the wind veered
flames spread out in the shape of an open fan.
Tongues torn by gusts stretched and leapt.
In the sky clouds of cinders lit red with the blaze.

Some choked, some burned, some barely escaped.
Sixteen great officials lost houses and
very many poor. A third of the city burned;
several thousands died; and of beasts,
limitless numbers.

Men are fools to invest in real estate.

Three years less three days later a wind
starting near the outer boulevard
broke a path a quarter mile across
to Sixth Avenue.
Not a house stood. Some were felled whole,
some in splinters; some had left
great beams upright in the ground
and round about
lay rooves scattered where the wind flung them.
Flocks of furniture in the air,
everything flat fluttered like dead leaves.
A dust like fog or smoke,
you could hear nothing for the roar,
            bufera infernal!
Lamed some, wounded some.
This cyclone turned southwest.

Massacre without cause.

Portent?

The same year thunderbolted change of capital,
fixed here, Kyoto, for ages.
Nothing compelled the change nor was it an easy matter
but the grumbling was disproportionate.
We moved, those with jobs
or wanting jobs or hangers on of the rest,
in haste haste fretting to be the first.
Rooftrees overhanging empty rooms;
dismounted: floating down the river.
The soil returned to heath.

43

I visited the new site: narrow and too uneven,
cliffs and marshes, deafening shores, perpetual strong winds;
the palace a logcabin dumped amongst the hills
(yet not altogether inelegant).
There was no flat place for houses, many vacant lots,
the former capital wrecked, the new a camp,
and thoughts like clouds changing, frayed by a breath:
peasants bewailing lost land, newcomers aghast at prices.
No one in uniform: the crowds
resembled demobilized conscripts.

There were murmurs. Time defined them.
In the winter the decree was rescinded,
we returned to Kyoto;
but the houses were gone and none
could afford to rebuild them.

I have heard of a time when kings beneath bark rooves
watched chimneys.
When smoke was scarce, taxes were remitted.

To appreciate present conditions
collate them with those of antiquity.

Drought, floods, and a dearth. Two fruitless autumns.
Empty markets, swarms of beggars. Jewels
sold for a handful of rice. Dead stank
on the curb, lay so thick on
Riverside Drive a car couldn't pass.
The pest bred.
That winter my fuel was the walls of my own house.

Fathers fed their children and died,
babies died sucking the dead.
The priest Hoshi went about marking their foreheads
A, Amida, their requiem;
he counted them in the East End in the last two months,
fortythree thousand A's.

Crack, rush, ye mountains, bury your rills!
Spread your green glass, ocean, over the meadows!

Scream, avalanche, boulders amok, strangle the dale!
O ships in the sea's power, O horses
on shifting roads, in the earth's power, without hoofhold!

This is the earthquake, this was
the great earthquake of Genryaku!

The chapel fell, the abbey, the minster and the small shrines
fell, their dust rose and a thunder of houses falling.
O to be birds and fly or dragons and ride on a cloud!
The earthquake, the great earthquake of Genryaku!

A child building a mud house against a high wall:
I saw him crushed suddenly, his eyes hung
from their orbits like two tassels.
His father howled shamelessly—an officer.
I was not abashed at his crying.

Such shocks continued three weeks; then lessening,
but still a score daily as big as an average earthquake;
then fewer, alternate days, a tertian ague of tremors.
There is no record of any greater.
It caused a religious revival.
Months . . .
Years . . .
. . . .
Nobody mentions it now.

This is the unstable world and
we in it unstable and our houses.
A poor man living amongst the rich
gives no rowdy parties, doesnt sing.
Dare he keep his child at home, keep a dog?
He dare not pity himself above a whimper.

But he visits, he flatters, he is put in his place,
he remembers the patch on his trousers.
His wife and sons despise him for being poor.
He has no peace.

If he lives in an alley of rotting frame houses
he dreads a fire.
If he commutes he loses his time
and leaves his house daily to be plundered by gunmen.

The bureaucrats are avaricious.
He who has no relatives in the Inland Revenue,
poor devil!

Whoever helps him enslaves him
and follows him crying out: *Gratitude!*
If he wants success he is wretched.
If he doesnt he passes for mad.

Where shall I settle, what trade choose
that the mind may practise, the body rest?

My grandmother left me a house
but I was always away
for my health and becase I was alone there.
When I was thirty I couldnt stand it any longer,
I built a house to suit myself:
one bamboo room, you would have thought it a cartshed,
poor shelter from snow or wind.
It stood on the flood plain. And that quarter
is also flooded with gangsters.

One generation
I saddened myself with idealistic philosophies,
but before I was fifty
I perceived there was no time to lose,
left home and conversation.
Among the cloudy mountains of Ohara
spring and autumn, spring and autumn, spring and autumn,
emptier than ever.

The dew evaporates from my sixty years,
I have built my last house, or hovel,
a hunter's bivouac, an old
silkworm's cocoon:

46

ten feet by ten, seven high: and I,
reckoning it a lodging not a dwelling,
omitted the usual foundation ceremony.
I have filled the frames with clay,
set hinges at the corners:
easy to take it down and carry it away
when I get bored with this place.
Two barrowloads of junk
and the cost of a man to shove the barrow,
no trouble at all.

Since I have trodden Hino mountain
noon has beaten through the awning
over my bamboo balcony, evening
shone on Amida.
I have shelved my books above the window,
lute and mandolin near at hand,
piled bracken and a little straw for bedding,
a smooth desk where the light falls, stove for bramblewood.
I have gathered stones, fitted
stones for a cistern, laid bamboo
pipes. No woodstack,
wood enough in the thicket.

Toyama, snug in the creepers!
Toyama, deep in the dense gully, open
westward whence the dead ride out of Eden
squatting on blue clouds of wistaria.
(Its scent drifts west to Amida.)

Summer? Cuckoo's *Follow, follow*—to
harvest Purgatory hill!
Fall? The nightgrasshopper will
shrill *Fickle life!*
Snow will thicken on the doorstep,
melt like a drift of sins.
No friend to break silence,
no one will be shocked if I neglect the rite.
There's a Lent of commandments kept
where there's no way to break them.

A ripple of white water after a boat,
shining water after the boats Mansami saw
rowing at daybreak
at Okinoya.
Between the maple leaf and the caneflower
murmurs the afternoon—Po Lo-tien
saying goodbye on the verge of Jinyo river.
(I am playing scales on my mandolin.)

Be limber, my fingers, I am going to play *Autumn Wind*
to the pines, I am going to play *Hastening Brook*
to the water. I am no player
but there's nobody listening,
I do it for my own amusement.

Sixteen and sixty, I and the gamekeeper's boy,
one zest and equal, chewing tsubana buds,
one zest and equal, persimmon, pricklypear,
ears of sweetcorn pilfered from Valley Farm.

The view from the summit: sky bent over Kyoto,
picnic villages, Fushimi and Toba:
a very economical way of enjoying yourself.
Thought runs along the crest, climbs Sumiyama;
beyond Kasatori it visits the great church,
goes on pilgrimage to Ishiyama (no need to foot it!)
or the graves of poets, of Semimaru who said:

> *Somehow or other*
> *we scuttle through a lifetime.*
> *Somehow or other*
> *neither palace nor straw-hut*
> *is quite satisfactory.*

Not emptyhanded, with cherryblossom, with red maple
as the season gives it to decorate my Buddha
or offer a sprig at a time to chancecomers, home!

A fine moonlit night,
I sit at the window with a headful of old verses.

Whenever a monkey howls there are tears on my cuff.

Those are fireflies that seem
the fishermen's lights
off Maki island.

A shower at dawn
sings
like the hillbreeze in the leaves.

At the pheasant's chirr I recall
my father and mother uncertainly.

I rake my ashes.

                    Chattering fire,
soon kindled, soon burned out,
fit wife for an old man!

Neither closed in one landscape
nor in one season
the mind moving in illimitable
recollection.

I came here for a month
five years ago.
There's moss on the roof.

And I hear Soanso's dead
back in Kyoto.
I have as much room as I need.

I know myself and mankind.
· · · · · · ·
I don't want to be bothered.

(You will make me editor
of the Imperial Anthology?
I don't want to be bothered.)

You build for your wife, children,
cousins and cousins' cousins.
You want a house to entertain in.

A man like me can have neither servants nor friends
in the present state of society.
If I did not build for myself
for whom should I build?

Friends fancy a rich man's riches,
friends suck up to a man in high office.
If you keep straight you will have no friends
but catgut and blossom in season.

Servants weigh out their devotion
in proportion to their perquisites.

What do they care for peace and quiet?
There are more pickings in town.

I sweep my own floor
—less fuss.
I walk; I get tired
but do not have to worry about a horse.

My hands and feet will not loiter
when I am not looking.
I will not overwork them.
Besides, it's good for my health.

My jacket's wistaria flax,
my blanket hemp,
berries and young greens
my food.

(Let it be quite understood,
all this is merely personal.
I am not preaching the simple life
to those who enjoy being rich.)

I am shifting rivermist, not to be trusted.
I do not ask anything extraordinary of myself.
I like a nap after dinner
and to see the seasons come round in good order.

Hankering, vexation and apathy,
that's the run of the world.
Hankering, vexation and apathy,
keeping a carriage wont cure it.

Keeping a man in livery
wont cure it. Keeping a private fortress
wont cure it. These things satisfy no craving,
Hankering, vexation and apathy . . .

I am out of place in the capital,
people take me for a beggar,
as you would be out of place in this sort of life,
you are so — I regret it — so welded to your vulgarity.

The moonshadow merges with darkness
on the cliffpath,
a tricky turn near ahead.

Oh! There's nothing to complain about.
Buddha says: 'None of the world is good.'
I am fond of my hut . . .

I have renounced the world;
have a saintly
appearance.

I do not enjoy being poor,
I've a passionate nature.
My tongue
clacked a few prayers.

CHARLES TOMLINSON

Paring the apple

There are portraits and still-lives.

And there is paring the apple.

And then? Paring it slowly,
From under cool-yellow
Cold-white emerging. And . . . ?

The spring of concentric peel
Unwinding off white,
The blade hidden, dividing.

There are portraits and still-lives
And the first, because "human"
Does not excell the second, and
Neither is less weighted
With a human gesture, than paring the apple
With a human stillness.

The cool blade
Severs between coolness, apple-rind
Compelling a recognition.

Observation of facts

Facts have no eyes. One must
Surprise them, as one surprises a tree
By regarding its (shall I say?)
Facets of copiousness.

The tree stands.

The house encloses.

The room flowers.

These are fact stripped of imagination:
Their relation is mutual.

A dryad is a sort of chintz curtain
Between myself and a tree.
The tree stands: or does not stand:
As I draw, or remove the curtain.

The house encloses: or fails to signify
As being bodied over against one,
As something one has to do with.

The room flowers once one has introduced
Mental fibre beneath its elegance,
A rough pot or two, outweighing
The persistence of frippery
In lampshades or wallpaper.

Style speaks what was seen,
Or it conceals the observation
Behind the observer: a voice
Wearing a ruff.

Those facets of copiousness which I proposed
Exist, do so when we have silenced ourselves.

Up at La Serra

THE shadow
       ran before it lengthening
              and a wave went over.
Distance
       did not obscure
              the machine of nature:
you could watch it
       squander and recompose itself
              all day, the shadow-run
the sway of the necessity down there
       at the cliff-base
              crushing white from blue.
Come in
       by the arch
              under the campanile parrocchiale
and the exasperation of the water
       followed you,
              its *Soldi, soldi*
unpicking the hill-top peace
       insistently.
              He knew, at twenty
all the deprivations such a place
       stored for the man
              who had no more to offer
than a sheaf of verse
       in the style of Quasimodo.
              Came the moment,
he would tell it
       in a poem
              without rancour, a lucid
testament above his name
       Paolo
              Bertolani
—*Ciao, Paolo!*
       —*Ciao*
              Giorgino!

He would put them
        all in it—
                Giorgino going
over the hill
        to look for labour;
                the grinder
of knives and scissors
        waiting to come up, until
                someone would hoist his wheel
on to a back, already
        hooped to take it,
                so you thought
the weight must crack
        the curvature. And then:
                Beppino and Beppino
friends
        who had in common
                nothing except their names and friendship;
and the sister of the one
        who played the accordion
                and under all
the *Soldi, soldi,*
        sacra conversazione
                del mare—
della madre.
        Sometimes
                the men had an air of stupefaction:
La Madre:
        it was the women there
                won in a truceless enmity.
At home
        a sepia-green
                Madonna di Foligno
shared the wall
        with the October calendar—
                Lenin looked out of it,
Mao
        blessing the tractors
                and you told

the visitors:
>*We are not communists*
>>*although we call ourselves communists*
>*we are what you English*
>>*would call . . . socialists.*

He believed
that God was a hypothesis,
>that the party would bring in
>>a synthesis, that he
would edit the local paper for them,
>or perhaps
>>go northward to Milan;
or would he grow
>as the others had—son
>>to the putana-madonna
in the curse,
>chafed by the maternal knot and by
>>the dream of faithlessness,
uncalloused hands,
>lace, white
>>at the windows of the sailors' brothels
in the port five miles away?
>*Soldi—*
>>*soldi—*
some
>worked at the naval yards
>>and some, like him
were left between
>the time the olives turned
>>from green to black
and the harvest of the grapes,
>idle
>>except for hacking wood.
Those
>with an acre of good land
>>had vines, had wine
and self-respect. Some
>carried down crickets
>>to the garden of the mad Englishwoman

56

who could
     not
          tolerate
crickets, and they received
     soldi, soldi
          for recapturing them . . .
The construction
     continued as heretofore
          on the villa of the Milanese dentist
as the evening
     came in with news:
          —We have won
the election.
     —At the café
          the red flag is up.
He turned back
     quickly beneath the tower.
          Giorgino
who wanted to be a waiter
     wanted to be commissar
          piling *sassi*
into the dentist's wall.
     Even the harlot's mother
          who had not dared
come forth because her daughter
     had erred in giving birth,
          appeared by the *Trattoria della Pace.*
She did not enter
     the masculine precinct,
          listening there, her shadow
lengthened-out behind her
     black as the uniform of age
          she wore
on back and head.
     This was the Day
          which began all reckonings
she heard them say
     with a woman's ears;
          she liked

the music from the wireless.
    The padre
       pulled
at his unheeded angelus
     and the Day went down behind
       the town in the bay below
where—come the season—
    they would be preparing
      with striped umbrellas,
for the *stranieri* and *milanesi*—
    treason so readily compounded
      by the promiscuous stir
on the iridescent sliding water.
    He had sought
      the clear air of the cliff.
—*Salve, Giorgino*
    —*Salve*
     Paolo, have you
heard
    that we have won the election?
     —*I am writing*
a poem about it:
    it will begin
     here, with the cliff and with the sea
following its morning shadow in.

A death in the desert

in memory of Homer Vance

There are no crosses
on the Hopi graves. They lie
shallowly
under a scattering
of small boulders. They sky
over the desert

with its sand-grain stars
and the immense equality
between
desert and desert sky,
seem
a scope and ritual
enough to stem
death and to be its equal.

'Homer
is the name,' said
the old Hopi doll-maker.
I met him in summer. He was dead
when I came back that autumn.

He had sat
like an Olympian
in his cool room
on the rock-roof of the world,
beyond the snatch
of circumstance
and was to die
beating a burro out of his corn-patch.

And nobody climbs
the dry collapsing ledges
down to the place
to stand
in solitary, sharpened reflection
save for that swaying moon-face.

Somebody
finding nobody there
found gold also:
gold gone, he
(stark in his own redundancy)
must needs go too
and here, sun-warped
and riddled by moon, decays
his house which nobody occupies.

Las Trampas U.S.A.

for Robert and Priscilla Bunker

I go through hollyhocks
in a dry garden, up
to the house,
knock, then ask
in English for the key
to Las Trampas church.
The old woman
says in Spanish: I
do not speak English
so I say: Where
is the church key
in Spanish.
—You see those
three men working: you
ask them. She
goes in, I
go on
preparing to ask
them in Spanish:
Hi, they say
in American. Hello
I say and ask
them in English
where is the key
to the church and they
say: He has it
gesturing to a fourth
man working
hoeing a corn-field
nearby, and to him
(in Spanish): Where is
the church key? And he:
I have it.—O.K.

they say in
Spanish-American:
You bring it (and
to me in English)
He'll bring it. You
wait for him
by the church door.
Thank you, I say and they
reply in American
You're welcome. I go
once more and
await in shadow
the key: he
who brings it is not
he of the hoe, but
one of the three
men working, who
with a Castilian grace
ushers me in
to this place
of coolness out
of the August sun.

Mr. Brodsky

I had heard
before, of an
American who would have preferred
to be an Indian;
but not
until Mr. Brodsky, of one
whose professed and long
pondered-on passion
was to become a Scot,
who even sent for haggis and oatcakes
across continent.

Having read him
in Cambridge English
a verse or two
from MacDiarmid,
I was invited
to repeat the reading
before a Burns Night Gathering
where the Balmoral Pipers
of Albuquerque would
play in the haggis
out of its New York tin.
Of course, I said
No. No. I could *not* go
and then
half-regretted I had not been.
But to console
and cure the wish, came
Mr. Brodsky, bringing
his pipes and played
until the immense, distended
bladder of leather seemed
it could barely contain its water—
tears (idle
tears) for the bridal of Annie Laurie
and Morton J. Brodsky.
A bagpipe in a dwelling is
a resonant instrument
and there he stood
lost in the gorse
the heather or whatever
six thousand
miles and more
from the infection's source,
in our neo-New Mexican parlour
where I had heard
before of an
American who would have preferred
to be merely an Indian

Idyll

Washington Square, San Francisco

A door:
>PER L'UNIVERSO
>>is what it says

above it.
>You must approach
>>more nearly

(the statue
>of Benjamin Franklin watching you)
>>before you see

La Gloria di Colui
>*che tutto muove*
>>PER L'UNIVERSO

—leaning
>along the lintel—
>>*penetra e risplende*

across this church
>for Italian Catholics:
>>Dante

unscrolling in rhapsody.
>Cool
>>the January sun,

that with an intensity
>the presence of the sea
>>makes more exact,

chisels the verse with shade
>and lays
>>on the grass

a deep and even
>Californian green,
>>while a brilliance

throughout the square
>flatters the meanness of its architecture.
>>Beyond

there is the flood
>which skirts this pond
>>and tugs the ear

63

towards it: cars
          thick on the gradients of the city
               shift sun and sound—
a constant ground-bass
          to these provincialisms of the piazza
               tasting still
of Lerici and Genova.
          Here
               as there
the old men sit
          in a mingled odour
               of cheroot and garlic
spitting;
          they share serenity
               with the cross-legged
Chinese adolescent
          seated between them
               reading, and whose look
wears the tranquility of consciousness
          forgotten in its object—
               his book
bears for a title
          SUCCESS
               in spelling.
How
          does one spell out this
               che penetra e risplende
from square
          into the hill-side alley-ways
               around it, where
between tall houses
          children of the Mediterranean
               and Chinese element
mingle
          their American voices? . . .
          The dictionary
defines idyllium
          as meaning
               'a piece, descriptive

chiefly of rustic life';
  we
     are in town: here
let it signify
   this poised quiescence, pause
     and possibility in which
the music of the generations
   binds into its skein
     the flowing instant,
while the winter sun
   pursues the shadow
     before a church
whose decoration
   is a quotation from *Paradiso*.

TED HUGHES

October Dawn

OCTOBER is marigold, and yet
A glass half full of wine left out

To the dark heaven all night, by dawn
Has dreamed a premonition

Of ice across its eye as if
The ice-age had begun its heave.

The lawn overtrodden and strewn
From the night before, and the whistling green

Shrubbery are doomed. Ice
Has got its spearhead into place.

First a skin, delicately here
Restraining a ripple from the air,

Soon plate and rivet on pond and brook;
Then tons of chain and massive lock

To hold rivers. Then, sound by sight
Will Mammoth and Sabre-toothed celebrate

Reunion while a fist of cold
Squeezes the fire at the core of the world,

Squeezes the fire at the core of the heart,
And now it is about to start.

Pike

Pike, three inches long, perfect
Pike in all parts, green tigering the gold.
Killers from the egg: the malevolent aged grin.
They dance on the surface among the flies.

Or move, stunned by their own grandeur,
Over a bed of emerald, silhouette
Of submarine delicacy and horror,
A hundred feet long in their world.

In ponds, under the heat-struck lily pads—
Gloom of their stillness:
Logged on last year's black leaves, watching upwards.
Or hung in an amber cavern of weeds.

The jaws' hooked clamp and fangs
Not to be changed at this date;
A life subdued to its instrument;
The gills kneading quietly, and the pectorals.

Three we kept behind glass,
Jungled in weed: three inches, four,
And four and a half: fed fry to them—
Suddenly there were two. Finally one

With a sag belly and the grin it was born with.
And indeed they spare nobody.
Two, six pounds each, over two feet long,
High and dry and dead in the willow-herb—

One jammed past its gills down the other's gullet:
The outside eye stared: as a vice locks—
The same iron in this eye
Though its film shrank in death.

The pond I fished, fifty yards across,
Whose lilies and muscular tench

Had outlasted every visible stone
Of the monastery that planted them—

Stilled legendary depth:
It was as deep as England. It held
Pike too immense to stir, so immense and old
That past nightfall I dared not cast

But silently cast and fished
With the hair frozen on my head
For what might move, for what eye might move.
The still splashes on the dark pond,

Owls hushing the floating woods
Frail on my ear against the dream
Darkness beneath night's darkness had freed,
That rose slowly towards me, watching.

Thrushes

TERRIFYING are the attent sleek thrushes on the lawn,
More coiled steel than living—a poised
Dark deadly eye, those delicate legs
Triggered to stirrings beyond sense—with a start, a bounce, a stab
Overtake the instant and drag out some writhing thing.
No indolent procrastinations and no yawning stares,
No sighs or head-scratchings. Nothing but bounce and stab
And a ravening second.

Is it their single-mind-sized skulls, or a trained
Body, or genius, or a nestful of brats
Gives their days this bullet and automatic
Purpose? Mozart's brain had it, and the shark's mouth
That hungers down the blood-smell even to a leak of its own
Side and devouring of itself: efficiency which
Strikes too streamlined for any doubt to pluck at it
Or obstruction deflect.

With a man it is otherwise. Heroism on horseback,
Outstripping his desk-diary at a broad desk,
Carving at a tiny ivory ornament
For years: his act worships itself—while for him,
Though he bends to be blent in the prayer, how loud and above what
Furious spaces of fire do the distracting devils
Orgy and hosannah, under what wilderness
Of black silent water weep.

Ghost Crabs

At nightfall, as the sea darkens,
A depth darkness thickens, mustering from the gulfs and the
                                        submarine badlands,

To the sea's edge. To begin with
It looks like rocks uncovering, mangling their pallor.
Gradually the labouring of the tide
Falls back from its productions,
Its power slips back from glistening nacelles, and they are crabs.
Giant crabs, under flat skulls, staring inland
Like a packed trench of helmets.
Ghosts, they are ghost-crabs.
They emerge
An invisible disgorging of the sea's cold
Over the man who strolls along the sands.
They spill inland, into the smoking purple
Of our woods and towns—a bristling surge
Of tall and staggering spectres
Gliding like shocks through water.
Our walls, our bodies, are no problem to them.
Their hungers are homing elsewhere.
We cannot see them or turn our minds from them.
Their bubbling mouths, their eyes
In a slow mineral fury
Press through our nothingness where we sprawl on our beds,
Or sit in our rooms. Our dreams are ruffled maybe.

Or we jerk awake to the world of our possessions
With a gasp, in a sweat burst, brains jamming blind
Into the bulb-light. Sometimes, for minutes, a sliding
Staring
Thickness of silence
Presses between us. These crabs own this world.
All night, around us or through us,
They stalk each other, they fasten on to each other,
They mount each other, they tear each other to pieces,
They utterly exhaust each other.
They are the powers of this world.
We are their bacteria,
Dying their lives and living their deaths.
At dawn, they sidle back under the sea's edge.
They are the turmoil of history, the convulsion
In the roots of blood, in the cycles of concurrence.
To them, our cluttered countries are empty battleground.
All day they recuperate under the sea.
Their singing is like a thin sea-wind flexing in the rocks of a headland,
Where only crabs listen.

They are God's only toys.

Out

I
The dream time

My father sat in his chair recovering
From the four-year mastication by gunfire and mud,
Body buffeted wordless, estranged by long soaking
In the colours of mutilation.
                                    His outer perforations
Were valiantly healed, but he and the hearth-fire, its blood-flicker
On biscuit-bowl and piano and table-leg,
Moved into strong and stronger possession
Of minute after minute, as the clock's tiny cog

70

Laboured and on the thread of his listening
Dragged him bodily from under
The mortised four-year strata of dead Englishmen
He belonged with. He felt his limbs clearing
With every slight, gingerish movement. While I, small and four,
Lay on the carpet as his luckless double,
His memory's buried, immovable anchor,
Among jawbones and blown-off boots, tree-stumps, shellcases and craters,
Under rain that goes on drumming its rods and thickening
Its kingdom, which the sun has abandoned, and where nobody
Can ever again move from shelter.

II

The dead man in his cave beginning to sweat;
The melting bronze visor of flesh
Of the mother in the baby-furnace——
Nobody believes, it
Could be nothing, all
Undergo smiling at
The lulling of blood in
Their ears, their ears, their ears, their eyes
Are only drops of water and even the dead man suddenly
Sits up and sneezes—Atishoo!
Then the nurse wraps him up, smiling,
And, though faintly, the mother is smiling,
And it's just another baby.

As after being blasted to bits
The reassembled infantryman
Tentatively totters out, gazing around with the eyes
Of an exhausted clerk.

III
Remembrance Day

The poppy is a wound, the poppy is the mouth
Of the grave, maybe of the womb searching—

A canvas-beauty puppet on a wire
Today whoring everywhere. It is years since I wore one.

It is more years
The shrapnel that shattered my father's paybook

Gripped me, and all his dead
Gripped him to a time

He no more than they could outgrow, but, cast into one, like iron,

Hung deeper than refreshing of ploughs

In the woe-dark under my mother's eye—
One anchor
Holding my juvenile neck bowed to the dunkings of the Atlantic.
So goodbye to that bloody-minded flower.

You dead bury your dead.
Goodbye to the cenotaphs on my mother's breasts.

Goodbye to all the remaindered charms of my father's survival.
Let England close. Let the green sea-anemone close.

Pibroch

The sea cries with its meaningless voice
Treating alike its dead and its living,
Probably bored with the appearance of heaven
After so many millions of nights without sleep,
Without purpose, without self-deception.

Stone likewise. A pebble is imprisoned
Like nothing in the Universe.
Created for black sleep. Or growing
Conscious of the sun's red spot occasionally,
Then dreaming it is the foetus of God.

Over the stone rushes the wind
Able to mingle with nothing,
Like the hearing of the blind stone itself.
Or turns, as if the stone's mind came feeling
A fantasy of directions.

Drinking the sea and eating the rock
A tree struggles to make leaves——
An old woman fallen from space
Unprepared for these conditions.
She hangs on, because her mind's gone completely.

Minute after minute, aeon after aeon,
Nothing lets up or develops.
And this is neither a bad variant nor a tryout.
This is where the staring angels go through.
This is where all the stars bow down.

Wodwo

What am I? Nosing here, turning leaves over
Following a faint stain on the air to the river's edge
I enter water. What am I to split
The glassy grain of water looking upward I see the bed
Of the river above me upside down very clear
What am I doing here in mid-air? Why do I find
this frog so interesting as I inspect its most secret
interior and make it my own? Do these weeds
know me and name me to each other have they
seen me before, do I fit in their world? I seem
separate from the ground and not rooted but dropped
out of nothing casually I've no threads
fastening me to anything I can go anywhere
I seem to have been given the freedom
of this place what am I then? And picking
bits of bark off this rotten stump gives me
no pleasure and it's no use so why do I do it

me and doing that have coincided very queerly
But what shall I be called am I the first
have I an owner what shape am I what
shape am I am I huge if I go
to the end on this way past these trees and past these trees
till I get tired that's touching one wall of me
for the moment if I sit still how everything
stops to watch me I suppose I am the exact centre
but there's all this what is it roots
roots roots roots and here's the water
again very queer but I'll go on looking

CHRISTOPHER MIDDELTON

The thousand things

Dry vine leaves burn in an angle of the wall.
Dry vine leaves and a sheet of paper, overhung
by the green vine.
From an open grate in an angle of the wall
dry vine leaves and dead flies send smoke up
into the green vine where grape clusters go
ignored by lizards. Dry vine leaves
and a few dead flies on fire
and a Spanish toffee spat
into an angle of the wall
make a smell that calls to mind
the thousand things. Dead flies go,
paper curls and flares,
Spanish toffee sizzles and the smell
has soon gone over the wall.

A naked child jumps over the threshold,
waving a green spray of leaves of vine.

China shop vigil

Useful these bowls may be;
what fatness makes the hollows glow,
their shadows bossed and plump.

Precisely there a wheel whirling backward
flattens them. Knuckles whiten on copper:
headless men are hammering drums.

Cup and teapot may be such comforters:
small jaws mincing chatter
over the bad blood between us once.

When baking began, the air in jugs frothed
for milk, or lupins. Now mob is crushed
by mob, what fatness but in wild places,

where some half dozen dusty mindful men
drinking from gourd or canvas huddle,
and can speak at last of the good rain.

Five psalms of common man

'Je n'aime pas le dimanche'

1

Whisky whipping g-string Jaguar megaton
sometimes a 'purely rational human being'

it's me they tell of yonder sea devoid of amber
it's me they tell of column and haunting song

noncommittal me my mumble eaten
by the explosions of clocks and winds without routine

not fountains not millennia of light inextinguishable
ebbing through column and throat with its
    wombwombwomb

come my pet my demagogue excruciate me watching
yonder fountain douse the yolky dunes

2

THE creatures of coal have looked for you all over;
the creatures of tea heard a snatch of song, it was not you.

The creatures of smoke have looked for you all over;
the creatures of tar saw a tree, it was not you.

The hand was not you, nor the hairy ear;
the belly was not you, nor the anklebone.

The eyeball was not you. Tongue and teeth
and jawbone were not you. The creatures of hair

have looked for you all over; the creatures of snow
touched a locked door, it was not you.

The creatures of paper have looked for you all over;
the creatures of steel smelled thick wallets, it was not you.

These creatures wanted to be free to look for you;
and all the time you looked to be free of their want for you.

3

W. N. P. Barbellion (pseudonymous)
March 1915
sees 'on the top of an empty omnibus
a little heap of dirty used-up bus tickets
collected by chance in the corner'

felt sick
the number of persons
the number of miles
the number of buses

at all times
the number of voices
the number of voices not speaking to one another
perplexity without surprise

Avenues Madison Shaftesbury Opéra
the number of heart beats
without number

the sick one is he on whom his desire advances asking
      why
the sick one is he who has begun all over again
not waiting not
'waiting that hour which ripens to their doom'

he speaks (Adolf Eichmann April 1961)
'in starchy, clerkish language
full of abstractions
pedantry
euphemism'

4

My blind wife kicking in her flesh of flies.
My blind wife in her ring of ribs beating me flat.
But no shard of keg shall cool my last bones.

The flies were dancing in their ring.
Their ring was dancing in the flies.
The ring desired by the nature of flies.

Stomach eyes packing it all in tight.
Knotted wings kicking in a glue film.
Ghosted in glue was the nature of eyes.

Revolt severe if sieved for its ghost of motive.
Air without motive rubbing in the arid throat.
My blind wife I warm to the coolness of bones.

5

Order imagined against fear is not order.
Saith man. Fear imagined against order.
only negates or does not negate existing order.
Out of a rumbling of hollows an order is born
to negate another existing order of fear.

Nights broken before they end, interrupting
the millennia of my vigilance, saith man.

The nights of past time never slept to the end
re-enact themselves in the existing order of fear.

Another order of fear is chaos.
Images of chaos variously coordinated
by disparate imaginations accord or do not accord
to their seasons in time enacting the indeterminations.
The orders revolve in the ring or do not evolve.

The orders revolve as improvisations against fear,
changed images of chaos. Without fear, nothing.
Let me, saith man, take another look at the sea again.
And in his ear begin the rumblings of keels again.

January 1919

What if I know, Liebknecht, who shot you dead.
Tiergarten trees unroll
staggering shadow, in spite of it all.
I am among the leaves; the inevitable
voices
have left nothing to say, the holed head
bleeding across a heap of progressive magazines;
torn from your face,
trees that turned around,
we do not sanctify the land with our wandering.
Look upon our children, they are mutilated.

Young woman in apathy

Something, the sandwich and the coffee—
but her look (if you knew) could blind. Soon
something may crack inside it—listen:

over her cup, still as desolate, the misty
ovals make nothing of her trees and men; unholed
ice, and she shooting under the ice out of no-

where; no star (to feed on sandwich), not
a faint star, even, who'll sneak into
averted vision—caryatid!—

what in all the world is company? what is it?
Blood bawling its lies back at an impromptu 'O
I am so unhappy,' or some such? Even 'it's

me' pretends, fools
no one, lets
go the least sound

collapsing the pediment,
and she—suffocated in a heap
under her stone gods.

Disturbing the tarantula

The door a maze
of shadow, peach leaves
veining its wood colour,

and cobwebs broken
breathing ah ah
as it is pushed open—

two hands
at a ladder shook
free the tarantula, it slid

black and fizzing to a rung
above eye-level,
knees jack knives,

a high-jumper's, bat mouth
slit grinning
into the fur belly—

helpful: peaches
out there, they keep growing
rounder and rounder

on branches wheeled low
by their weight over
roasted grass blades; sun

and moon, also, evolve
round this mountain
terrace, wrinkling now

with deadly green
emotion: All things
are here, monstrous convulsed

rose (don't anyone
dare come), sounding through
our caves, I hear them.

Poem written after contemplating the adverb 'primarily'

This is the room. Those windows
admit swift revolutions
of sunlight, moonlight. So swift they form
the mass. That is the smell. With a spoon
we could not stir it.

The room is called the hub. Hub. There he goes
—those points all equidistant from the churning
(where the darkness
leans all around the wheel, see?)—
the assistant. What he does

we describe as bearding. Notice
his routine. Incessant
innumerable
ingenious ploys hazarded
to attenuate the light (or what

could we be inhabiting?). It is
the same
in each room.
There are many rooms. Each called
the hub.

You should be there when the master comes.
He strides through the thudding diameters.
He reaches the assistant.
He floors the assistant with one blow.
Out he goes again, wearing his old grin.

The assistants are
changed. And the master. The master
with a little
less
frequency.

Octobers

They watch the big vats bubbling over.
They walk forward, fists dig
into hip bags and sweep in silver arcs
the seed. They put ready
files that will rush from room
to room when the crisis breaks.

They rake the pear leaves into piles
on lawns. Among square mounds
of air bricks they prepare foundations.
They return, with faint tans, to renew

their season tickets. They are giving
again the first of last year's lectures.

They remember Spring. It is the walk
of a woman otherwise quite forgotten.
Wondering if it is for the last time,
they drive through the red forests.
They control the conference tables
with promises of mutual destruction.

They put the cat out with unusual caution.
They clean the flues. They fall
flat on their tough backs off mustangs.
They visit the rice and the apple barns.
They man the devices with fresh crews.
They like the o in the middle of the name.

The Historian

Things might not be so bad if I did not always have to write it in a hurry.
The historian, after all, should move at a leisurely pace among the objects
of his investigation, as a dog might, in a forest of lamp-posts, a lucid dog,
that is, one who knows the pleasure of dragging pleasure out. What a
magical forest this history has been, even then: first I wrote the official
history of the trees, singly and in their concert, the wars, laws, public
achievements and transactions, in the manner bequeathed to me by my
illustrious forebears. Then, as my hours of sleep grew shorter, with
anxiety more than with age, I set about writing the Secret History, at
night, as I have indicated, when the servants were asleep in the cellars,
only a few shouts in the street below, but still in fear of that man in the
black raincoat, belted and hatted, who would one night appear in my
doorway and ask, with his smile: "Working late again, Procopius?"—
and then I would have no time to stuff my papers under the flagstone
beside my littered, but not inhospitable, writing table.

What more can be said of that girl and the two valets whose tongues
were cut out, whose bodies were chopped into little pieces, packed into
sacks and dropped into the sea? What of the poet expelled from the

city, living now in the woods (with his second wife)—when he told the story of his friend's ludicrous funeral, the coffin too heavy, the factions struggling with flags and wreaths to claim the corpse as an advocate of their particular lies, was he laughing or crying?

I wrote the Histories in order to buy time for the writing of the Secret History. And the Secret History had to be told in a hurry; I cannot exist in this suspense for long, though it can be, for an old man, almost as exhilarating as an early love-affair, all the same. How two-faced one is, especially when facing oneself. The doctor says that I am ill. Yes. They said this of that other poet, in whose will it was written: "Let no man say that I perished because of some sickness during these years. It was their brutality which killed me, the torment of their lies, the fear which stopped my heart whenever a door would creak."

I remember Theodosius well, not a pleasant fellow, to be sure; but it was an injustice to tie him up in that cell like a donkey, with the tether tight around his throat, four months at a manger, standing there in his excrements. Once he had gone safely mad, they let him go; and he died. I am told that Theodora used to come and bray at him, when she could find the time, lift up her skirts and wiggle her bottom at him, and she had him flogged if he declined to look at her: lack of due respect.

I cannot help laughing when I think of the astrologers whom they mounted on camels and drove through the streets for the mob to jeer at. Old men. Justinian's face is said to turn, at times, into a shapeless lump of flesh: no eyes, eyebrows, nose or anything. To think of that lump buzzing with plans for the killing of thousands. They uproot entire populations, weeping children, the tenderness of old women, worshippers of different gods, gods of the streams, winds, of the earth, and march them at planting-time from their villages into faraway camps of special huts where there is nothing to do but die. No, he does not even plan it. He does whatever comes into the lump, according to the circumstances. In the name of the laws. For the acquisition and storage of riches. For the few and no questions. It all makes the young men and women somewhat more irrational than is good for our society. Our society is probably destroyed, anyhow. Never again to sleep, never again to screw, in security. Was he laughing, or was he crying, that man in his hide-out, when he told the story of the funeral?
It is still mysterious here, still real, here in this room of mine. They are

still clattering about down there in the street. Tomorrow the blue dust
will go on rising, the new towers along the sea-shore too, built there
to shove back the sea which licks at their palaces. The thought still
bothers me, that, instead of writing, I might have changed the

Found poem with grafts 1866

To the north-east
    is the park of Mousseaux.
The Baths & Gardens of Tivoli
    & the slaughter-house du Moule must be seen.
Tivoli, near the Chaussée d'Antin
    contains forty acres of ground.
It is quite equal to your Vauxhall by night
    & is much superior in daylight.

But who is the man in the rusty black shapeless felt hat
    pointing south-west?

The walks are ornamented
    with roses honeysuckles & orange trees.
Amid the copses are seen
    rope dancers & groups riding at the ring or playing at shuttlecock.

All around are arbours filled with people
    enjoying the sight of the various amusements.
There is in the middle of the garden a theatre
    on which two hundred couple might dance at the same time.
There are also artificial mounts from which people descend
    in a species of car with incredible velocity.

But who stands in the huge overcoat that had once been brown
    & now is stained with large green patches?
Who is this in the trousers that are too short,
    revealing blue socks?

There are many canals
    in which the public amuse themselves in boats.

In the evening
    the illumination presents a lively spectacle.
All sorts of dances
    commence then,
& after the vocal & instrumental concert the evening concludes
    with the exhibition of splendid fireworks.

Is he not the man who cooks
    hideous mud in the Rue Beautreillis?
Who says: The day will come
    when a single original carrot shall be pregnant with revolution.
Whose wallpaper groans with addresses in the childish script
    of nudes he throws downstairs cursing through his teeth?
And I am aglow, he says,
    with all the hues of the infinite.

Jindrichuv Hradec

This is the chapel of the holy
    spirit he said and lifted
        the old yard-long iron latch

while in the castle courtyard
    outside raindrops were smacking
        old stone roses around the rim

of the fountain so in we went
    and from an organ loft with pious mien
        detected under the dust

a conference of upright chairs
    occurring in the chancel
        a leather sofa in the apse

and heaped around the font
    several curious brown closets
        so we ask him simply tell us

Who dismantled the organ pipes?
    Who presided with a pen in his fist?
        Who howls here when the moon shines in?

GEORGE MacBETH

Drop

Sky was the white soil you
Grew in. When the fourth stick broke
      Into thistledown
At the crack of a whistle, streaked brown

From the crutch out with a crust
Of fear it was like an orgasm to
      Fork into air.
I could see why they'd nicked that nylon

Rip-cord 'the release'. We
Spread like a leprosy on their clean
      Sun to the wogs. You
Could see their screwed heads grow up

Like dry coal we'd got
To clap a match to. Christ it was good
      To feel the sick
Flap of the envelope in the wind:

Like galloping under a stallion's
Belly. Half of Africa flushed
      Out and cocked
Up: you could piss in its eye. You could want to

Scream the Marseillaise like a
Hymn. And then it was all gone.
      Splum. You were sinking
In a hot bog you'd never wrench

Clear of alive. Soaked,
Vomiting, jelly-marrowed, afraid
        To spit. No life
Left but that leg-breaking drop on a

    Split stockade where they'd have your
Genitals off. You were strung up like Jesus
        Christ in the strings
Of your own carriage: lynched by the Kosher

    Sluts who'd packed your chute.
It couldn't work. You were on your own.
        The stick had died
In the screws or never dropped. When the ground

    Slammed you at eighteen feet
Per second you were out skedaddling for the first
        Tree with your harness
Cut: the sten jammed whore-

    hot yammering out of your
Groin. You were implementing the drill
        Balls: it was flog
On till you blacked out dead.

Early warning

Lord god of wings, forgive this hand
That stole from thee. These holy bones
Where thy long shadow ran I give
Thee back, repentant. From thy dead
Steel bird's ripped belly I and four
Doomed ice-men took them out, eight hands

Fouling thy sacred felled limbs. Two
Dropped bones I stooped and kicked. Forgive
Me, god. I never knew thy bones,

Delivered from the ice, could rise
And kill four men. I thought thou wast
Mortal as I. Thy lofty skull,

Smoothed by the Greenland wind, I stole
With my scarred hands. I thought last night
That whale-fat poured in thy round eyes
Would staunch the wind. If my hut stands
And others fell, no other cause
I seek for that. So when at dawn

Four ice-men died, burnt up by thy
Bones' wrath, I thought: this jealous god's
Enduring skull, strong thigh-bone, I
Must give back safe, wise helps, sure harms
For cruel men. Forgive me, god,
For what I did. Those men thou burned

With inward hell that made them twist
In wrangling heaps were faithless. I
Repent my sin. If I should carve
A cross for thee, draped with a fish
Nailed through its hanging tail, wouldst thou
Dismiss this plan? I feel it come

Below the eyes, inside my head,
As they all said it came. Forgive
My theft. I give thee back thy skull,
Thy scalding thigh-bone, god. Thou shalt
Own all I have, my hut, my wife,
My friendly pack of dogs, if thou

Wilt only tell why these green scars
Ache in my cheeks; why this grey mould
Forms on my herring pail; why this
Right hand that touched thy head shrinks up;
And why this living fish I touched
Writhes on that plank, spoiled food for gulls?

The twelve hotels

I

He examined the length of his thin body through the grey glass of dirty water: the strange hollow in his chest, half filled with hair, which was perhaps the consequence of some accident at birth: the thickening wiry growth towards his groin: and beyond this the world of blurred edges in which he always had to live without his spectacles on. He moved against the sandpapery sides of the old porcelain and felt the metal ball above the plug-chain clonk on his bony knee. In a way he could scarcely explain, it seemed right to be starting here, in the bath-room of a run-down Edwardian hotel, in Toulouse.

II

It came to him in the four-poster that he had better make notes. There was always a chance of accident. As he lay and savoured the cool pistachio sheets he began to write in his mind. He would need paper. Perhaps that stock with the dolphin from the place in Biarritz would see him through. He reached out to his bed-side table for another spangle. The main thing was to keep cool.

III

He heard the high floating squeal before he woke. From a dream of axes he came out into heat and darkness. There was only one thing for it. He lay quite still, listening. Again there was the high squeal and the brush of a little wing against his ear. He flexed his body violently. So this was luxury.

IV

In the afternoon the bites on his ankles began to itch again and he scrubbed his feet hard on the barley-sugar legs of his chair. In a few moments the chamber-maid would come in to draw back the bed-covers. He swallowed the last grape and wrapped the wet stalk in his paper napkin. Out of the corner of his eye he could see an old man with a schnauzer disappearing round the corner of the cathedral.

V

He walked on the very edge of the pavement to keep his head in shadow. The black lacquer of his sun-glasses was folded over his two middle fingers. Behind him, he could hear the chock-chock of a girl's high-heeled shoes. Pausing beneath the brick wall of the Museum on the corner, he looked back at her, disguising the movement under the appearance of consulting his Baedeker. The girl walked past, swaying evenly from her hips in a print dress. He felt the familiar prickling begin. She was French.

VI

The sun burned through the glass back of the bus outside the terminus. He loosened the cheap Woolworth's links in his sleeves and let the soiled whites of his cuffs hang loose. There was a cool draught as the bus moved, and he felt the sweat dry on his neck. He wiped his brow on his handkerchief. Things were going well. He would soon be in Albi.

VII

Against his shoulder he could feel the soft warmth of human flesh. He remembered Gilbert saying you could always tell if it was a woman. There was a strong smell of garlic. As the bus bucketed up the hill towards the pass he attempted to crane his neck round without moving his arm. The pregnant gypsy was leaning her bare leg against the edge of his seat. So that was it. He bent forward and, reaching for his jacket, slid his arm back into the rough mohair. He was gratified to feel the offensive pressure diminish.

VIII

Outside the bus station the hail had started. Big ice drops began to hiss and jump in the gutter. He eased himself in his nylon raincoat against the door. He remembered the trout hatchery on the frontier. If only one could turn and swoop like a fish! He considered for a second the possibility of making a run for it. Across the road the girl in braids was still in the chemist's. The park might be anywhere. He decided to stick it out. After all, he was still dry. Be thankful for *something,* he said to himself, as he watched the big driver pulling his gloves on.

IX

He was walking now on dense cones between the pine-trees. Through the dappled sunlight he could see the German tourist at the edge of the lake. That Tyrolean hat and the lederhosen were unmistakeable. But why should the man need to carry his dispatch case for a day in the mountains? The problem bothered him, but he knew it made no difference. He felt for the slack knot of his tie and had started to straighten it before he remembered where he was. For the first time in Andorra he smiled.

X

When the chance came he went down on one knee in the gravel, remembering to flick his precise crease away from the point of pressure. He closed his left eye, sighted along the parapet. Somewhere below him a man's voice was shouting in Italian. He could feel his hands quiver and pressed them more tightly together to hold the cool metal steady. The four towers were clearly outlined inside the yellow rectangle. He swung to his left. The priest had quickened his step. He was almost running now. There would scarcely be time before he reached the barbican. Without thinking, he squeezed the button. It closed with a slow hizz. He looked down at the dial. The distance needle was fixed at eight inches. The priest was already as far as the first tower. God damn those bloody snails, he thought.

XI

It was getting late. Below and to his left a man stood up in his seat, waving his arms and occasionally slapping his fist in his hands as if making a speech. Two or three cushions had already been thrown into the ring. He felt for the packet of polo mints in his pocket and slit off the top one with a circular incision of his nail. He would have to try almost immediately. He watched Zurito go in over the horns and come out again with the sword still in his hand. He slipped the mint between his teeth. It was now or never. He rose, flung his coat to the other shoulder and began to edge along the row. Two pairs of silk, stockings. A child's bare knees. A kilt. He had passed the point of danger almost before he noticed it. The Spaniards were still waiting for the kill.

XII

What was he trying to do, he asked himself, as the train moved way from the platform. Create a mystery out of nothing, was that it? Surely there was a line of Michael's about that. He tried to remember. The sweating woman opposite yawned, throwing her head back on the sticky leather. Across the aisle the girl was still looking down into her lap. It helps, he thought, it helps. Outside the window the black grids of the Hydro-Electric Plant at Foix were silhouetted against the sunset.

Against the sun

Malta 1565/1940

I

     So they laid oars
Along the sea, as if in blessing. To
The airs of lashes, and their alms, they moved
In scent of sweat.
    I see them strike and fail,
Recovering, strike and fail.
      On sterns of teak
Where harsh drops rake their awnings, two preside
In silk, inviolate. To the pull of oars
Along the bare thwarts, altering the world,
They crush the grape.
     The sun goes down the sea
Plating their East with blood. And still they row,
Wounding the wave.
     White in their hospital

The cold bread served on silver to the sick
Shines in the light. I see the long bells pitch
Over the islands, and the pious kneel,
Praying.
           Under their awnings here they kneel,
Doing some service.
                  The long whips lick at them
With tongues of night. Wine soaked in Christian bread
Absolves their lips. If any spit or die
Their bodies marry salt. In all that sweat,
In order, and rebellion, sick in soul,
The slaves are power.
                  So the galleys move
Into what wind there is.

II

                  I hear their wings
Freshening over Corsica. The guns
Along the grey ships arch and waver. To
The scream of air soon lead will fall like rain
And pit the stone.
             I see their clean grey eyes
Behind the wings, mounting in honour. One
Lifts a gloved hand.
              The screws turn. Black as crows
Against the sun, they mount the beaten sky,
Drilling the clouds with fire to clear the sea
And lead their ships.
            With paired wings, three remain
Holding the gold walls.
            Empire was all for them
Whom these oppose. Unclassed by age or skin
Their duty moves in eye and ear. All dive
As one in slow flight.
           Now, below crossed arms
I see the skeleton of one stripped bare
And made a show. No stones, no shells remain
Richer in bare defiance.

III

And so in brine
They sank the bridge of chains.

From fort to fort
The brass links bore their chill defiance to
The fire of Asia.

This shall rise, and rust,
Only when every flag I see in the East
Rots in our Sacristy, he swore, and crossed
The bare steel in his groin.

Under the waves
It dredged and fell, blocking the harbour. There,
Locked up in calm, the Christian ships lay, beached
With splayed oars, like split melon.

One
With gouged pits down its hull had weathered fire
In quelling Tunis. One had lain in Rhodes
Gored by the shells. There, blood of Turkey lurked
Under the hatches, gobbling to be clear
And rise in crescent fury.

Shrink their feed,
He said, *and screw them from the sun.*

I give
This isle a cross, another said. *Its flame*
Withstood a night of wings.

Against their heart
All pluck and wear it, hearing in the sun
The wings descending, once again the wings
Descending.

IV

There, where the lightning struck
And ranged all day, the cold star still remained,
Fish on the stone.

Salt licked their lips, the sea
Sprayed them with shells.

If any still believed
His oar might cross the stiff bay, he was bone

Crossed in the water when he sailed.
                                    At their posts
Men drank and burned, staunching their wounds with
    brine
And sterile cloths. Where surgeons lived, they came
With cautery and metal.
                            If the surgeons died,
They pitched their bodies in the trench. Unburied,
The rotten flesh swelled, burning in the sun
Against their pummelled clay.
                                    And wind,
Lifting hot silks, connived with death. Disease,
Essence of slow death, spiralled.

V

                            On the floor of the nave
Where knights in coloured stone lay in their arms
Two dropped a body. There it was dark, and stale
As lard with burnt out wax.
                            An old woman paused,
Lighting a candle, to look up.
                                    It was
His nephew, one said, and ran back.
                                        Between
The flags, beyond the coil of guns,
Hands parted, he was penned in tactics. *He*
Is dead, he died well, someone said.
                                    He came
In marred steel, breathless. As he crossed himself
Beside the dead skin, she held up her flame
Over the face.
                    One effigy of war
In wax and blood, with rough hands gripped in grief,
Stuck in his mind from Rhodes. A man could paint
The Baptist with his hacked head off, and miss
A mother in the shade.
                        He touched her hand,
Sour in the groin with dead seed. *For your pains,*

He said, and gave her gold.

                              Outside, the war
Beat on the stained glass. Here, her candle stirred
Above a lost boy.

                    As he rose, and knelt
Towards the altar, she reached out, and kissed
His hand.

                 Unheeding, he walked back, scarring
The bared arms in the aisles.

                                  To war and plans,
Immune from pity, it was honour breached
As cold air in the dry lungs dying meant
For all his line, he moved in action.

                                          All
The river of his nephew stilled in stone
Sank over plots to future prayers.

                                      He
Was building shells, fresh bastions.

                                        She knelt,
Honouring Victory.

VI

                  So when it came
The streets were filled with horses. Men walked down
The Kingsway with their hats off. Women, decked
In flagrant roses, watched from windows.

                                            There were fights
Between friends, foreign daggers worn
As open trophies.

                    After that blazing air
The silence was the strange thing.

                                      No-one knew
Who was dead, who had lived.

                                Everyone moved
In the calm dream of honour. There were stones
To be laid back on stones, bodies to bury,
Hopes to be fulfilled.

                        And, after all
That holocaust of starved withdrawal, wounds

Licked and re-opened, ordinary grief
At private scores.
                        Watching the last few gulls
Grey in the dockyard, hearing bald-headed men
Telling the stories, I return again
To the Armoury.
                        Here the heroic wars
Blaze in their oiled shields.
                        Here the impregnable dream
Halts on the islands in its final haze.

At Hunegg

on the Thunersee, circa 1901

1

                        Meanwhile, the Baron Albert
Emil Otto von Parpart
rose from the left side
of his brass bed
and walked (first drawing
the curtains embroidered with blue thistles)
to the window, which he opened.
                        Stepping through
onto a stone parapet, he stretched,
naked, in the cool air.
                        Across the lake
he could see the peak of Niesen,
above Spiez.
                        It was a fine day.
                        Turning,
he re-entered his bedroom.

2

                        Meanwhile, his wife,
the Baroness Adelheid Sophie

Margaretta née von Bonstetten,
rose from the right side
of his brass bed,
which was also hers, and walked (first drawing
the curtains embroidered with blue thistles)
to her dressing-room.
                    There,
beneath a cylindrical, brass chandelier
fashioned with rosettes, she waited,
seated naked at her white dressing-table,
until such time as the Baron should have washed.

                                        (There was
only one bathroom.)

3

                    Meanwhile, the Baron,
having greeted the day, proceeded
to the glory of his ablutions.
                    Passing
through the first of several mahogany doors, he arrived,
almost a little breathless,
on the upper level of his bathroom.
                              There he settled,
with some ceremony, his naked buttocks
on the lowered oak
of his English water-closet.
                    Evacuating
at his bare ease, the detritus of the evening's brilliance
into clear water, he rose
(as Christ) a second time, and flushed
what was left of himself
to the lake of Thun.
                    Through a linked series
of ingenious pipes, it fell
down forty feet of landscaped elegance
to amaze the perch.

4

                    Meanwhile, the Baron,
unmindful of these metallic services,

bent down
to the sheet steel
of his hip-bath.
                    Kneeling in this,
as to the pew in their chapel his ancestors,
he absolved himself,
with much grunting, and a little exercise,
of the body's dirt,
which is the sins of the flesh.
                              So cleansed,
upright at the mirror
above the hand-basin, in a white bath-robe,
the Baron shaved.
                    A little blood
flecked the marble
as he picked off some alert prominence
in the noble chin.
                    He dabbed
at the shorn skin.

5
          Meanwhile, his wife,
having thought over the day's impressing obligations,
containing her luxuriant wastes, as best she might,
on plaited cane,
grew restive.
          He was longer than usual.
                                   She
sulked.

6
          Meanwhile, the Baron,
having freed the temple of his deserts, the body,
of the night's adhesions,
descended to the second level
of his bathroom.
               Throwing aside the bath-robe,
he began the slow process
of powdering himself.
               Thereafter,

100

again naked,
he strode to his dressing-room.

On the glass-topped table,
beside his riding-boots,
a manual of Gymnástic Exercises lay open.

He tugged
the tasselled bell-pull in the door-way
to inform his wife
her way was clear.

With a sigh, she moved,
at some speed, and in perfumed openness,
to the seat of her relief.

Meanwhile, the Baron

7

(I draw a veil
over his wife's commensurate exertions, she was
no longer young)
extended his frame
in the morning lists of health.

So flushed
and bronzed, steeped
in a warm glow of remembered muscularity,
the Baron dressed.

As was his custom,
selecting without warrant of valet or chambermaids
the minimal tweeds
for the day's toilings, he hummed
a few bars of *La Vie Bohème,* as he moved
between press and dressing-table.

8

Meanwhile, his wife,
now washed, and restored
to some fine ghost
of her former splendid narrowness, withdrew,
once more, to her dressing-room.

Whether maids,

masseurs, or her own mere sleight of hand,
had achieved such miracles as had been achieved,
discretion conceals.
             In her clothes,
thrown on with care, though quickly,
she presented a firm spectacle.

9

                         Meanwhile, the Baron,
returning in waxed magnificence
for the day's affrays,
humming and calm
passed through the curtains
embroidered with blue thistles.
                    Admiring his wife,
he kissed her.
                    Turning, he then strode,
with some purpose, and in high fettle,
along the mahogany corridor
towards the landing.
                    To his left he nodded
to his first Mucha,
a girl clothed, who drew
her sheet up to her coy neck.
                    To his right
he winked at his second Mucha,
a girl naked, who drew
the sheet down to her wanton waist.
                         He felt

peckish.

10

        Meanwhile, before him,
his double stairway with the wrought-iron flowers,
and the lamp-standards,
plunged like the Trummelbach Falls through its naked rock
towards the smell of kippers.
                    The Baron descended,

as do the angels, even, sometimes,
to the satisfaction of the fleshly appetites.

                              On the shell terrace,
in the sound of falling water,
the Baron attended, opening his letters
with an ivory paper-knife,
to all intents and purposes amused,
his wife's delayed arrival.

                      It was the year
of Jugendstil.

             A vase by Lalique
drooped a florescence of contrived water-lilies
above his bending head.

11

                Meanwhile, his wife,
already tapping the yew balustrade in some distemper
with her manicured nails,
was on her way to join him.

                  Knowing this,
and the minutiae of her habits to the last detail,
the Baron rose.

               Ringing for breakfast,
he allowed the perfect Swiss clock of the world
to resume motion,
as it would continue to do,
without interruption,
for exactly thirteen years,
four months, and one day.

                Knowing this, too, perhaps,
or having arranged it, as so many other things,
the Baron ate, without sparing,
cheese, rolls, marmalade, eggs, meat and honey-cake,
and, when he had finished,
wiped his mouth on his napkin,
belched, and, with a perfect conscience,
shot himself through the brain.

                        Meanwhile, his wife,
the Baroness Adelheid Sophie
Margaretta née von Bonstetten,
having arrived, and eaten,
rose, and with a faint ruffle of her fastidious cuffs,
rang for the maid, who would, with some care
clear the table.
                 It was a fine day.
                            She opened her letters.

GAEL TURNBULL

Twenty words/Twenty days

I

at a certain hour of the morning of a certain day
of the week—
                  time, like a bonus, to be expended,
not used—
            a depth, a largess—
                              and within such
magnificence, nothing for it but to dilly-dally,
fritter—
         as a BOOMERANG—
                          thrown overhand to spin
vertically, will curve up and to the left, circle,
then glide back—
                  an effect discovered by observation
and refined by error, not deduced from principles—

the arms at right angles or less, each surface pared
smooth (but with a thickness on one side at the
leading edge of rotation)—
                            in the air, a phenomenon
and a byword—
              to be understood in both senses: as
'rebound to hurt' and as 'restore to safety'—
                                              so
this moment, in a gust of days, hovers—
                                          in which
I mess with the car, clean the guinea-pigs' cage,
fix the girls' byke, walk with Jonnie on the pier—
from where we can watch the surf riders on their
boards, the sea very still, with long slow, very

slow breakers—
                    coiling, uncoiling, recoiling—
returning, turning upon the shore—

II

going to the Art Centre in the next town in a rush,
and we get there too early, a mistake in the time, and
the children are patient, even eager, despite—
                                              the
hospital calling, can't find anyone to help with a
case and wouldn't I?—
                            but I can't (and they manage
just as well. after all)—
                            an afternoon frayed at the
edges, but without irritation—
                            let go as it may—
                                                  not
quite paying attention—
                            and the girls dance, a Round,
arms linked, legs swinging, something peasant—
                                              the
music draping them in long skirts of thick weave, with
smocked blouses, the music giving them bare feet, the
music turning the hardwood floor into dark earth, well
stamped—
                nimble to the throb of it, gay, approximate—

and I move also and am moved, in vague unison, and
throw back my head to let all go to that pulse—an
implication of soot, of grease, of uncombed hair—
                                                  a
stale odour, almost rancid—
                            but a comfort in the dusk,
in the thickness, the sun dropped behind the hills, the
air abruptly cold—
                as if abandoned, as if gone into
next year already—
                a SLATTERN—
                                    inconsequential, not

106

straight in the eye—
                    lacking something—
                                        if not
lacking charm—

III

a world awry as I read—
                    a letter from a friend—

". . . from a presbyterian standpoint what I'm doing is
unthinkable—from a French standpoint it's simply
poorly handled—but from the standpoint of authentic
something or other it's right and I don't regret . . ."

and myself snagged, almost throttled, as if I had
been the one—
                    but which one?—
                                        ". . . we hiked all
through the Sierras, living for three weeks off the
fish . . . attempted to break it off, but she had restored
to me a sense of joy and I was at a loss without her . . .
to see my wife suffering was also unbearable . . ."
                                                    as a
cord pulled together—
                    a DRAWSTRING—
                                        and I, in reply,
tumbling words, with nothing to say, nothing—
                                        except,
"Yes, of course . . . of course, yes . . . and I know . . . and
I couldn't . . . and can . . ."
                                    eager, eager for the bait,
that source and lure, there at the bottom of the bag—

the loop pulled tight, lifted into dark by the hand of
the hunter—
                    the fabric taut as I strain—
                                        myself taken,
snared—
            by a thin line straggled on paper—

IV

grape-like, a cluster—

        the technical word: a MORULA—

a condition of growth occurring after the first divisions
of the embryo but before the blastula, before any
structure is apparent—

        an interim, at a certain density—

clumped, almost ready to start the first breakdown, the
first cavitation—

        but as yet all intact, each cell
equally present—

        unlike this day, already gone beyond
any balance, already beginning to liquefy in places—
a deliquescence, and of event, as I remember—

                how I
held the baby, feeling her tremble as she drew, making
circles in pairs, over and over, elated at herself—

and remonstrated with Carol after Joan's anger had
detonated, the echoes lurking—

        and read Mead's pamphlet,
the first proofs, and wrote to Newcastle to say,
"Remember, a date!" and "Yes, how handsome!"—

              and
watched a child nearly choking during a tonsillectomy,
lips and ears cyanotic, with blood clots in its pharynx,
and had pleasure in my skill as I cleared the airway
deftly and re-inserted a tube—

        and collapsed on the
bad at 5:30, my knees aching, almost nauseous—

               with
the islands visible under low clouds, smudged with
graphite—

        the sea like a puddle, a huge rain-freshened,
rain-muddled puddle—

V

my daughter, gone into her own world, already cut off,
sitting out on the front steps in the dark—

                                        a cold
evening, in a thin dress, staring intently but not
seeing us—

                    locked in battle with . . . with what I can
only guess . . . where I can't come—

                                        and I resent this,
resent her, almost hate—

                            who sits there, barricaded
against us in desperation—

                                    voyaging where she must,
assuaging what she must, hurting whom she must—

                                                        there
being no sequence of words, no means of saying, "Yes,
of course . . . and having secured *that,* then *this* moves
into place . . . and the rest foreseen . . . and so forth . . ."

no domino count end to end, no source or destination
explicit—

                however hard one tries to demarcate its
parts, however closely one searches for some cleavage—

INDIVISIBLE—

                        as reduced to an element, each element
such by definition, beyond which there can be no
further process of fraction—

                                    or, touch at one place,
at any, and the whole edifice trembles—

                                        as the
depolarisation and the chemical change occurring with
the passage of an impulse along a nerve is associated
in such a way that it is not practical to ascribe
cause or effect to one or the other—

                                    an experience,
obdurate and yet perhaps equally yielding, affording
no access upon itself—

109

and the soldiers cast lots
for Christ's cloak, there being no seams to unravel—

VI

after the radio voices, television faces, all clatter,
flicker and stippled print, berating us with headlines,
bulletins—
   impaling the day with words—
         blood: bullets:
assassination—
     as one struck, so all struck—
          the
children too, on edge, shaken, aware of an adult world
disrupted by an inexplicable . . . by a . . . by what can be
named but not identified—
      a grief, undirected—
         yet
become direct, threatening and revealing—
        that persists,
is everywhere—
    a nausea in the air as of some sort of
gas leaking—
    and implying . . . no, more than that . . .
insisting upon a realisation of our
       UNDERVALUATION
         of
all that 'other', that unbelievable and extraneous, that
fairy-tale of king's daughters and wicked magicians that
is history—
    now grubby with detail—
       smeared on the
seat of a car, soaked into the pleats of a skirt—
         in
bright sunlight—
    what was so surely meaningless, no
longer supposed that—
      become, of a sudden, a membrane
lining the throat, an adhesion in the cavity of the
mouth—
   a cramp in the tongue—

VII

urgent, requires an answer, a query:

"... can you think of some
gay title for the reading ...?"

at once, it's no problem—

but instead, I think of my forefathers, namesakes, Borderers,
near Jedburgh and Melrose, and one day every tenth man
hanged for cattle stealing, on 'general principles' and
'as a caution'—

that father mine, was he one of the nine-
in-between, his luck good?—

ah, great luck, to survive to
write this and foresee—

myself, in a far place, a future
time—

an APPARITION—

a thousand miles, a few weeks hence,
all planned, where and when, and I anticipate—

that self,
there, genial, speaking as if with knowledge, to whom others
attend, a public occasion, with crowded faces—

asking to
be shown ... to be held ... to be astonished ...—

as birds
in migration—

as cattle thieves—

and to be gay—

that
is: apt, which means both relevant to the material and
having an impulse within itself, an identity as to phrase—

a pressure and a presence—

and happy, that is: containing
joy and contained by—

as this evening: the sunset, a fine
twilight, clear air, with a cobblestone drift of rose-petal
clouds—

as my thought moves, is able—

appears obvious,

hits square—

        fills out the sky of this paper—

                and replies—

VIII

described by Miss Ann Dart, as he was visiting Bristol,
while still a youth: Turner—

                ". . . not like other young
people but singular and very silent . . . no facility for
friendship but never other than pleasant . . . seemed
uneducated, difficult to understand . . . sometimes going
out sketching before breakfast and again after supper . . .
desirous of nothing but improvement in his art . . ."

                                      a

VALENCY—

        defined as: an expression in terms of small
digits of an ability to unite with other like integers—

a ratio, denoting specificity, an exaction—

                and at
approximately 5:45 p.m. a child brought in to the
hospital that had tripped, struck her head—

                  not much
more than dazed at first, then slowly lapsing, until
rapidly depressed, the breathing almost arrested—

"linear fracture of the skull in the left temporo-
parietal area"

        a decision, and with decision—

                to
surgery, each of us in place, to accomplish what must
be—

    an incision—

        at 4:17 p.m. the fault exposed, a
torn artery ligated, a clot removed, the brain free to
expand—

      without words or only of trivia—

                bonded by

our intent and intent upon it—
                              made explicit though
unspoken—
              an obligation assuaged, as discovered—
and a unison—

IX

at ease on my back, dozing, I look up—
                              into a sky
which becomes a ground from which all pigment has been
absorbed, leaving only a fine dust, an indeterminate
bleach—
              a purity, of a sort—
                              then the air fragmented
by diesel engines, bulldozers and earthmovers, on an
adjacent hill, cutting roads, leveling terraces—

masticating the dirt, excreting—
                              acromegalic locusts
with rumplestiltskin secrets—
              GARGOYLES—
                              as corbel
stones, carved at variance, obscene or ludicrous,
upon a sanctuary—
              then later at dusk as I walk on a
strand of rocks, the waves pulsing, the sun as if
corroded by salt and annealed into the horizon, but
the air still flushed, still holding trickles of
radiance—
              among the pebbles, one pebble, small, seen
from afar, as if arc-lit, a brilliant rose colour,
halting my glance—
                              as if ignited, as if conduit for
all the brilliance drained from the twilight—
                                                but
closer: pitted, chalky, with filaments of slate-grey—

taken home to lie on the table among the supper
dishes—

and become dun, grotesque, eroded into sworls,
almost a parody of the foam that shaped it—

                                and cold,
inappropriate—
               unyielding—

X

did I dial the right number? did I dial it correctly? or
if dialed, did the number go through? and etcetera . . .

                                        at
war with distance, and a gadget—
                            in quest? or on a
ramble?—
               to find a place knowable, circumscribed, having
identity—
               perhaps a VILLAGE—
                          within range of a good
shout, "Hello, Hello" and a direct reply, "Yes, I hear . . .
I hear you . . ."
                   where all needful may be found by a stroll,
and one face missing is a clarion—
                        a comfort too, that
might smother, against which it might be necessary to
rail, to muutter, "Damn them . . . *must* they . . .?"
                              who are but
us, behind partly drawn curtains or in half opened
doorways, peering out, anxious to miss nothing, as if
anything could happen—
                   seeing all that is within range—

a constriction, and a perspicacity—
                        to which and from
which there is a lane, an access and an exit, always open,
between hedgerows—
               as the Past might be invoked, summoned,
in exorcism, to contain the Present—
                   against disparities—
and the long distance telephone call—

XI

". . . a white object floating on the river, though its
whole surface is light against the water, yet the
reflection has not any light but on the contrary is
dark . . .

      and not only darker, but the reflection appears
longer than the object which occasions it . . ."

                                  perhaps
often seen but not hitherto remarked—
                        a peculiarity—

as a catalyst, the reaction proceeding—
                        IRREVERSIBLE—

and heat, as a bonus supplied, an excess of energy
liberated—
      or absorbed—
               and I, with a friend, suddenly
aware that I'm talking more rapidly than I was, as if to
convince someone (perhaps myself) of an opinion that
I've swallowed, a refrain—
               of injustice in the courts,
a man hung in error, documented, palpable, gross, and not
yet even partially acknowledged—
              with conviction as fuel,
as acceleration, my face flushed, and my words—
                     a
reflection of light—
        now dark—
            disproportionate—
                 past
recall—

XII

of or having to do with a method of helping to bring out
ideas latent in the mind—
       from the Greek, literally,
'obstetric'—

forceps needed on occasion, the child willing
to come, and willed, but yet unable—

or, "Push, you've
got to push! A deep breath and hold it! Then relax, you
must relax in between, until the next one!"

and also the
value of a long black cigar, smoked to maximal savour (that
is, to a measured pace)—

doing nothing, with precision—

and this evening, by chance, as we visit some friends, their
voices, the sound of guid scots—

and the taste of it—

MAIEUTIC—

our tongues loosened—

animated, almost garrulous
and then surprised, "Did I say that? Or said, did I mean?
And if meant, then . . .?" and "No, it couldn't . . . but . . ."

and laughter bursting, at such recognition—

". . . a shame to spoil by diluting . . . and if you don't care
for the flavour, why take it at all?"—

taking a glass
together—

or, perhaps, looking at, reading the glass to
foretell the weather—

or through a glass, to approach
detail—

or just in the glass, a long look at oneself—

then
faltering, with gaps, reticences—

unable to speak, and
listening—

to the pauses, their conception, the gestation,
their deliverance—

that nothing hinder—

that all come forth—

116

XIII

bloated from over-eating, picked bones on a plate—

and the fallen leaves too damp to burn properly,
smouldering, the smoke like resentment contaminating
the air—
        yet a deep smell, as of a completion, to
be inhaled, a savour—
               the year too, shrinking,
seeking another level—
            a CARCASS—
                  and on the
wireless, a jetliner down, just north from Montreal,
118 people aboard—
                "... seemed to explode ... just
came apart in mid-air ..."
              in a driving rain, near
freezing, masses of mud, with no survivors to be
expected—
        and I go out, restless, to try to walk it
off, a thick taste in my throat—
              on the front steps,
the remains of a mouse that the cat hadn't finished,
just one leg and an ear, some whiskers, that I carry
to the dustbin—
          to go off scuffing the weeds, down
back lanes, along a railway line, past shops gone
out of business—
         by a scrap yard, with rust like
scabbed ulcers, speckled ochre, eating away the
metal—
     desultory—

XIV

obviously how it must be—
              you really knew all the
time but just tried to pretend—
            go at it how you may,

it will end up the same—
                     strident, a voice from a box:
". . . a man protection, the effective protection he needs,
with three times the power of any other deodorant . . ."

did you *have* to be told?—
                     a NINCOMPOOP!—
                              and Jean-Louis
Barrault, in 'Les Enfants du Paradis', lugubrious, in
front of a raucous crowd, with unguent limbs, drooping
sleeves, pantaloons—
                     moving as if to move were to
betray all (and yet his only hope . . . his hope of what?)—
and his eyes as if the lids were shut tightly but
behind rather than in front of his eyeballs so that at
first glance he appeared to be looking out but in fact
was looking in, and had shut his eyes at that sight—

yes, there he was, a posture!—
                     and you, where have
you been . . .? nodding . . .?—
                     a silly ass, to suppose that
the answers aren't given at the back of the book—
                                        an
utter goof, to expect anything—
                     more than the obvious—

XV

                     "I'm sure I can find
                     a thing of some kind,
                     a good kind of thing
                     to do with my string"

the forward path of the poet into the labyrinth—
                                        not
a poet, be it noted, but *the* poet, that flourish—
                                        but
Theseus used his to find his way back—
                     an INTELLECTUALISM—

118

as a prism to spread the light for its parts (but looked
through one sees only a jumble)—

 a great fankle, sometimes,
to be unravelled—

 or a spider, hanging its web for what
might be snared, arrogant in patience, and sticky—

 or a
 or a
child, collecting bits of twine, knotting them end to
end—

 (how big will it get?)—

 "with a big ball of string
 I could do anything!"

XVI

awakening this morning, as the alarm rang, a guilt—

unexpectedly remembering a girl I met once years ago, while
on holiday, out walking in the Appalachians—

 how I came
upon her on the trail, high on the ridge, having seen no
one for two days: she in shorts, with rucksack, plodding the
same direction but more slowly, a student from some
university and taking . . . what was it? . . . geology?—

 and
she wanted to talk, so it seemed, a bit lonely too I
suppose, a gawky kid and more than slightly eccentric to
be way off there by herself—

 and I turned, turned from
her because my mind said that she was ugly, not attractive,
a physical aversion, a disdain, not the woman I imagined
for myself at such time and such place—

 and I walked on
ahead as quickly as I could, as if in flight, as if
actually pursued—

 as I flee the vague guilt, the regret
that follows me closely even to this moment—

 that I

should have feared such an ordinary smile, of someone out
there on that mountain, trudging the same route, sweating
the same pack, seeing the same endless trees—

                         assuaging
the same oppressions heavy on me—

                  yes, surely the same,
surely, however different—

           and yes, PRECONCERTED—

                           the
whole thing 'fixed', 'rigged', 'a set up'—

               granted the
facts of my birth, natural disposition, up-bringing, and
so forth—

        no escape; and all now escaped, gone—

                       before
I knew fully, without possibility of appeal—

                as I do
appeal, none-the-less, not knowing to whom—

               as gesture—
and indictment—

XVII

to prevent abrasion—

        DEMULCENT—

               an agent and an action—

and I, up half the night working, so today my eyesockets
burn, my lips tingle—

          my attention drifting in lapses,
despite effort, despite all resolve—

             with flushes, then
chills—

       clarity through a haze—

               nausea, upon euphoria—
and I cling to one strand . . . the next instant . . . and the
one after . . . and . . .

          and pause, to breathe deeply, and hear
within my ears, a sound—

         as if all carried by wheels on

rails—

      chuck, chuck . . . chock, chock . . . a pulse—

                            the
universe unfurled, sliding yonder where I was, where I
may be—

       to an end-point, to a fixity—

                     with sleep as a
pit—

     and fatigue: a mercy, an opiate—

                  and as reported
in the paper: the Wankel Engine, for the first time in a
commercial car, at the Motor Show—

                 essentially a single
rotary piston without reciprocating parts, attractive for
its simplicity and excellent torque—

            with an almost
complete lack of frictional surfaces at which wear could
occur—

XVIII

as against: ". . . . the first genius of our age . . ."

                     Turner,
according to a contemporary—

          this afternoon, reading a
magazine, a collection of poems by living authors, all
their writing, the mass of it—

         so prolix an effort—
and gloom, not that it can't be read, but can, so much
of it, so apt, with such singleness, such a pain to be
urgent—

     and I, busy as with a Meccano set, a language
of nuts, bolts and tin struts, contriving phrases as one
might improvise toys—

        for ingenuity, and as a pastime—

'Turn the handle. A string runs on a pulley. A hook
lifts a matchstick. It works!'—

         a LATTICE—

            of bits,

lacking better, a patchwork—

                         as against: Watercolour,
the 'English Medium'—

                    where the texture of the pigment
is determined not merely by the brush but by what is
given up as the strokes dry, by what is lost from the
paper—

           a purity; but in that, without body, without
protection against air, against light—

                         so that what
we have now in the galleries, mostly but hints—

                              even
Ruskin, in *his* old age, saying, ". . . have lost something
of their radiance, my Turners . . . though the best, in
that sort, are but shadows . . ."

                   of the day rising up,
of the sun shining through vapour . . . through interstices
of cloud . . . in crannies, the light precipitate as dew . . .
the colours flared . . .

               ". . . with blue and yellow close
together in some places, instead of green" one critic
grumbled, "as if *that* could fool anyone . . ."

XIX

Weyland Smith, worker in iron, shoer of horses, linker
of chain-mail, himself perhaps chained—

                   a captive, a
refugee, and said to be lame, perhaps hamstrung when
taken, who toils for a master—

              by the Ridgeway on the
Berkshire Downs, a ruined Long Barrow, ringed with elm,
once used as a forge and given his name, where the turf
is alive under foot and the granular stones, dark as rain
clouds on the horizon, lie half submerged where they
have tumbled—

            and I remember it today, Pay Day,
collecting my cheque, my ration, to be used and hoarded—

I sign for it, a slave's mark—

                  yet bread in my mouth,

and a roof—

a FAMILIARITY—

of disgust and of necessity—

and in that, a sort of reassurance, a persistence—

even
a pride, if not always of craft, then at least of a
certain minimal agility—

as if also at the anvil,
squeezing the bellows to heat the charcoal to incandescence,
the iron thrust deep until softened, to be hammered and
rehammered—

day upon day—

sweat dripping onto the metal,
sizzling in beads, engraving the surface with whorls, with
a lace-tracery pattern—

myself imaged and marked—

as
bondsman—

and contriver—

XX

last night, crying out in my sleep (so that Jonnie had to
prod me until I stopped), ". . . but it's murder . . ."

not
in fear, but amazement where I was—

a valley between
mountains, with boulders, bracken, straggled clouds
down to tree top, tents, canopies, dripping guy-ropes,
banners—

and men: hulking, spare of words, their eyes
bloodshot from urgent travel and the smoke of charcoal
braziers, with rich brocade under their jerkins—

inhaling each others thought as one might scent—

their
inmost being finding sustenance far down, as plants
with long tap-roots growing out of a shale slope—

a

world imagined, become immanent—

                              but not mine and
blundered into as I slept—

                    Powys (John Cowper) and his
book *'Porius'*—

                read so long ago and so ill remembered,
yet unmistakable—

                    never POOR—

                        but a plethora, a
gallimaufry—

                and this evening, the baby, as she fell
asleep after happy struggle in a corner of her crib,
almost upside down, so abruptly, she was so tired, with
one last wail as if tumbled into a chasm—

                                    puir wee
thing—

            and I remember an Edinburgh room and one saying,
when I asked what he'd done that day, how much—

                                        " I tore
it up . . . I wisnae pure enough when I wrote . . . I wisnae
pure enough ..."

ROY FISHER

City

On one of the steep slopes that rise towards the centre of the city
all the buildings have been destroyed within the past year: a
whole district of the tall narrow houses that spilled around what
were a hundred years ago outlying factories has gone. The streets
remain, among the rough quadrilaterals of brick rubble, veering
awkwardly towards one another through nothing; at night their
rounded surfaces still shine under the irregularly-set gaslamps, and
tonight they dully reflect also the yellowish flare, diffused and
baleful, that hangs flat in the clouds a few hundred feet above the
city's invisible heart. Occasional cars move cautiously across this
waste, as if suspicious of the emptiness; there is little to separate
the roadways from what lies between them. Their tail-lights vanish
slowly into the blocks of surrounding buildings, maybe a quarter
of a mile from the middle of the desolation.

And what is it that lies between these purposeless streets? There
is not a whole brick, a foundation to stumble across, a drainpipe,
a smashed fowlhouse; the entire place has been razed flat, dug
over, and smoothed down again. The bald curve of the hillside
shows quite clearly here, near its crown, where the brilliant road,
stacked close on either side with warehouses and shops, runs out
towards the west. Down below, the district that fills the hollow is
impenetrably black. The streets there are so close and so twisted
among their massive tenements that it is impossible to trace the
line of a single one of them by its lights. The lamps that can be
seen shine oddly, and at mysterious distances, as if they were in a
marsh. Only the great flat-roofed factory shows clear by its bulk,
stretching across three or four whole blocks just below the edge of
the waste, with solid rows of lit windows.

Lullaby and Exhortation for the Unwilling Hero

A fish,
Firelight,
A watery ceiling:
Under the door
The drunk wind sleeps.

The bell in the river,
The loaf half eaten,
The coat of the sky.

A pear,
Perfume,
A white glade of curtains:
Out in the moonlight
The smoke reaches high.

The statue in the cellar,
The skirt on the chairback,
The throat of the street.

A shell,
Shadow,
A floor spread with silence:
Faint on the skylight
The fat moths beat.

The pearl in the stocking,
The coals left to die,
The bell in the river,
The loaf half eaten,
The coat of the sky.

The night slides like a thaw
And oil drums bang together.

A frosted-glass door opening, then another.
Orange and blue *décor.*
The smoke that hugs the ceiling tastes of pepper.

126

What steps descend, what rails conduct?
Sodium bulbs equivocate,
And cowls of ventilators
With limewashed breath hint at the places
To which the void lift cages plunge or soar.

Prints on the landing walls
Are all gone blind with steam;
A voice under the floor
Swings a dull axe against a door.

The gaping office block of night
Shudders into the deep sky overhead:

Thrust down your foot in sleep
Among its depths. Do not respect
The janitors in bed,
The balustrades of iron bars,
The gusty stairwells; thrust it deep,
Into a concrete garage out of sight,
And rest among the cars
That, shut in filtered moonlight,
Sweat mercury and lead.

Subway trains, or winds of indigo,
Bang oil-drums in the yard for war:
Already, half-built towers
Over the bombed city
Show mouths that soon will speak no more,
Stoppered with the perfections of tomorrow.

You can lie women in your bed
With glass and mortar in their hair.
Pocket the key, and draw the curtains,
They'll not care.

Letters on a sweetshop window:
At last the rain slides them askew,
The foetus in the dustbin moves one claw.

And from the locomotive
That's halted on the viaduct
A last white rag of steam
Blows ghostly across the gardens.
When you wake, what will you do?

Under the floorboards of your dream
Gun barrels rolled in lint
Jockey the rooms this way and that.
Across the suburbs, squares of colour gleam:
Swaddled in pink and apricot,
The people are 'making love'.

Those are bright points that flicker
Softly, and vanish one by one.
Your telegraphic fingers mutter the world.
What will they reach for when your sleep is done?

The hiss of tyres along the gutter,
Odours of polish in the air;
A car sleeps in the neighbouring room,
A wardrobe by its radiator.

The rumbling canisters beat for you
Who are a room now altogether bare,
An open mouth pressed outwards against life,
Tasting the sleepers' breath,
The palms of hands, discarded shoes,
Lilac wood, the blade of a breadknife.

Before dawn in the sidings,
Over whose even tracks
Fat cooling towers caress the sky,
The rows of trucks
Extend: black, white,
White, grey, white, black,
Black, white, black, grey,
Marshalled like building blocks:

Women are never far away.

In the century that has passed since this city has become great, it
has twice laid itself out in the shape of a wheel. The ghost of the

older one still lies among the spokes of the new, those dozen highways that thread constricted ways through the inner suburbs, then thrust out, twice as wide, across the housing estates and into the countryside, dragging moraines of buildings with them. Sixty or seventy years ago there were other main roads, quite as important as these were then, but lying between their paths. By day they are simply alternatives, short cuts, lined solidly with parked cars and crammed with delivery vans. They look merely like side-streets, heartlessly overblown in some excess of Victorian expansion. By night, or on a Sunday, you can see them for what they are. They are still lit meagrely, and the long rows of houses, three and four storeys high, rear black above the lamps enclosing the roadways, clamping them off from whatever surrounds them. From these pavements you can sometimes see the sky at night, not obscured as it is in most parts of the city by the greenish-blue haze of light that steams out of the mercury vapour lamps. These streets are not worth lighting. The houses have not been turned into shops—they are not villas either that might have become offices, but simply tall dwellings, opening straight off the street, with cavernous entries leading into back courts.

The people who live in them are mostly very old. Some have lived through three wars, some through only one; wars of newspapers, of mysterious sciences, of coercion, of disappearance. Wars that have come down the streets from the unknown city and the unknown world, like rainwater floods in the gutters. There are small shops at street corners, with blank rows of houses between them; and taverns carved only shallowly into the massive walls. When these people go into the town, the buses they travel in stop just before they reach it, in the sombre back streets behind the

Town Hall and the great insurance offices.

These lost streets are decaying only very slowly. The impacted lives of their inhabitants, the meaninglessness of news, the dead black of the chimney breasts, the conviction that the wind itself comes only from the next street, all wedge together to keep destruction out; to deflect the eye of the developer. And when destruction comes, it is total: the printed notices on the walls, block by block, a few doors left open at night, broken windows advancing down a street until fallen slates appear on the pavement

and are not kicked away. Then, after a few weeks of this, the
machines arrive.

The entertainment of war

I saw the garden where my aunt had died
And her two children and a woman from next door;
It was like a burst pod filled with clay.

A mile away in the night I heard the bombs
Sing and then burst themselves between cramped houses
With bright soft flashes and sounds like banging doors;

The last of them crushed the four bodies into the ground,
Scattered the shelter, and blasted my uncle's corpse
Over the housetop and into the street beyond.

Now the garden lay stripped and stale; the iron shelter
Spread out its separate petals around a smooth clay saucer,
Small, and so tidy it seemed nobody had ever been there.

When I saw it, the house was blown clean by blast and care:
Relations had already torn out the new fireplaces;
My cousin's pencils lasted me several years.

And in his office notepad that was given me
I found solemn drawings in crayon of blondes without dresses.
In his lifetime I had not known him well.

These were the things I noticed at ten years of age;
Those, and the four hearses outside our house,
The chocolate cakes, and my classmates' half-shocked envy.

But my grandfather went home from the mortuary
And for five years tried to share the noises in his skull,
Then he walked out and lay under a furze-bush to die.

When my father came back from identifying the daughter
He asked us to remind him of her mouth.
We tried. He said 'I think it was the one'.

These were marginal people I had met only rarely
And the end of the whole household meant that no grief was seen;
Never have people seemed so absent from their own deaths.

This bloody episode of four whom I could understand better dead
Gave me something I needed to keep a long story moving;
I had no pain of it; can find no scar even now.

But had my belief in the fiction not been thus buoyed up
I might, in the sigh and strike of the next night's bombs
Have realised a little what they meant, and for the first time been afraid.

North area

Those whom I love avoid all mention of it,
Though certain gestures they've in common
Persuade me they know it well:
A place where I can never go.
No point in asking why, or why not.
I picture it, though—
There must be dunes with cement walks,
A twilight of aluminum
Among beach huts and weather-stained handrails;
Much glass to reflect the clouds;
And a glint of blood in the cat-ice that holds the rushes.

The edge of the city. A low hill with houses on one side and
rough common land on the other, stretching down to where a
dye-works lies along the valley road. Pithead gears thrust out above
the hawthorn bushes; everywhere prefabricated workshops jut
into the fields and the allotments. The society of singing birds
and the society of mechanical hammers inhabit the world together,
slightly ruffled and confined by each other's presence.

By the pond

This is bitter enough: the pallid water
With yellow rushes crowding toward the shore,
That fishermen's shack,

The pit-mound's taut and staring wire fences,
The ashen sky. All these can serve as conscience.
For the rest, I'll live.

Brick-dust in sunlight. That is what I see now in the city, a dry
epic flavour, whose air is human breath. A place of walls made
straight with plumbline and trowel, to dessicate and crumble in
the sun and smoke. Blistered paint on cisterns and girders,
cracking to show the priming. Old men spit on the paving slabs,
little boys urinate; and the sun dries it as it dries out patches of
damp on plaster facings to leave misshapen stains. I look for
things here that make old men and dead men seem young. Things
which have escaped, the landscapes of many childhoods.

Wharves, the oldest parts of factories, tarred gable ends rearing
to take the sun over lower roofs. Soot, sunlight, brick-dust; and
the breath that tastes of them.

At the time when the great streets were thrust out along the
old highroads and trackways, the houses shouldering towards
the country and the back streets filling in the widening spaces
between them like webbed membranes, the power of will in
the town was more open, less speciously democratic, than
it is now. There were, of course, cottage railway stations, a
jail that pretended to be a castle out of Grimm, public urinals
surrounded by screens of cast-iron lacework painted green and
scarlet; but there was also an arrogant ponderous architecture
that dwarfed and terrified the people by its sheer size and
functional brutality: the workhouses and the older hospitals,
the thick-walled abattoir, the long vaulted market-halls, the
striding canal bridges and railway viaducts. Brunel was welcome
here. Compared with these structures the straight white blocks and
concrete roadways of today are a fairground, a clear dream just
before waking, the creation of salesmen rather than of engineers.
The new city is bred out of a hard will, but as it appears, it shows
itself a little ingratiating, a place of arcades, passages, easy
ascents, good light. The eyes twinkle, beseech and veil themselves;
the full, hard mouth, the broad jaw—these are no longer made
visible to all.

A street half a mile long with no buildings, only a continuous
embankment of sickly grass along one side, with railway signals
on it, and strings of trucks through whose black-spoked wheels you
can see the sky; and for the whole length of the other a curving
wall of bluish brick, caked with soot and thirty feet high. In it, a
few wicket gates painted ochre, and fingermarked, but never open.
Cobbles in the roadway.

A hundred years ago this was almost the edge of town. The goods
yards, the gasworks and the coal stores were established on tips
and hillocks in the sparse fields that lay among the houses. Between
this place and the centre, a mile or two up the hill, lay a continuous
huddle of low streets and courts, filling the marshy valley of the
meagre river that now flows under brick and tarmac. And this was
as far as the railway came, at first. A great station was built,
towering and stony. The sky above it was southerly.
The stately approach, the long curves of wall, still remain, but
the place is a goods depot with most of its doors barred and pots of
geraniums at those windows that are not shuttered. You come
upon it suddenly in its open prospect out of tangled streets of small
factories. It draws light to itself, especially at sunset, standing still
and smooth faced, looking westwards at the hill. I am not able
to imagine the activity that must once have been here. I can see no
ghosts of men and women, only the gigantic ghost of stone. They
are too frightened of it to pull it down.

The sun hacks

The sun hacks at the slaughterhouse campanile,
And by the butchers' cars, packed tail-to-kerb,
Masks under white caps wake into human faces.

The river shudders as dawn drums on its culvert;
On the first bus nightworkers sleep, or stare
At hoardings that look out on yesterday.

The whale-back hill assumes its concrete city:
The white-flanked towers, the stillborn monuments;
The thousand golden offices, untenanted.

133

At night on the station platform, near a pile of baskets, a couple embraced, pressed close together and swaying a little. It was hard to see where the girl's feet and legs were. The suspicion this aroused soon caused her hands, apparently joined behind her lover's back, to become a small brown paper parcel under the arm of a stout engine-driver who leaned, probably drunk, against the baskets, his cap so far forward as almost to conceal his face. I could not banish the thought that what I had first seen was in fact his own androgynous fantasy, the self-sufficient core of his stupor. Such a romantic thing, so tender, for him to contain. He looked more comic and complaisant than the couple had done, and more likely to fall heavily to the floor.

A café with a frosted glass door through which much light is diffused. A tall young girl comes out and stands in front of it, her face and figure quite obscured by this milky radiance.

She treads out on to a lopsided ochre panel of lit pavement before the doorway and becomes visible as a coloured shape, moving sharply. A wrap of honey and ginger, a flared saffron skirt, grey-white shoes. She goes off past the Masonic Temple with a young man: he is pale, with dark hair and a shrunken, earnest face. You could imagine him a size larger. Just for a moment, as it happens, there is no one else in the street at all. Their significance escapes rapidly like a scent, before the footsteps vanish among the car engines.

A man in the police court. He looked dapper and poker-faced, his arms straight, the long fingers just touching the hem of his checked jacket. Four days after being released from the prison where he had served two years for theft he had been discovered at midnight clinging like a tree-shrew to the bars of a glass factory-roof. He made no attempt to explain his presence there; the luminous nerves that made him fly up to it were not visible in daylight, and the police seemed hardly able to believe this was the creature they had brought down in the darkness.

In this city the governing authority is limited and mean: so limited that it can do no more than preserve a superficial order. It supplies fuel, water and power. It removes a fair proportion of the refuse, cleans the streets after a fashion, and discourages fighting. With these things, and a few more of the same sort, it is content. This could never be a capital city for all its size. There is no mind in it, no regard. The sensitive, the tasteful, the fashionable, the intolerant and powerful, have not moved through it as they have moved through London, evaluating it, altering it deliberately, setting in motion wars of feeling about it. Most of it has never been seen.

In an afternoon of dazzling sunlight in the thronged streets, I saw at first no individuals but a composite monster, its unfeeling surfaces matted with dust: a mass of necks, limbs without extremities, trunks without heads; unformed stirrings and shovings spilling across the streets it had managed to get itself provided with.

Later, as the air cooled, flowing loosely about the buildings that stood starkly among the declining rays, the creature began to divide and multiply. At crossings I could see people made of straws, rags, cartons, the stuffing of burst cushions, kitchen refuse.

Outside the Grand Hotel, a long-boned carrot-haired girl with glasses, loping along, and with strips of bright colour, rich, silky green and blue, in her soft clothes. For a person made of such scraps she was beautiful.

Faint blue light dropping down through the sparse leaves of the plane trees in the churchyard opposite after sundown, cooling and shaping heads, awakening eyes.

The hill behind the town

Sullen hot noon, a loop of wire,
With zinc light standing everywhere,
A glint on the chapels,
Glint on the chapels.

Under my heel a loop of wire
Dragged in the dust is earth's wide eye,

135

Unseen for days,
Unseen days.

Geranium-wattled, fenced in wire,
Caged white cockerels crowd near
And stretch red throats
Stretch red throats;

Their cries tear grievous through taut wire,
Drowned in tanks of factory sirens
At sullen noon,
Sullen hot noon.

The day's on end; a loop of wire
Kicked from the dust's bleak daylight leaves
A blind white world,
Blind white world.

The populars

Where the road divides
Just out of town
By the wall beyond the filling-station
Four lombardy populars
Brush stiff against the moorland wind.

Clarity is in their tops
That no one can touch
Till they are felled,
Brushwood to cart away:

To know these tall pointers
I need to withdraw
From what is called my life
And from my net
Of achievable desires.

Why should their rude and permanent virginity
So capture me? Why should studying

These lacunae of possibility
Relax the iron templates of obligation
Leaving me simply Man?

All I have done, or can do
Is prisoned in its act:
I think I am afraid of becoming
A cemetery of performance.

Starting to make a tree

First we carried out the faggot of steel stakes; they varied in
length, though most were taller than a man.

We slid one free of the bundle and drove it into the ground, first
padding the top with rag, that the branch might not be injured
with leaning on it.

Then we took turns to choose stakes of the length we wanted, and
to feel for the distances between them. We gathered to thrust them
firmly in.

There were twenty or thirty of them in all; and when they were in
place we had, round the clearing we had left for the trunk, an
irregular radial plantation of these props, each with its wad of
white at the tip. It was to be an old, downcurving tree.

This was in keeping with the burnt, chemical blue of the soil, and
the even hue of the sky which seemed to have been washed with
a pale brownish smoke;

another clue was the flatness of the horizon on all sides except the
north, where it was broken by the low slate or tarred shingle roofs
of the houses, which stretched away from us for a mile or more.

This was the work of the morning. It was done with care, for we
had no wish to make revisions;

we were, nonetheless, a little excited, and hindered the women at
their cooking in our anxiety to know whose armpit and whose

groin would help us most in the modelling of the bole, and the thrust of the boughs.

That done, we spent the early dusk of the afternoon gathering materials from the nearest houses; and there was plenty:

a great flock mattress; two carved chairs; cement; chicken-wire; tarpaulin; a smashed barrel; lead piping; leather of all kinds; and many small things.

In the evening we sat late, and discussed how we could best use them. Our tree was to be very beautiful.

Yet whenever I see that some of these people around me are bodily in love, I feel it is my own energy, my own hope, tension and sense of time in hand, that have gathered and vanished down that dark drain; it is I who am left, shivering and exhausted, to try and kick the lid back into place so that I can go on without the fear of being able to feel only vertically, like a blind wall, or thickly, like the tyres of a bus.

Lovers turn to me faces of innocence where I would expect wariness. They have disappeared for entire hours into the lit holes of life, instead of lying stunned on its surface as I, and so many, do for so long; or instead of raising their heads cautiously and scenting the manifold airs that blow through the streets.

The city asleep. In it there are shadows that are sulphurous, tanks of black bile. The glitter on the roadways is the deceptive ore than shines on coal.

The last buses have left the centre; the pallid faces of the crowd looked like pods, filled by a gusty summer that had come too late for plenty.

Silvered rails that guide pedestrians at street corners stand useless. Towards midnight, or at whatever hour the sky descends with its full iron weight, the ceilings drop lower everywhere; each light is partial, and proper only to its place. There is no longer any general light, only particular lights that overlap.

138

Out of the swarming thoroughfares, the night makes its own streets
with a rake that drags persuaded people out of its way: streets
where the bigger buildings have already swung themselves round
to odd angles against the weakened currents of the traffic.

There are lamplit streets where the full darkness is only in the
deep drains and in the closed eyesockets and shut throats of the
old as they lie asleep; their breath moves red tunnel-lights.

The main roads hold their white-green lights with difficulty,
like long, loaded boughs; when the machines stop moving down
them their gradients reappear.

Journeys at night: sometimes grooves in a thick substance,
sometimes raised weals on black skin.

The city at night has no eye, any more than it has by day, although
you would expect to find one; and over much of it the sleep is
aqueous and incomplete, like that of a hospital ward.

But to some extent it stops, drops and congeals. It could be broken
like asphalt, and the men and women rolled out like sleeping
maggots.

Once I wanted to prove the world was sick. Now I want to prove
it healthy. The detection of sickness means that death has
established itself as an element of the timetable; it has come
within the range of the measurable. Where there is no time there
is no sickness.

The wind at night

The suburb lies like a hand tonight,
A man's thick hand, so stubborn
No child or poet can move it.

The wind drives itself mad with messages,
Clattering train wheels over the roofs,

Collapsing streets of sound until
Far towers, daubed with swollen light,
Lunge closer to abuse it,

This suburb like a sleeping hand,
With helpless elms that shudder
Angry between its fingers,
Powerless to disprove it.

And, although the wind derides
The spaces of this stupid quarter,
And sets the time of night on edge,
It mocks the hand, but cannot lose it:

This stillness keeps us in the flesh,
For us to use it.

I stare into the dark; and see a window, a large sash window of
four panes, such as might be found in the living-room of any
fair-sized old house. Its curtains are drawn back and it looks out
on to a small damp garden, narrow close at hand where the kitchen
and outhouses lead back, and then almost square. Privet and
box surround it, and the flowerbeds are empty save for a few
laurels or rhododendrons, some leafless rose shrubs and a giant
yucca. It is a December afternoon, and it is raining. Not far from
the window is a black marble statue of a long-haired, long-bearded
old man. His robes are conventionally archaic, and he sits, easily
enough, on what seems a pile of small boulders, staring intently
and with a look of great intelligence towards the patch of wall just
under the kitchen window. The statue looks grimy, but its exposed
surfaces are highly polished by the rain, so that the nose and the
cheekbones stand out strongly in the gloom. It is rather smaller
than life-size. It is clearly not in its proper place: resting as it does
across the moss of the raised border, it is appreciably tilted forward
and to one side, almost as if it had been abandoned as too heavy by
those who were trying to move it—either in or out.

Walking through the suburb at night, as I pass the dentist's house
I hear a clock chime a quarter, a desolate brassy sound. I know
where it stands, on the mantelpiece in the still surgery. The chime
falls back into the house, and beyond it, without end. Peace.

I sense the simple nakedness of these tiers of sleeping men and women beneath whose windows I pass. I imagine it in its own setting, a mean bathroom in a house no longer new, a bathroom with plank panelling, painted a peculiar shade of green by an amateur, and badly preserved. It is full of steam, so much as to obscure the yellow light and hide the high, patched ceiling. In this dream, standing quiet, the private image of the householder or his wife, damp and clean.

I see this as it might be floating in the dark, as if the twinkling point of a distant street-lamp had blown in closer, swelling and softening to a foggy oval. I can call up a series of such glimpses that need have no end, for they are all the bodies of strangers. Some are deformed or diseased, some are ashamed, but the peace of humility and weakness is there in them all.

I have often felt myself to be vicious, in living so much by the eye, yet among so many people. I can be afraid that the egg of light through which I see these bodies might present itself as a keyhole. Yet I can find no sadism in the way I see them now. They are warm-fleshed, yet their shapes have the minuscule, remote morality of some mediaeval woodcut of the Expulsion: an eternally startled Adam, a permanently bemused Eve. I see them as homunculi, moving privately each in a softly lit fruit in a nocturnal tree. I can consider without scorn or envy the well-found bedrooms I pass, walnut and rose-pink, altars of tidy, dark-haired women, bare-backed, wifely. Even in these I can see order.

I come quite often now upon a sort of ecstasy, a rag of light blowing among the things I know, making me feel I am not the one for whom it was intended, that I have inadvertently been looking through another's eyes and have seen what I cannot receive.

I want to believe I live in a single world. That is why I am keeping my eyes at home while I can. The light keeps on separating the world like a table knife: it sweeps across what I see and suggests what I do not. The imaginary comes to me with

as much force as the real, the remembered with as much force as
the immediate. The countries on the map divide and pile up like
ice-floes: what is strange is that I feel no stress, no grating
discomfort among the confusion, no loss; only a belief that I
should not be here. I see the iron fences and the shallow ditches
of the countryside the mild wind has travelled over. I cannot enter
that countryside; nor can I escape it. I cannot join together the
mild wind and the shallow ditches, I cannot lay the light across
the world and then watch it slide away. Each thought is at once
translucent and icily capricious. A polytheism without gods.

The park

If you should go there on such a day—
The red sun disappearing,
Netted behind black sycamores;

If you should go there on such a day—
The sky drawn thin with frost,
Its cloud-rims bright and bitter—

If you should go there on such a day,
Maybe the old goose will chase you away.

If you should go there to see
The shallow concrete lake,
Scummed over, fouled with paper;

If you should go there to see
The grass plots, featureless,
Muddy, and bruised, and balding—

If you should go there to see,
Maybe the old goose will scare you as he scared me

Waddling fast on his diseased feet,
His orange bill thrust out,
His eyes indignant;

Waddling fast on his diseased feet,
His once-ornamental feathers
Baggy, and smeared with winter—

Waddling fast on his diseased feet,
The old goose will one day reach death; and be unfit to eat.

And when the goose is dead, then we
Can say we're able, at last,
No longer hindered from going;

And when the goose is dead, then we
Have the chance, if we still want it,
To wander the park at leisure;

—Oh, when excuse is dead, then we
Must visit there, most diligently.

IAN HAMILTON FINLAY

ring of waves
row of nets
string of lights
row of fish
ring of nets
row of roofs
string of fish
ring of light

le circus!!

smack

K47

and crew

also

corks

nets

etc.

on the left, a green blinker

on the right, a red blinker

they

leap

BARE-BACK

through

the

rainbow's

hoop

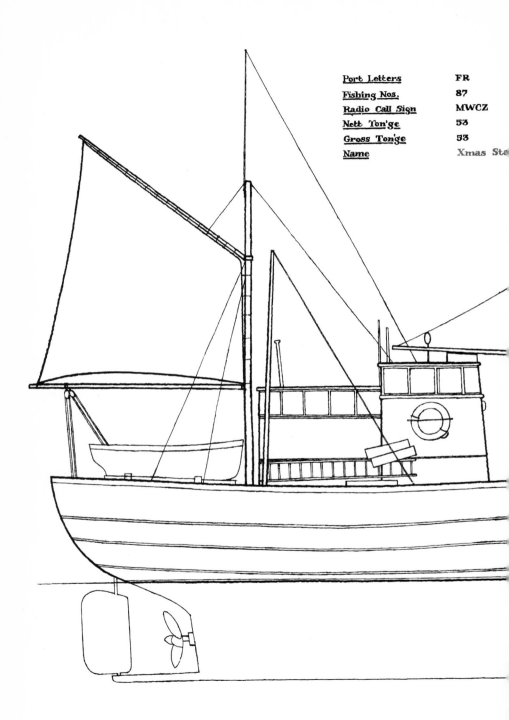

Port Letters	FR
Fishing Nos.	87
Radio Call Sign	MWCZ
Nett Ton'ge	53
Gross Ton'ge	53
Name	Xmas Sta

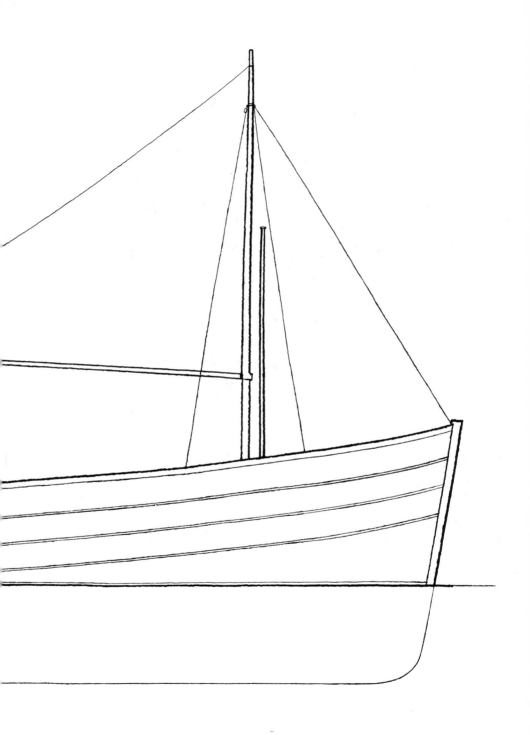

STAR FAITHFUL LIGHT ONWARD GUIDING STAR WOOD NORRARD STAR OF FREEDOM KINDRED STAR DAY STAR UNIVERSAL STAR RADIANT STAR CONSTANT STAR DIVINE FORTUNE STAR MORNING STAR OF PEACE STAR

THE LAND'S DRIFT TRAWL RING SEINE SHADOWS

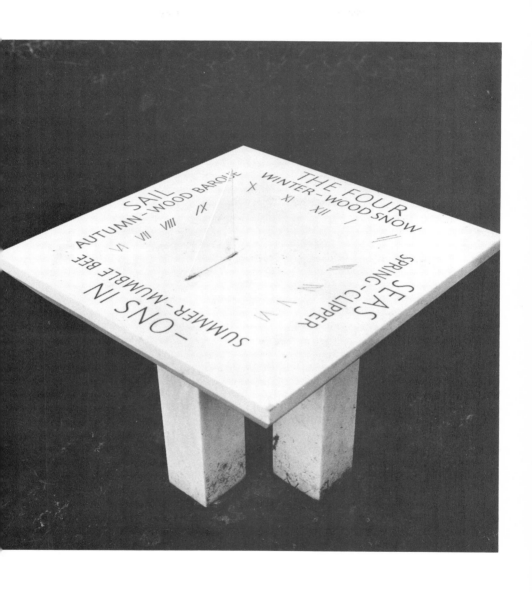

stack net

ring net

seine net

salmon net

drift net

trawl net

herring net

planet

liner
longliner longliner longliner
liner
longliner longliner longliner
longliner longliner longliner longliner longliner

Note: liners & longliners are line-fishing boats

Green Waters

Blue Spray

Grayfish

Anna T

Karen B

Netta Croan

Note: these are the names of actual trawlers, fishing from
Aberdeen, Lowestoft, and other ports.

Constant Star

Daystar

Starwood

Starlit Waters

Moonlit Waters

Drift

CHRISTOPHER LOGUE

Two sections from *Patrocleia* (Book XVI of Homer's *Iliad*)

I

    Now hear this:
While they fought around the ship from Thessaly,
    Patroclus came crying to the Greek.
    "Why tears, Patroclus?" Achilles said.
'Why hang around my ankles like a child
Pestering mother, wanting to be picked up,
Expecting her to stop what she is doing, and,
In the end, getting its way through snivels?
    You have bad news from home?
Is someone dead, Patroclus? Your father? Mine?
But news like that is never confidential.
If it was true, you, me, and all the Myrmidons
Would cry together.

    It's the Greeks, Patroclus, isn't it?
You weep because some Greeks are beaten dead beside their ships!
But did you weep when those same Greeks condoned my wrongs?
If I remember rightly you said nothing . . . Yes?"

    And Patroclus:
"Save your hate, Achilles. It will keep.
Our cause is sick enough without your grudging it my tears.
You know Odysseus and Diomede are wounded?
Eurypylus, too—his thigh—and even Agamemnon.
And you still ask '*Why tears?*' Ach,
    Is there no end to your obdurate grudge?
No. Don't shrug me off. Remember who is asking.
Not Agamemnon. Not the smart Ithacan. No one save me—

And God forbid I share the niceness of a man who,
When his friends go down, sits tight
And claims their punishment as just amends
For the wrongs they did him.
   They are dying, Achilles. Dying like flies.
If you can't think of them, think for a moment
Of those who will come after them, what they will say:
'*Achilles The Grudgebearer*'—can't you hear it?—or,
'*Achilles The Strong*'—and just as well for that,
Because his sense of wrong was heavy—or,
'*Some people say Lord Peleus and Thetis,*
Lovely among the loveliest of women,
Were his folk. But if you want the truth,
His mother was a long bleak rock
That after centuries was moved
By the even bleaker, always disconsolate
Pestering of the Sea, until she had a son,
Achilles.'
   Why make me talk to you this way?
If it is true that God or your sainted Mother
Whisper persuasive justifications for desertion in your heart,
It's also true they do not mention me.
Let me go out and help the Greeks, Achilles?
Let me take our troops? Half of them, then!
And let me wear your weapons . . .
   Man, it will be enough!
Me, dressed as you, leading the Myrmidons . . .
The sight of us will make Troy hesitate, saying
'*It's him*'; a second look will check them, turn them,
Give the Greeks a rest (although war has no rest)
And, once they have turned, nothing will stop us till
They squat inside their walls."

   In this way, in words
Something like those written above,
   Patroclus begged for death.

   And Achilles:
"Better to ask yourself if you're my friend or not,
Than speculate which god, or whether God himself,

Or could it be that my mother has put
The cheap excuses in my mouth that you see fit
To mention to my face.
Excuses? What excuses? And you,
You mind your tongue,
And not make God sound like a fool
Servicing my resentment.
Why not add Agamemnon to your arguments?
Vain, fretful, insolent King Agamemnon!
Why don't you mention him, Patroclus—eh? Go on . . .
'He was a sick man at the time, Achilles.
He did it to avoid unpleasantness, Achilles.
Achilles, he was not too well advised.' "

And they stared each other down until he said:

"O, Patroclus,
I'm so full of resentment that I ache.
Tell me, have I got it wrong?
Didn't he take the girl I won?
And didn't all my so-called friends agree that she was mine
Who cut a town in half to get her?—
(That was something!)—yet,
When it comes to it, they side with him,
The Royal thief
Who robs the man on whom his commonwealth depends.
But done is done; I cannot grudge forever, love.
Take what you want: men, horses, cars, the lot."
You could see the grudge was almost gone,
Him saying:
"Muster the troops and thrust them, hard,
Just here"—marking the sand—"between the enemy
And the fleet. Aie! . . . they are impudent,
These golden Trojans.
They stroke our ships,
Fondle their slim black necks and split them—
Yes! Agamemnon makes me absent.
My absence makes them brave. And so, Patroclus,
Dear Agamemnon makes his enemies secure. All right:
If not Achilles, then his vicar.

166

Forget the spear. It's not your weight. Take this"—
   Choosing one half as long—"instead.
You say Diomede is out? That's bad. And Ajax too?
He's all that's left then . . . No wonder all I hear is
Hector, Hector, Hector, everywhere Hector,
As if he was a god split into sixty!
Hurry, Patroclus, or they will burn us out—
No. Wait. Listen to me. You're listening? Good.
   Here's what I want.
Win my apologies. My rights and my apologies.
That's all. You hear? I want the Greeks saved, yes,
And then I want to see them at the tent here,
Every single one, with Briseis, virgin, in the front.
And many other gifts. You're clear on that?
Good. And one more thing before you go:
   Don't overreach yourself, Patroclus.
Without me you are something, but not much.
Let Hector be. He's mine—God willing—
In any case he'd make a meal of you
And I don't want you killed, you hear?
But neither do I want to see you shining
At my expense. So, here's my order.
No matter how, how much, how often, or how easily you win,
Once you have forced the Trojans back, you stop. That's clear?
The mercenaries can do the mopping up.
   There is a certain brightness in the air
Which means the Lord Apollo is too close
For you to disobey me and be safe.
You know Apollo loves the Trojans, and you know
That even God the Father hesitates
To tamper with him . . .
   O, my sweet friend,
How splendid it would be if all of them—
Greeks, Trojans, Allies, Confederates—were dead.
And thou and I were left to rip Troy down alone!"

II

It is true that men are clever.
But the least of gods is cleverer than their best.
   And it was here, before God's hands

(Moons poised either side of the world's agate)
You overreached yourself, Patroclus.

    Yes, my darling,
Not only God was out that day but Lord Apollo.
"You know he loves the Trojans. So,
No matter how, how much, how often, or how easily you win,
Once you have forced them back, you stop."

    Remember it, Patroclus? Or was it years ago
Achilles cautioned you outside his tent?
Remembering or not you stripped Sarpedon's gear,
That glittered like the sea's far edge at dawn,
Ordered your borrowed Myrmidons to drag him off
And went for Troy alone.

    And God turned to Apollo, saying:
"Mousegod, take my Sarpedon out of range
And clarify his wounds with mountain water.
Moisten his body with tinctures of white myrrh
And the sleeping iodine; and when these chrysms dry,
Fold him in minivers that never wear
And lints that never fade,
And call my two blind footmen, Sleep and Death,
And let them carry him to Lycia by Taurus
Where his tribe, playing stone chimes and tambourines,
Will consecrate his royal death,
Before whose memory even the stones shall fade."

    And Apollo took Sarpedon out of range,
And clarified his wounds with mountain water.
Moistened his body with tinctures of white myrrh
And the sleeping iodine, and when the chrysms dried
The Mousegod folded him in minivers that never wear
And lint that never fades,
And fetched the two blind footmen, Sleep and Death,
And saw they carried him, as fits a man
Before whose memory the stones shall fade,
To Lycia by Taurus.

    While this was done Achilles' overreaching vicar killed,

Eckelus, of whom nothing is known;
Perimas, the son of Meges; Sistor, an
Egyptian horse dealer; Keth and San,

slaves to the former; Krates, a silver-
smith from Cyme; Doron, a regular;
Pilarty, a cook; Fanes, Geyan, & Mastor,
farriers; Toris, a merchant slaver.

Three times Patroclus climbed Troy's wall.
Three times his fingers scraped the parapet.
Three times and every time he tried it on
The smiling Mousegod flicked him back.
But when he came a fourth, last time,
The smile was gone.

Instead, from parapet to plain to beach-head, on,
Across the rucked, sunlit Aegean, the Mousegod's voice—
Loud as ten thousand crying together—
Cried

"Greek,
Get back where you belong!"

So loud
Even the Yellow Judges passing sentence
Half of the world away, paused—

"Get back where you belong
Troy will fall in God's good time
But not to you!"

Banner behind slatted banner,
Blue overwhelming gold, gold over blue,
It was Patroclus' turn to run
Wide-armed, staring into the fight, and desperate
To hide (to blind that voice) to hide
Behind the moving blades.

And as he ran
Apollo dressed as Priam's brother
Settled beside the inner gates
And strolled with Hector for a while, and took his arm
And, mentioning the ways of duty, love, good-conduct,
And the other perishable joys infecting men,
Dissolved his cowardice with promises.

169

Think of it: They stand like brothers, man and god,
Chatting together on the parapet that spans the inner gate.
The elder points. The other nods. And the plumes nod
Over them both. Patroclus cannot see
The Uncle's finger leading Hector's eye
Towards his heart. Nor does he hear Apollo whispering
"Achilles' heart will break . . ." And neither man
Imagines that a god discusses mortals with a mortal.

So Hector mounts. Half of each pair of gates swings up,
And with the sun across his shoulders like a metal stole
   Hector comes out.

The daylight weakens. Up on the hillside
Women waist-deep in dusk sing while working.
The first movement of sunset turns the blue air
   Darker blue.

Patroclus fought like dreaming.
His head thrown up, his mouth—wide as a shrieking mask—
Sucked at the air to nourish his infuriated body,
And the Trojans seem to be drawn to him,
Locked round his waist, red water, washed against his chest,
And laid their tired necks beside his sword like birds,
—Is it a god? Divine? Needing no tenderness?—
Yet instantly they touch he butts them,
Cuts them back.

You know from books and talking pictures,
How people without firearms set about
Killing a tiger that has grown too old
To prey on antelope or zebra and
Must confine its diet to the slower
Animals like man. Following its spoor,
They rig a long funnel of netting up
On spikes (like pointed clothes-props) and the lean
Striped beast is driven down its throat by gongs.
The net is shut. And when the beast is tired out
The humans kill it in their own good time.
But if the net breaks many humans die.

Likewise Patroclus broke among the Trojans.
A set of zealous bones covered with flesh,
Finished with bronze, dipped in blood,
And the whole being inspired by ferocity.

−Kill them!

My sweet Patroclus,

−Kill them!

As many as you can,
For
Coming behind you in the dusk you felt
—What was it?—felt the darkness part and then

Apollo!

Who had been patient with you,
Struck.

His hand came out of the east,
And in his wrist lay eternity.
And every atom of his mythic weight
Was poised between his fist and bent left leg,
And it hit the small of your back, Patroclus . . .

Your eyes leant out. Achilles' helmet rang
Far and away beneath the cannon-bones of enemy horses,
And Achilles' breastplate (five copper plys
Mastered with even bronze) split like a pod.
And you were footless . . . staggering . . . amazed
Between the clumps of dying, dying yourself,
Dazed by the brilliance in your eyes
And the noise, like weirs heard far away.

So you staggered, blind eyes open,
Dabbling your astounded fingers in the vomit
On your chest.

And all the Trojans lay and stared at you,
Propped themselves up and stared at you,

Feeling themselves as blest as you felt cursed.
All of them just lay and stared
Except a boy called Euphorbus.

    He took his chance and cast.
The javeline went through both your calves,
Stitching your knees together, and you fell
(Not noticing the pain) and tried to crawl
Towards the fleet, and—even now—snatching
Euphorbus' ankle—Ah!—and got it? No . . .
Not a boy's ankle that you got,
But Hector's

    Standing above you,
His bronze mask smiling down into your face,
Putting his spear through . . . ach, and saying,
    "Why tears, Patroclus?
Did you hope to melt Troy down
And make our women carry home the ingots for you?
    I can imagine it!
You and your marvellous Achilles sitting,
Him with his upright finger wagging, saying,
'Don't show your face in here again, Patroclus,
Unless it's red with Hector's blood.'
    You fool.
You weak, impudent, silly little fool."
    And Patroclus,
Shaking his voice out of his body, says
    "Big mouth,
Remember it took three of you to kill me.
A god, a boy, and last of all, a hero!
    I can hear Death
Calling my name and yet,
Somehow it sounds like *'Hector'*
    And when I close my eyes
I see Achilles' face with Death's voice coming out of it."

    Saying these things Patroclus died.
And as his soul went through the sand like water,
Hector withdrew his spear and said
    "Perhaps."

from *Pax* (Book XIX of the *Iliad*)

Rat,
pearl,
onion,
honey:
these colours came before the sun
   lifted above the ocean
                    bringing light
   alike to mortals and immortals.

And through this falling brightness
through the by now
   mosque,
   eucalyptus,
   utter blue,
         came Thetis,
   gliding across the azimuth,
with armour the colour of moonlight laid on Her forearms,
   palms upturned towards the sun,
                    hovering above the fleet,
   Her skyish face towards her son,

   Achilles,
gripping the body of Patroklos naked and dead against his own,
   weeping terribly,
            while Thetis spoke:
   'Son . . .'
The soldiers looking on;
   looking away from it; remembering their own:
'Grieving will not change what Heaven has done.
Suppose you throw your hate after Patroklos' soul,
Who besides Troy will be the gainers?
   See what I've brought.'
And as she laid the moonlit armour on the sand
it chimed;
      and the sounds that came from it,
followed the light that came from it,
   like sighing,
            saying,
   Made In Heaven.

And those who had the neck to watch Achilles weep
could not look now. Nobody looked. They were afraid.

Except Achilles. Looked,
lifted a piece of it between his hands; turned it;
tested the weight of it; then,
spun the holy tungsten like a star between his knees,
slitting his eyes against the flare, some said,
by other thought the hatred shuttered by his lids,
    made him protect the metal.

His eyes like furnace doors ajar.

When he had got its weight
and let its industry console his grief a bit,
    'I'll fight'
he said. Simple as that. 'I'll fight.'

    And so Troy fell.

'But while I fight what will become of this'—
Patroklos—'Mother?
    'Inside an hour a thousand slimy things will burrow.
And if the fight drags on his flesh will swarm like water boiling.'
    And She:
'Son, while you fight
        Nothing shall taint him,
Sun will not touch him,
        Nor the slimy things.'

Promising this she slid
rare ickors in the seven born openings of Patroklos' head,
    making his carrion radiant.
And her Achilles went to make amends,
walking alone beside the broken lace that hung
    over the sea's green fist.

The sea that is always counting.

Ever since men began in time, time and

Time again they met in parliaments,
Where, in due turn, letting the next man speak,
With mouthfuls of soft air they tried to stop
Themselves from ravening their talking throats;
Hoping enunciated airs would fall
With verisimilitude in different minds,
And bring some concord to those minds, soft air
Between the hatred dying animals
Monotonously bear toward themselves,
Only soft air to underwrite the in-
Built violence of being and meld it to
Something more civil, rarer than true forgiveness.
No work was lovelier in history;
And nothing failed so often: knowing this
The Army came to hear Achilles say:
'Pax, Agamemnon.' And Agamemnon's 'Pax.'

Now I must ask you to concede reality,
to be a momentary bird above those men
and to watch their filings gather round
the rumour of a conference until
magnetic grapevines bind them close.
    From a low angle the Army looks oval, whitish centred,
split at one end, prised slightly open, and,
opposite to the opening, Achilles
(whom they had come to hear) with hard-faced veterans
on either side, lance-butts struck down,
and here and there a flag. Even the chariot mechanics,
cooks, priests, helmsmen, heralds and whores came up
    to hear the Lords say pax.

And as men will, they came, the limping Kings;
Odysseus first, chatting to Diomede, into the ring,
sitting them down; and after them, a trifle slow
but coming all the same, doomed Agamemnon,
King of Kings, his elbow gummed with blood,
walking as if he'd got five legs,
and sitting—rather wearily—beside Odysseus.

The ring is shut. Enormous quiet.

King Agamemnon and Achilles face each other
as different as polygon and circle.

Somebody coughs.

ACHILLES: 'King,
I have been a fool.
The arid bliss self-righteousness provokes
addled my heart.'
Odysseus nods.
'Remembering how I took her City,
and how its women offered me their bodies,
like simple creatures looking for a passage to the sea,
it would have been much better for us both
if Artemis had pinned her to the gates.
And as their mouths filled up with dust
doubtless the Greeks who died for our black amnesty
remembered me re-creating my exalted grudge each morning.
Yet I'm a man; I like my own.
And if another man—my King, what's more—
takes what is mine and lets the Army know it,
what are they both to do?
Kings can admit so little.
Kings know, what damages their principality endangers everyone.
If he is inconsiderate,
he is the King; if greedy, greedy King;
aoi! . . . if at noon the King says: *It is night,*
behold, the stars!
What if he damages the man on whom his principality depends?
He's still the King. His war goes on. The man must give.
But if the man in question cannot give
because the god in him that makes the King his chief dependant
is part and parcel of the god that cries revenge when he is wronged—
what happens then?
Stamp on my foot, my heart is stunned;
I cannot help it; it is stunned; it rankles—
here,' touching his chest.
'I am not angry anymore.
My heart is broken. Done is done, it says.
And yet the pain can only mask my rancour.

So let pride serve.
    When all is said and done—I am Achilles.'

    And the Army love their darling,
and they cry
    'Achil! Achil! Achil!'
louder than any counting sea,
    and sentries on the eastern walls of Troy
    sweat by their spears.

MATTHEW MEAD

The barbarians

If the victors were magnificent!
They are dazed by a splendour of broken palaces;
Cracked floors are the smoothest they have walked.
More beautiful than their goddess
(I have seen her in effigy, scowling)
And our underfed women (bitches!)
                    the common girls
They keep in their quarters.

Their commander is a squat devil,
Strong and cunning in a shabby coat;
He rides the city
With an armed guard and a rumour.

I think they will stay here,
Learning the streets, picnicking by the lake.
The wind drops and the dust settles.
They will walk among old tombs
Looking for ancestors.

From *identities*

I

After Paeschendale
After Katyn
After Auschwitz
After Kronstadt
We stand here

After Asquith
After Beria
After Noske
We stand here

What footfall?
What valley what field what forest
What streets in the morning sun
After the streets of Nagasaki?
Mask, persona,
Alias, pseudonym;
We stand here.

Why should we flee Jahveh?
    Where are the lightnings,
    The scorched prophets?
'In millions of hearts
'burns the inextinguishable
'flame of his word.'.
Apollo: carven flame.
Christ by candlelight.

And that he mount the unbuilt steps
To the unraised altar
        with sky for roof
        and star for pinnacle
        sumus in fide

We stand here.
We stand in the press.
We stand here alone.

IV

We stand here.
Statisti.

My pills are good pills
rustle and chink
container and carton and can

179

all cars are good cars
but our cars are *sacred*
the next scream you hear will be MAN.

'there is no such THING
         as saturation point'

My pills are good pills
interim interim
dreams you can drive in your sleep
hand washes hand
our after-death service
washes bone-white and bone-deep.

'for Christ's sake, Stan,
         TRY and be a merchant'

Buy it today
that agglutinous yellow
matches the STYLE of your heart
our workers sweat
at contented machine tools
producing the part of a part.

'buy him and THEN he'll buy you'

Mixed in a minute
served in a second
slashes the stomach for days
interim interim
listprice and discount
traders must follow the phrase.

'for all practical purposes
         YOU ARE the product'

My pills are good pills
my self's a good self
complete with a soul to consume
last thing at night

don't just say 'Dreadful' say 'Doom'.

We stand here
for all practical purposes
for christ's sake or near offer.
At our heels a question-mark
      in our heads the moon.

VII

My verses, Ochkasty, and your music,
Your mathematical progression
To the door of Terpsichore's boudoir,
These brought us a summons to dine
At the groaning table of Paren,
To wolf his steak, to guzzle his wine,
To play 'feet' with his wife (beneath table)
To ogle his sister.

The hordes of the East are unfed.
I felt them, Ochkasty,
Their hunger a wolf-pack,
Round the broken meats of that board.
Wolf-faces, wolf-bellies,
Landless, arms like sticks.
Most terrible were the eyes of the children,
Heirs to famine; Romulus, Remus unsuckled.

You would share your bread with them and perish,
Remembered by 'Tone Poem: Hunger'.
I am 'aware of the problem'.
See, it clutters a poem.

I weigh our undoubted genius
Against the million-death headline.
I spoon up my onion soup
And know that I am not God.

The hordes of the East are unfed.

If Io herself has failed them
          let us despatch
With teats and feeding bottles
          Paren to lands of morning

He serves a very good dinner.

He may meet cannibals.

From *the administration of things*

I

No days but these,
No Praesidium but this,
No silence but my own.
Drift of dead mind
In mind, noon its own spectre.
And what the dead men saw I see—
Girls on the lawn beneath a female sun,
Breasts, thighs, the prison of bright shade,
The certain shape of death.

Learn what is taught,
Learn only what is taught:
The same stiff dialect,
The revelation fixed;
Brittle as bone,
Stopped short like breath.
The whole summer archaic.

No age but this,
Shaped by the dead;
What they destroyed
          rebuilt as what they built,
A future traced in palms like parchment.
The silence mine, as if a dead man spoke
Or pondered in a sunlit interval
The dark from which he came.

II

Never clear, never simple
nor sharp in sunlight
and made straight;
long rain, a harvest rotting,
the report 'harvest rotting',
this report read, the discussion,
techniques of drying-out
and nameless fear.

Yet more approximate—
memories of an unknown;
all that a symbol masked
bare of a sudden;
a wall fallen, emptiness
an unending step.
The report read.
This read between the lines.

We move with the dead in mind.
Give us something easy to run
like Adelkhanov's shoe factory;
bankrupt shoe-makers begging for jobs,
unions hardly heard of.

VI

Riot, tumult, anticipated disturbances
or ice
or war
acts of god, enemies, pirates

at these risks

restraint of princes, rulers, peoples
quarantines, lockouts, strikes, combinations
fire on board, in hulk or craft

at this peril, these perils

183

or from any act, neglect, default whatsoever
or ice
or war
proceeding by any route, however circuitous
or as near thereto as she may safely get.

Send us on something easy like a run to Ithaca.

VIII

Sword or stealth, strength or ancient blood,
Conqueror, elect or heir—however you come,
Have no compassion. Curl the lip,
Let the eye grow cold.

Who more brutal than we
Who less compassionate
What colder eyes than ours
Who more unflinching
Facing the endless faces

Ours the command
The calm of copper noon
The Sind in blossom
An ante-natal clinic
In Deolali South

To rule. A grievous scourge.
We move with the dead in mind.
Time kills the dead,
Time and the death of memory.
A dark: simplicities
of Adieu and Anon.

To redistort a Weltanschauung

The new mirage emerges, right,
Heartrending, stubborn, slow to change.

MICHAEL ROBERTS

Out of the broken
morning   out of
the sunrise
                who
now
            dew on
the stiff curl
            races
the dawn wind and
his golden shadow
to stand
in the blear
and stir of our
half-woken day?

who should?

we are sleepers
plotters of stars
men for the ill-
kept night-watch

(cold ash
        of the phoenix)

we have stared
into darkness
for light
a light
born of light
would offend us.

Who from the 'motherless'
fire
     now leaps to burn

bleached curl
and profiled
flame

down the cold dawn
of our day
         to set
for everlasting day
a light on earth?

The dayspring bubbled.
We spat into it.

They sit with primitive nuclear weapons
aimed on Lepsinsk Kopal

That they may not

    in mucksweat
    coat-skirts aswirl
    chophaired and
    almond-eyed

that they may not

    bravado masking an awe
    of supermarket-temples
    diffidence thrust aside
    and all else to be slaked
    that they may not arrive

      distance and death
      in their eyes

the 'defenders of Europe
'for four hundred years'

sit between them and us.
Africa
at our back

black comely haunches
glutting the cradles
'many a digger'
Smith the last hero
and the victor
    he with the bloodiest spear.

Bodies are rolled from bed to scuffed slippers
and day stiff-jointed; in sense repetition;
in spring one more spring; the figure
in a worn carpet traced with a dull eye.

And the house old, the wind's sound, each ache
lent art and length, given due weight
the dragging footfall. For this are we bent
and gnarled and wrinkled—to cross the room.

And as at sunset what a high sun lit
—windows at morning, other people, earth—
takes back the darkness as a low sun sinks
and lights, at last, only itself

(the burst veins on the visage of the sky)
so here the shadows flicker in a face
as word and flesh sag in a sleepy chair
and dream beyond the poem and the child

of some deliverance—not day renewed,
hauled up the man that was, the girl aroused
in the cold chamber where the thin crone lies
(the child tottering, the pile thick)

but day done, time completed, a room
with a threadbare carpet crossed.

When you lie
to me
     as you will
          lie
with élan
deceive me
with a laugh
meet my eyes
steadily
when you lie
to me
     as you should
          lie
as if truth
were told

     I need not
     truly know
     all (invent
     that other
     half of truth
     with care)
          lie
as if oaths
were new
     and by no
     kiss betrayed
          lie
with more skill
tomorrow.

You shall not hope to break
the bond of earth nor rise
against the tyranny of the rose;
the green tree shall not fall
     by your treason
nor the west wind perish
     on your barricade;
though street-fighters mob the stars
     and squadroned thinkers
     turn the flank of the sky,

Gentlemen where is the rhythm
or one man to stand unaided
upon three feet of air?

You shall not forswear your day
for gardens beyond catastrophe
nor say 'We shall not die'
nor say 'Well if we die
'tomorrow is worth our deaths'.
The tides ebb and the tides flow
what coup d'état could change this?
We sweat, we shiver;
would you riot against the hoar-frost
or behead high noon?

Comrades, you are to know limits.
You are to be yourselves,
in your time, in your pain.
You are breakers of stone;
there is stone to be broken.
No life is too long to waste
    in waiting for disaster
and earth turns
and a vlast of honeysuckle
fills a garden and firm
is the diktat of flesh.

Neither as we saw
nor as we were seen
nor as we saw ourselves
in a glass darkly
outfacing the shiftless stare
like the blind standing
before a railed-off sculpture;
Nor the eyes evasive, cold,
altered, turned aside
('the plains are empty of horsemen
'there are no horsemen
'I will not look');
Nor the attempt to add nothing,

the tilth an artefact, the ruin
                only rebuilt.
Nor that sockets have cradled
             the flame
above parchment cheeks;
nor the lip painted, the nipple
              rouged,
a love draped in an artifice of light;
but to pluck green from the spectrum.
Sheba dances her triumph
within a darkened hall.
The ruins triumph
When no man walks among them.

Rose-coloured spectacles,
smoked glass, stained glass,
dawn in a haze
   of halo-filtered glory;
through a corrective lens
the sharp, false vision;
dogma defined with desire
in an esteem of mirrors.

          We were the lagging
          shadows after moon-set

          Dark on the dark
          in the dark

          We learned in the dark
          the darkness in us

          as clear as light
          more simple
          more specific

          We were shadows
             before sunrise
          waiting for
             sunrise

Negative, capable,
to be cast.

Day renews day, 'our' day but uncommanded;
a taut habit of waking to windows stressed with light.
Blood and the will of man (the frail boast)
burn in a tolerance of air.

Or light excels without object
folding no form in gold
in lazy splendour
nor swift in the slash of air
quick limbs leap and turn
as men like gods in sunlight
race down to the clear water;
and no face feels the light
burning and firm upon it,
no eye seeks the line of hills.

Or light has no likeness
born of the same fire,
no eye seeks the line of hills
nor follows unthinking grace
nor tongue trembles to truth
   '. . . . like gods to clear water'.
Nor is pride. Nor the heart sick.
Nor a name covered with darkness.

We have loved the clear phantom of summer,
the clean edge under the dazzle;
the same fire in the red dance of flame.

Earth without men; no footfall,
the empty yellow of sunlight as at parting.

D. M. THOMAS

Elegy for an android

At the last moment I
thought of the Neanderthals
pouring their flint arrows
into the rough grave
with its skins, haunch of meat, and
the wedding-ring I did
fling down onto your
casket was like a
lifebuoy, but where could I
possibly pretend that you were
going? I think that if I could
have paid more for you,
there would have been more persons
standing above that hole.

Bion and Theocritus
seeing your straight limbs,
classic grace of feature and gold
dazzling curls would have
unhitched their pipes but
chancing to see the
tiny emblem *'made in
U.S.A.'* in the whorl of your
navel would have
shuddered and walked
on. Yet I loved you,
Vanessa, passing the love of
women.

O my America

'O my America, my Newfoundland!"

What worked
for Donne—their Tu-
dor lips
hooked by that fine-
spun line
—a dozen reefs
to pil-
grim through, then More,
—freezes
Jan to an Ellis

Island
glaze. —Christ! she says,
Christ! do
you think my thighs
Broadway,
do you think my
love's a
Wall Street stock? Gee,
thanks for
nothing, fella!

(She speaks
like that despite
her First
in History—it's
put on) . . .
Ah well—I try
that vir-
gin globe designed
to break
virginities. . .

Christ! she
says, Christ! that whore
the moon,
that poxy cat
raddled
alternately

193

by Reds
and neo-Fasc-
ist jerks.
Oh swell—that's me!

—whirls down
the road . . . prospect-
ing night,
gloating on quartz,
lets stream
her fine washed gold. . .
I throw
my last, call her
bright star.
Her laughter rings,

Am I
no more? boy, how
you flat-
ter me! She points
a gay
finger at faint
star-dense
Andromeda.
In there's
a billion Jan's!

—O Jan,
you are more wild,
untouch-
able, than New-
foundland,
than moon, than star!
Only
a quasar is
so rad-
iantly beyond

us. —Christ!
says Jan. Christ! (ten-
derly)

L A B Y R I N T H

```
es-conveniently-easy
o                    t
g                    h
e     e has spun t   e
h     h          h
-                e   line
o     sa noos        t
t                t   o
                 h
m           stirred
i           d    e
h           na da t  b
d                h
l  ti tsaeb gnipeels e
                     w
                     o
                     u
                     n
                     d

            up by a man
```

```
                VED YOU
        O          HE
        L          E
es conveniently easy O
g  NOT EVEN        F      t
e  U  e has spun  F      h
h  O  h           E      e
o  Y      HE      R   line
t  D   sa NooS    D
m  E   E   A   t  T O WAIT WHILE
i  V   H   I   h  o           E
h  O   T   D stirred    b     I
d  L       d     e  t   e
           Ina da   h   w     WENT
d  I THGUOHT        e   o
l  ti tsaeb gnipeels    u
                        n
   FFORP-TI DELLIK DNA NI
   E             R        up by a man
   R             O
   D ME HIS  S   W
```

```
WRITHE-AND W
             H
        YM HCI
D               HANDS        ved you
N               A                o
A               N                l          h
T              eS COnveniently easy         e
S               N
I   g         noT even          fTO THINK
W              AIN              fer  h
T   i           e  has spun     t e      T
      e   u  e                  h d       H
H   o     h                     e         A
C   t         he   sa noos      e  line   T
I   i       d        a      t o wait Whil
H   m     e  v       h  i       h      o  e
W   h     h  o     t  d stirred  I NE     i
N        d   l         d            b
I           ina da     t   Pe       i
         d i thguoht        h   L    A   went
         l ti tsaeb gnipeels    A   Yo   t
                 fforp ti dellik dna ni  Eu
AW EZA            e           r        A Dn
S      M         r           o         ASup by a man
A   D  S         e           w
A   A            d me his    s         A
LRE  IHT DNALSI  SIHT NO DLIHC
```

FOURTH MONTH

```
                    DARKNESS
     writhE  and w        THE GROUND          A  EVO
          H      h                 T       N     L
     d    Tym hci                  D
     n                             R
     a    Nh            ved you    E   HA
          Ia              o        M   TYRAN
     t    n               l    TH MY BODY
     s    Pd                   A  h    L
     i    DEEs conveniently easy       WOULD
     w       o      n              o
     t    G  g   not even         fto think        K
     i    N      ain              fer h      t     I
          I  e u e has spun       te e       ha    L
     h    R  h o h                h d        h a   L
     c    R  o      he            e   line   t
     i    I  t   sa noos          t                A
     h    T  d          e   a     t o wait whilN
     w    S  e          h   i     h       o h  eD
     n    UOY l         t   d stirred    i ne
     i    Y  h          ina da       t   b  LLIK
     t        d i thguoht          h  l   M w
     l    LEEF I               e  awEVYSEL
     i       l ti tsaeb gnipeels      yo A  nF
     u                            eu S  OT
     b       fforp ti dellik dna ni
     aw eza   e        r         a
     s y  m   r        o      sup by a man
     d        e        w
     a a  s   d me his s       a
     lre iht dnalsi siht no dlihc
```

LEAVING YOU LOOK W
          darkness **E**   a evo
N writhe and w   **LL IF THERE I** n l
O   h   h the ground t **S** d
    d   tym hci   r**A**   i
C n   e**NYTHING Y**
I a   nh   ved you   m   a t**O**
N t   ia   o   th my body tyran**U**
O s   n   l   a h   l e
C i   pd   eneb se   **N**
A i   dees conveniently easy   would**E**
L w   o   n   o   **E**
    t   g g not even   fto think   k**D**
E   n   ain   fer h   t   i
R i   ie u e has spun t e e   h   l
A   r h o h   h d   a   l
    h   r y   he   e   line t
S c i o   sa noos   t   a
D i t t d   e a   t o wait whiln
R h s   e   h i   h   o h ed
O w   m v   t d stirred i ne
W   u i o   d   e   b llik
    n o h l   ina da t pe
S i y   h   l   m w
I   d i thguoht   e   awevysel
H **T** leef   yo a nf
   L   l ti tsaeb gnipeels eu s ot
    M E   dn
UG Y **D** **DNU**fforp ti dellik dna ni
  b **I**   **O**e   r   a
aw eza **H** OT F**r**   o   sup by a man
s y m   e   **HE WALKS**
  d   **E HAS**d me his s   a
a a s **H**   **W**
lre iht **DNALSI** siht no dllhc
        EHT NO EM HT

SIXTH MONTH

```
leaving you look w
        darkness e                    a evo
  n writhe and w    ll if there i  n    l
OOM EH  h      h the ground  t   s d        i
N   d T  tym hci                  r   a        i
S c n                              e nything y
i a  R   nh          ved you    m    a    to
n   O  ia        o    th my body tyranu
Mo t    n          l    a h   l    e          n
Y c s E pd   SS eneb se              n
  a i Cdees conveniEntly easy        woulde
Sl w A    o    n    N    o                    e
O t Fg g not evenI    fto think        kd
Re      n      ain  LENOLfer h      t    i
Rr i Yi e u e has spun t e    e      h    l
Oa   R r h o h          Eh d      a    l
W  h Gr    y      he    He    line t
I s cNi o    sa noos    T Ht              a
N d iAt t d      e   a      tTo wait whiln
Gr o h s    dev      h i    hIW STo h  ed
Mw  ws Su io  m v    t d stirred Si ne
O    n Ro h l        d   e    R b  llik
T s i H y          ina da  t Upe
Hi T    d i thguoht          h Bl    m w
Eh t leef                  e  awevysel
R  lA    l ti tsaeb gnipeels Leu s ot
  iF M e                      Udn
C ug YNd  dnufforp ti delliK dna ni
O  b Ui      oe        r    Sa
l aw ezaSh ot fr          o      sup by a man
Ls y m      e      he walksY
S d  E e hasd me his s      Ma
  a a sHTh                  w
Slre  iht dnalsi siht no dliHc
T                eht no em htT
RETCH OUT TO FILL THE LABYRIN
```

```
leaving you look w                    UND ALL
          darkness e          Oa evo P
n writhe and w   ll if there iRn  l  O
oom eh  h     h the ground t  sGd    I
n  dt  tym hci              r IAR     N
'c  n                    eLnything yT
si  a  r  nh    VED YOU FAMI   a  toL
 n   o  ia     O    th my body tyranuE
mo   t    an    L    ah   l  e       S
yc  s  e  pd      ss eneb se       nS
 a  i cdeés convenlently easy     woulde
sl  w  a  o   n    n    o         eM
o   t fg g NOT EVENi  fto think   kdY
re    n    ain  lenolfer  h  t  i
rr  i yi e Ue has spun t e     hD AL  L
oa    rr h O h       eh d      aN EL  I
w  h gr  Y    HE     he  line tI Y  F
is c ni o  sa nooS  t ht       LB A E
nd i at t D   e A    tto wait whiln
gr  h  s    O  h   I  hiw st o h  ed
 o  w  s  mV   t  D stirred si ne
mw  iu i O     d    e   r b  llik
o  n ro h L    Ina da t upe
ts  i ey            h  bl  m w
hi  h  d I THGUOHT    e  awevysel
eh  t tleef            lyo a  nf
r  l a  l ti tsaeb gnipeels leu s ot
  i fm e             udn
c  ug ynd dnufforp ti dellik dna ni
o   b  ui  oe      r   sa
iaw ezash ot fr       o     sup by a man
ls  y  m    e    he walksy
s  d  e e hasd me his s   ma
 a  a  shth          w
slre  iht dnalsi siht no dlihc
t           eht no em htt
retch out to fill the labyrin
```

```
leaving you look w              und all
        darkness e                oa evo p
  n writhe and w    ll if there irn    l o
oom eh  h    h the ground t  sgd        i
n   d t  tym hci          riar        i n
'c   n     OF YLL              elnything yt
si   a  r   nhR    U ved you fami   a    tol
 n    o  iaM    F  o    th my body tyranue
mo    t    nE      l   a h   l      e      s
yc  s  e  pdD      ss eneb se            ns
 a  i cdees conveniently easy      woulde
sl  w  a  oON n      n     o              em
o   t fg gWhot eveni    fto think     kdy
re      n     ain    lenolfer h    t  i
rr  i yi eSu e has spun t e e      hd al l
oa    rr hHOUh        eh d        an el i
w   h gr   yL    he      he    line ti y  f
is  c ni o Dsa noos    t ht        lb a  e
nd  i at  t dE   e    a    tto wait whiln
gr  h  s   eRINGh   i   hiw st o  h  ed
 o   w s  m v   t  d stirred si ne
mw    iu i o   A    d   e TTr b   llik
o   n ro h l      ina da StAupe
ts  i ey       PATH B      AhUbl   m w
hi    h  d i thguohtU      PeT awevysel
eh  t tleef      RSTING    lyo a   nf
r   l a  l ti tsaeb gnipeelsMleu s ot
    i fm e              CSUudn
c   ug ynd  dnufforp ti deLlik dna ni
o   b   ui    oe        r E  sa  pRES
iaw ezash ot fr        o S I SUP bySa man
ls  y  m      e    he walksy SEIRC    O
s   d   e e hasd me his s     maY      W
 a  a   shth              w  O   UT OF
slre  iht dnalsi siht no dlihcU   O
t                      eht no em htt
retch out to fill the labyrin W  DAERHT
                              IND UP THE
```

UOY MORF TIXE ON SI EREHT EM ENOG EVAH U
R leaving you look w **ANDS FOR** und all O
darkness e **H RELBA O**ᵀ oa evo pY
B n writhe and w ll if there irn l o
Ioom eh h h the ground t sgd iH
Rn d t tym hci riar i nG
T c n of yll elnything ytU
Hsi a r nhr u ved you fami a tolO
n o iam f o th my body tyranueH
Rmo t ne l a h l e sT
Oyc s e pdd ss eneb se ns
U a i cdees conveniently easy woulde T
Nsl w a oon n n o e M
Do t fg gwnot eveni fto think kd U
re n ain lenolfer h t i Y A
Err i yi esu e has spun t e e hd al L H
Voa rr hhouh eh d an el I
Ew h gr yl he he line ti y F U
Ris c ni o dsa noos t ht lb a E O
Ynd i at t de e a tto wait whiln I Y
gr h s eringh i hiw st o h edS
Co w s m v t d stirred si ne H
Omw u i o a d e t tr b llikA T
Ro n ro h l ina da staupe N N
Nts i ey path b aheul m w N I
Ehi h d i thguohtu pet awevyselE R Y
Reh t tleef rsting lyo a nfM Y B
r l a l ti tsaeb gnipeelsmleu s ot P A
I i fm e csuudn T L
c ug ynd dnufforp ti dellik dna ni Y
So b ui oe r e sa press
Hiaw ezash ot fr o s i sup by a man
Als y m e he walksy seirc o
Ls d e e hasd me his s may w
L a a shth w o ut of
slre iht dnalsi siht no dlihcu o
St eht no em htt
Eretch out to fill the lanyrin w daerht
E **YOUR FACE** ind up the

ANSELM HOLLO

& how it goes

zoo day, today
.with the 2 young

"what animal
            did you like best?"
"that man"

she's three, more perfect
            than any future
                        I or any man
                        will lead her to

but now, to the gates
            & wait for the boat
                        by the Regent's Canal
we stand in a line
all tired, speechless

a line from Villon
            sings into my mind:
"paradis paint . . ."
            "a painted paradise
where there are harps & lutes"

yes & no children
but who say such pretty things
            for me to inscribe
                        in one of my notebooks
with the many blank pages
            marking the days
                        I feel as forsaken as
                                    balding François

who also found
in himself
the need to adore

as different as my stance is
here, in a line of moms & dads
down the green slope
to the canal

—when he wrote to the Virgin
hypocrite, setting his words
to the forgotten quavers
of his mother's voice

le bon Dieu
knows where he'd left her

at least
I'm holding her hand
she's here, my daughter
he is here
"my son

the lives of the poets
even the greatest, are dull
& serve as warnings"
to say this, suddenly
here, in the line
would no doubt be brave

he's half asleep,
clutching a plastic lion

"the thing is, they could not
get out of themselves
any better than these
who also wait
for a boat

—o that it were drunken

on what wild seas—
they didn't
      even try, just griped about it
         or made little idols
for brighter moments . . ."

the boat has arrived
    & there,
        the elephant's trumpet,
          farewell

her weight on my knees
his head on my shoulder
    here
     we
     go

we, best-loved animals
one, two, three
    & as Illuminated
    as we'll ever be

Instances

i

nice place ya got here
the Messenger said
to her whose island
it was

    but the boss
give an order:
let the guy sail
back to his own

ii
there he sat
by the shore

broken nose
missing teeth
balding
      old dog

thinking of elsewhere   as always
traveling hard   in his head

iii
where she was
a moment ago
there is only the wind
whirling up leaves
in her form

long train of leaves
carried by   known to be small
though invisible   hands
while someone is playing a tune on a reed

iv
o Athenaia
fixup the old dog
make him look good to her
again

      eating her famous
celery salads
drinking to her
with new eyes

      flexing
      his toes
    under the table

v
like a trajectory of tons
metal and flesh
hurled down the street
in the living light

his anima
drifting ahead

leading him into it   and through

when he got to the other side
people looked different than he had thought

vi
came up from the cave
patted him   told him
time now
             to go

"who said I wanted to go?"

vii
who walk in back of the back of the real
"beside you"
                  the term intersection
a crude imitation of what they are

your known dead are your gods
beautiful but inaccurate
metaphors of themselves

who comes
           has words for it
will be worshiped as men on horses
in Malinche's country.

Buffalo—isle of wight power cable

i
writing a letter he said
"this instant in time"
but what was that instant
if not where they were

she and the three
like plants with platinum petal hair
sprung from his head

ii
'in the Neverness Motels of the Bitter Country
lovers lie sleeping and loving in fits and starts'

iii
empty
     milky sky
above the building-brick town with its captive dogs
baying at night and in the mornings
the radiation
you opened the door and it hit you

air of metal and transmutations

iv
the cars kept flowing past and into the tower courtyard
but when they stopped no one got out of them
he was waiting for no one
whom did he want to hold
                 here in the next town

far away too

he had won the race but no one was cheering
slowly he drove up to the starting line

The charge

small metal box I was given
with a length of black string
     the fuse? no
   it won't light
      no fire
only his ashes of eighty years
into this hole in the ground.

burial
the law demands
in his cold country

can't keep your ancestors
            on a shelf nor give them to wind sun and rain
they must be dug under
mummies bones rotting flesh even ashes go
            into the ground.

hold the string gently
    it slides
across my palm
goes slack. *son*
            bury your father
is the law.

a scholar
he had the face of a chieftain
it haunts me
            the sense of that hole being far too small
to contain what I left there.

Bouzouki music

1
Odysseus was
ein Sitzriese

'a sitting giant'

one who looks tall
at table

see him now
through Nausicaa's eyes
shambling forth and into her eyes
out of those shrubs by the shore

2
we love you
by our defects you
tell us apart and
we
love you

3
'he had the funniest legs'
         —Calypso

4
a man's legs grow
straight out of his soul

who knows where they take him

5
heel and toe
and soul to sole

all that

       bouzouki music

Your friend

he said this
he said that
when pressed
as to which
he said nothing at all

in his country the weather
was mostly rainy

he tried to ride horses
they didn't go   or went
too fast

he punched them in the head
he fell off them

he tried to love women
tried to write poems

even his fellow men
their wives their children and cattle
he tried to love

but he didn't know
how or what was
or was good for him
at all

whatever it was
it kept punching him
in the head to make him
fall off

so he blamed them for it
all of them fellow men women
children cattle poems and horses

many a rainy
day you could hear him
yelling 'it's all
your fault'

after that things
were all right for a while
until the next try

On the occasion of becoming an echo

the goddess stands in front of her cave
waves me into the drawing   eyes
like an afterthought
dotted in   green

Gaia   drawn by a six-year-old
very clear

many more things in this room
books chairs a bed
at least two people
(how many more in their dreams)
but the signals are garbled
garbled

I mean (he says
who is I   who *is* I?)
mean well I want the whole world to love me
not need me at all

the goddess stands in front of her cave
not waving me in   just raising her hands
as if to say 'well   who's to tell you?'
once upon a time
my head says   there was a man he got very tired
he went to sleep and didn't dream
didn't even sleep but was gone

out
and out there
all things were clear

He she because how

one a.m.
                and she has been sleeping
two hours
                is still asleep

didn't marry him 'only to sleep'
but does now
                sleep

because she's tired because
he's been unkind? because

feeling her bones through her sleep
on the floor in their other room

because she's her kind of woman
because he's his kind of man

and because she is sleeping
                              he's writing
moving a few of his smaller bones

words like love and hurt
kindness unkindness blindness
ecstasy jealousy anger
sweetness
              that too
sweetness of making it with you

how do those words hang together
how does his hand move the pen

how do he (plus) she (equals) it hang together
on their still beautiful
(though in his case
                    slightly bent) frames?

two a.m. questions
now make him sleepy too

he'll go wake her up

they won't feel the same

Bison flower days

for Michael Rumaker

i

the day Jayne Mansfield died
        ... crossed Buffalo Main St.
     "buy a new shirt"
   "you *depressed?*"
           almost run over
          obtained
      a cut-rate bottle of bourbon

           one
       of a number of sunny days
   "Mr. Clarke"
   complained:
after-effects of too much prune juice
   "may we suggest you remove
     your blazer & cardigan"
        in the 80s
          (he *and* the temperature)
     but such a beautiful hat
     told one and all
        what a prick WBY was

      no doubt no doubt
     Odysseus   Oxygen
       how it connects

         a CRAZY machine

ii

gone to some lengths
such sonnets
   to some
as always
      sweet silly girl
   who once had the patience

        let her hair grow
    to an unusual length

he decided to purchase a radio
I
    that is
decided to buy a radio
it was that way
    (of variable
        lengths)

iii
taut
        this place
peopled by helpful intelligent
    vending machines

soldiers of Jesus Christ
    the cardinal said
        (Xmas eve 66)

sit staring into space
    and it goes out
                and out

we been talkin' about Jackson
ever since the fire went out

        while the very young
            move past
                and out

KEN SMITH

The street

I.M. Antonio Machado
And for Europe, 1936-45

leads nowhere, cannot be entered,
down which no one is walking

into the silence, the pure sea
of boats, cryings, scuffed quays.

The grey air is empty, built into
cloud-columns. Street of childhood,
     no one is calling.
In its doorways no person is standing
nor stares from one house to another.

     Things happen to us.
War boarded these windows, split walls
spilled in the held spaces.

In the growing dark only a sadness
presses the stairs to the stilled rooms

whose walls peel like maps. Here the guns
and the toys become one another. The war

has moved off. Who left can't return.
Who lived here has forgot the clear lines

the far buildings had, *it has happened*
we say, the sound bobs on the water.

Who stares at the great shadows, remembers
a voice, forgets whose, who watches

the sunlight fall, there, between high houses
themselves fallen, his feet don't lead back.

Who had a house now has a stone.

Beyond breath

i
Beyond breath labour bread—
he feels grass shake without wind—
a twig snaps with no footstep

Fields flecked by rain and yellow—
too long he wanted more—
his hands make a dismissal

She sweeps the dust out,
the smuts of the rain forests—
she sweeps words out of her mouth—
he sits with rats in the barn—
the silence cannot endure itself

ii
Tear up the map of your lands.
Let the foxes out hunting.
Fill the forms up with jokes.
Give the schools to the children.
Scrap the dead languages.
Prevent nothing, prevent nothing

Behind those who pile up the bread
come the armies

You will be accused, deny nothing

Facts

Reading about Machado
teaching in dreary Baez
I looked from my book
finding myself on the wrong bus
in the wrong road
in the wrong town

Elsewhere
walking through the gaslight
I was on the wrong platform
in the wrong country

It was still raining
on an evening in March
with the same wind blowing
but I stepped down
into the wrong century

the wrong planet
I said
looking at Russia and America

Well then, I accept
the wrong universe
but I do not attach myself;
my textbooks yawn up at me:
8 Henries, 6 wives.
I learn the facts
and don't count the dead
with no claim on us

And only afterwards think
how the sea makes a mouth
between continents
under the frail blown seeds of men
leaving for China,
and Columbus, stepping ashore,
who gaped at the wrong Indians

Old mill, Newton St. Cyres

Bring out number weight & measure in a year of dearth
                                             —Blake

Knowledge alone is no more than a weariness of the soul
                                    —Arthur C. Clarke

Always this pressing for shape—
paddlewheel, gear's tooth, millstone,
wood driven on water, the force
pushing through iron to stone and the stones
grinding to quiet the shudder of wheatfields.
Centuries of grain, centuries of water,
galaxies of dust mottling the sunlight
sheened their working flesh, dust
in the eyelid, chaff in the shoes.
Somewhere are numbers and graphs
for the mountains of bread, the fat loaves
rising in ovens: knowledge of soils,
rainfall, knowledge of mills, beams, joints,
or the tensions of water—for the curious
threading their beads of fact, those magpies.
Leave that old weariness
knowing or not knowing, the earth's water
is pressing out of shape, its denial gives
in its *no* the quick of renewal, a mere
gesture of water here and not here
like a going of air. I revolve doubt
around doubt in this certainty of things—
stone, metal, wood, the running grain
beaten to meal: show me a thin cook
or a poor baker, wherever I look
I might see only wheatfields, possibles
turning about without centre,
doubt at the axlehub driving the flour
into bread and the bread into sleek girls
measuring their waists in pale slices.
Crush the doubt under words, it

raises its ear, its signal for silence;
crush out the silence, it waits at the end
of our syllables, entered this mill
like an anthem. A quiet under sound,
the doubt back of certainties, there's hunger
for bread and hunger apart from the bread.
Measureless absence, hunger is no word
it is nothing in the mouth
but struggling to say. On Famine Ridge
the bones count out loud: rib bone,
shut mouth, dead genital,
stone sounding on stone, throat whispering
eat eat in the sour fields,
charity's ashes and lemonjuice, eat, eat,
devour the earth. To the last crumb

Inventory/Itinerary

Illinois, Iowa
Dead grass & maize stalks
Miles, miles, 4½ thousand
Timeshift 7 hours
2 continents, 1 ocean
Travelling, 4 days
1 good time, much being quiet
200 cigarettes, 1 bottle brandy
1 arrival in Iowa City
March 25th 1969, 6:00 pm
$3.38¢ in my pocket
1 cab-ride into the clapboard wilderness
1 return on foot carrying 2 bags
9 phone calls, 2 wrong numbers, 1 reply
Waiting, waiting
Hunger, loneliness, weariness, silence
1 poem written quickly holding things down
The durations of wind, cold, grainfields
Endless helpfulness, cheerfulness, on the nail
The bland faces, America America
And silence. And night
And wind blowing, right through the heart

The Amana Colonies

Founded 1855 in Iowa by a group calling themselves
Inspirationists originated in Germany about 1714.
The immigrants 'according to His laws and His
requirements in our own consciences' attempted a
community sharing work and wealth equally that
persisted up to the Depression but that exists
now as tourist bait close to Interstate 80:
"one of the midwest's most historic and recent
attractions".

1

Fortitude, endurance, *amana: remain faithful.*
We survive the sea and the great silences.
Under God and the blue sky we share all we have.
Amana—we put a spade to the wilderness.
Amana—skill of our hands on the new turned land.
Amana—the word is our breath, we share,
we survive the woods that are gone
where the redmen went hearing the rain speak.
Amana, the corn roots, cattle and vines,
mortise and tenon, coins and sweat run together.
Amana, our work and our bread.
Amana. The voice within each of us speaks

2

In the turning of wood or habit of speech
that old life may whisper, a black dress
fluttered in wind, wooden shoes in the snow,
poverty chewing its nails, winter and summer.
Will nothing of sharing survive, the cry
of what was weathered away in the guidebook.
Erosion is paint from an aerosol can, visitors
sniffing repeating *authentic authentic*—
a word in the mouth. We make and we sell,
We share our dead root, we dream of endurances

3

What prints mark butterchurn, spinning-wheel,
what is a scythe's use, how held, what sweats

stain the handles of tools? What sleeps
in the dropped vowels or survives
in the ticking of clocks? Why these names
and *amana,* this word, that remains, that endures?

Persistent narrative

The speaker opens his mouth.
The lovers lie down together.
The boy is sent to the war.

The last train leaves the city.
The sky clouds over with ruin.
The animals step back into shadow.

The speaker opens his mouth.
The fields are trampled by horses.
Children crouch down in the ashes.

Survivors wait at the frontier.
Two armies meet in a forest.
The lovers take off their clothes.

The speaker opens his mouth.
An earthquake topples the belltower.
The boy lies down in a cornfield.

Soldiers patrol all the streets.
The grocer has run out of flour.
The girl dreams of a wheatfield.

The speaker opens his mouth.
Now the woman sweeps out her house.
Now there is a christening.

The ship enters the harbour.
The girl waves her red scarf.
The lovers cry out in their love.

And at last it is still.
And the speaker says *I shall begin.*
The children are all asleep.

After a journey

When we wake
snow will lie on the sills. There are things
happening when no-one knows it

I returned from the west finding the trees bare.
With the first cold my children came,
I don't know where they learn their songs from

I know the dead have little to say to us,
but speak like they were still the same, like clocks
scuttling into the dark with the same nothings

Later perhaps they turn aside to a place
where they no longer need us to listen, or go out
when they are at peace like burned wicks

What we don't know yet is no matter.
I pray not to a god but to stone,
to the grass, to the running hooves of the horses

The stone poems

1.
A man's work
that he must bend for them,
in his lifting become
stone-shut
with a stone's presence

Stone of house, stone
of monument, deceptions,
nothing in their gift

Stone in a man's field
or a man's shoe—

225

piece of the earth's
wish to be idle, rid of us,
fraction of misery

Not as the sea is:
weeds, birdcries, a fish
glancing the sunk light

Sea changes totally,
stone rarely. The dead
form a new kind of stone

It will not alter. Snap
maybe, be nattered to dust
or the chafing of water

Part of the sea asleep
in its own shadow. Part
of its huge stone, growing

2.
Either he must shift it
or go round it

Dragged to the field's edges
to be grown over, useful there

Others rise later, chiselled
by rain, tossed up by boys

Arrive strangely by night
or happen as comets do. In New England
frosts force them out, stone's
on the move

Some lie continually
in the field's way,
finding their way back
like bleak malevolent creatures
wanting to sit in open fields

And the man keeps pelting them
in a backward whirlpool of stones
slewed over centuries

As if this were a battle: a man
hurling stones and the stones'
sad returns to their orbits

As if they would lie barearse
to the sun, giving nothing growth

3.

I

Sonecold we say.
In the blank faceless thing
nothing of our meanings
but that it outlasts us, holds up
the names that mean nothing

That it is stone, that
it is cold, that it is
chosen for sepulchres

Nothing in that: bones
picked clean as a stick
with the seasons drained out,
a stone flag,
a perpetual lament
for dead people

And nothing in that, nothing
can be stayed off: *a
stoney vision* we say,
amazed at the strange light
grown in the world

II

Absence of stones
in our cities;

only the stone scraped
to its usefulness

No miracles of gneiss
nor graining nor quartzstone,
neither the dross nor the eye
of volcanoes, no scourings
of rivers, blocks, puddingstones

Nothing in our way, nothing
that might grow wildly
or move oddly, or not move

Not the bull's darkness
nor the beasts' wonder
at their own birth

Not that. Only silences
after eleven, only the wind
smelling of forgotten country

City: a land gleaned clean,
yellow with absences, a soil
of misery. And never a stone

4.
All through, stone. Things
immersed in it
become stone

Without feature
save for the scrape
of a glacier, wind
or water

Anonymous,
not dreaming, not dancing

Intends nothing—
neither the good house

nor arrowhead, not even
inconvenience

But there, resisting,
holding on while the planet
shudders to bits

Nothing to do
but be grey boulder
or pebble

No inside, no outside, no centre.
No squatting like an animal.
No nesting like a bird

Not wanting to go back
into rock, not wanting
to enter the sea, not wanting
to be a small red flower
or a lost button

Not even likeable

Not bothered

5.
Turned in the hand, idly
to the contempt of the busy

Whatever it would be
to be brought to it

A man's say to be
pig, bird in flight
the tiny house of a small

A man's say. Stone is
its own place

That it may look

from the churchwall
a man sharpens chisells

From the bleak glance
of quarries footstools,
snarling waterspouts,
knights in stone armour,
the poor kneeling or stooping,
locked beasts, a man
peering, Siva's dance

The man's tools seek
a stone anaconda

But the stones, bunched in riverbeds,
abandoned on plains,
lie down anywhere

They will not answer
out of the strange mouth
of the dead

The silence
applauds them

PETER WHIGHAM

The orchard is not cut down

The orchard is gone. A space, con-
      ventionally like Paaschendaele,
      linearly framed by black rail-
ings, rises to a wide field on
which, inert, the milk-brown cows sun
      themselves and where the busy mail-
      van and the bus brightly curtail,
on the road sudden as a gun,
the field—the vanished grove.

                     No dream
      of priest or king can empower mind
      to seize the blossom on the wind;
only, in passing, I have seen

      swan leaning on confused swan
      fall inwards like a folding fan.

Erotion's death

Frontus, Father; Flacilla, Mother, extend
      your protection from the Stygian shadows.
The small Erotion (my household Iris)
      has changed my house for yours. See that the hell-
hound's horrid jaws don't scare her, who was no
      more than six years old (less six days) on the
winter day she died. She'll play beside you
      gossiping about me in child's language.
Weigh lightly on her small bones, gentle earth,
      as she, when living, lightly trod on you.

                 Martial, V.34;

from Catullus

2
Lesbia's sparrow!
                  Lesbia's plaything!
in her lap or at her breast
when Catullus's desire
                 gleams
and fancies playing at something,
                       perhaps precious,
a little solace for satiety
                when love has ebbed,
    you are invited to nip her finger
    you are coaxed into pecking sharply,
if I could play with you
                her sparrow
lifting like that my sorrow
                I should be eased
as the girl was of her virginity
when the miniature apple,
                gold/undid
her girl's girdle
           —too long tied.

8
Break off
        fallen Catullus
              time to cut losses,
bright days shone once,
        you followed a girl
            here & there
loved as no other
        perhaps
            shall be loved,
then was the time
        of love's *insouciance,*
            your lust as her will
matching.
        Bright days shone
           on both of you.

Now,

        a woman is unwilling.

           Follow suit

weak as you are

        no chasing of mirages

           no fallen love,

a clean break

        hard against the past.

           Not again, Lesbia.

No more.

        Catullus is clear.

           He won't miss you.

He won't crave it.

        It is cold.

           But you will whine.

You are ruined.

        What will your life be?

           Who will 'visit' your room?

Who uncover that beauty?

        Whom will you love?

           Whose girl will you be?

Whom kiss?

        Whose lips bite?

           Enough. Break.

Catullus.

        Against the past.

12

While everyone else is laughing & drinking

you extend

        a surreptitious claw,

Asinius,

        towards the table napkins

of the negligent . . .

        an unattractive habit

you misguidedly think funny.

You demur?

        I assure you

it is at once squalid & unattractive.

Ask Pollionus, your brother

a boy crackling with wit
who would give a substantial sum
to disembarrass himself of your talents.
Expect, Asinius, a bombardo
of 300 hendecasyllables, or
return my napkin—
   of small value itself,
but a memory of friends,
   Veranius & Fabullus,
who sent this set of fine table linen
from Spain,
   a present cherished by Catullus
as his own Veraniolus—
as Fabullus mine—must always be.

42
From the quarters of the compass
   gather round Catullus
indelicate syllables
   as many as you are,
a slippery whore has caught
   Catullus by the hairs.
She won't give me my pocket book back.
Come with Catullus
   follow her along the sidewalk
accost her on her beat
   insist she gives it back.
You ask, "Which one is yours?"
   The one parading in front
like a stage tart
   grinning like a French poodle.
Surround the little bitch
   insist she gives it back:
 "My pocket book unwholesome whore
 unwholesome whore my pocket book."
She looks the other way.
   "O tart of turpitude! O brothel lees!"
The brazen-faced bitch does not blush.
Approach again
   repeat in even louder tones:

"My pocket book unwholesome whore
unwholesome whore my pocket book."
We make no visible impression.
        The girl is totally unmoved.
Indelicate syllables
        to get our pocket book
we must adopt a change of front
        we must adopt new tactics
thus:
        Intact young lady and of nubile rectitude
        would you be so kind as
        to give me back my pocket book?"

Love poems of the VIth Dalai Lama

1
        This country girl
with skin like country cream
        looks with frankness
at me from the bed-furs.
        Her eyes watch me
put my rings on one side.
        They watch me
unlace my purse-belt.

5
A pattern of birds,
        crossed twigs,
& the last milestone
        have brought love
like luck
        to these two
met
        in this hedge-tavern,
where an old woman
        ladles out wine to them.

She will go on
        serving wine
on the periphery
        of their lives
at parting,
        at welcoming,
at childbirth.

8
Why does this pretty boy from Kong-po
buzz like a trapped bee?
He has been my bed-mate for three days,
and now he thinks only of God
& talks constantly of 'the future'.
                loquitur puella

11
In a season
        the shoots we planted
in last year's mud
        have become
handfuls of desiccated
        bent
fit for thatching.

In a season,
        the young men
have become stooped,
        their bodies curved
as the bent bows
        of the archers of Mu.

Who bends the bow?
Who loads youth with sudden age?

16
The old dog
        at the west postern
has a yellow beard
        and is discreet

236

as the discreet Mandarin
        whom he resembles,
he does not betray
        my dusk departure
nor my return
        at dawn.

The Lion Throne
        stands empty,
the stiff ceremonial robes
        are hidden
in a clothes closet.
        Here,
I am the best drinking
        comrade,
the consoler
        of fifty young women.

Into the bedroom
        with the first light
comes snow light,
        we look out
and snow has filled the streets.

Though my good Mandarin
        opens but one eye
a black snow-snake
        clamours
from downtown Lhasa
        all the way
to the Potala walls.

23
In summer
        this reed-patch
tainted
        the lakeside water
& couched
        the tranquil young goose

237

that nested here.
       Now,
winter crackling
       coats
the separate stalks,
       the reflection
of those days
       is like
white coal,
       & the young goose
lacking fire & a mirror
       stands dejectedly
on the bank.

26
In the oasis of the day
       she is with me
but I cannot,
       for reasons of circumspection,
touch her small hand
       too often
or let my eyes
       too lovingly rest
on her amber skin.

When night returns
       and sleep is a mirage
hands
       fresh from her touch
flutter before my eyes,
       eyes
in which hers are reflected
       ogle
ne from the darkness.

30
Frost
       lacing
late summer
       grass

gives warning
        of autumn
winds.
        The honeyed
season
        is over.
The bee
        takes leave
of the flower.
        I
bow myself
        from your bed.

from The ingathering of love

I

It was in one of those old stone houses in Monmouthshire
that we first met.
            The flagged kitchen
filled by a battered refectory table,
                            a whole family
sprawled there, gossiping . . .
                    and you walked in from a side door
—in a swathe of sunlight.

                Was it farm eggs?
or something about cutting a hedge?
or one of those dances we all went to?
                        I recall
the impatient sun
            through the low windows
describing your neck and chin;
                    I recall
how you walked
        & stood
free with your legs
            as girls who have no thought of getting married

walk and stand,
                    gauchely, a little astride,
a light cotton skirt loose on your hips.

It is used by our children, now, for dressing up.
Laughing immoderately
                    they stumble about in its neglected folds;
pausing fractionally, they hesitate,
                    when the cloth suddenly tears.

That laughter is caught like tears in the groin
as the swirling Usk catches Caerleon
as we first caught hold of each other
                    thoughtlessly
with our tongues' and fingers' ends.

We could have lived no other life but this.

The centre drives.
                    The reef forms.
Your acts & mine.
                    A network of peripheries.
Never still.
                    The coral blossoms.
The petals,
          in lovers' shoes,
in shopping baskets
                    up the Woodstock & the Banbury road.
A world refracted in spring wind & rain.
Wet pavements
                    lips & eyes
dissolving
          as the petals fall.

The weight of ocean,
                    almond & cherry
falling
          in the face of dreams.

We could have lived no other life but this.

II

Our bedroom darkens into light
                    the trees outside
their sap subsided
                    adopt black attitudes,
a remote light
                    looks in at the windows.
At this time,
          the flesh courses with fragmented images.
We enfold each other,
                    seed stirs in the man.
The woman's stomach grows warm.

                    The fuse lit,
in the flare,
          God blinks at the bed.

And another dawn shall find you,
                    dry,
like the fruit you are,
                    a carcass curled in this same bed,
your marred skin & eyes
glazed pools unstirred by otherness,
cloudy as these windows
where a brown haze now lies
in broad belts across the sky.
No light struck.
          No love.
Ash left with no fire.

And sunset & sunrise curtain the winter sky.
Here is love. And here is between hot bedclothes.
Here after all is where past & future lie.

III

The rolling heavens & the fire of time
consume this barrel body. Here,
the pitiably silent organs creep

241

blindly to decrepitude. The red water &
the blue gristle pale hourly,
                              —and somewhere/sometime
a fixed and ineluctable hour
an implacable and unavoidable wall
(on the other side of the bed
on the further side of the ward)—wait.
Strangers (indeed kind) must finally attend
this tiresome skinful, while self (as ever)
attends only the most idiot objects,
and the significance of the lifelong monologue
palls as life wanes.

                    One observes, then, affectionate sunlight
melt unreal sugar on afternoon cakes,
—*They whipped hers out just in time!*
Hey Presto! (What dates one like slang?)
one is aware of the smell of linoleum
(sticky) whose surface sends back the black bed-legs
(on castors),
            one watches a helicopter hovering in a nearby field;
or the young man across the street removes the
silencer on his motor bike . . .

. . . .
                    Nothing,
nothing can shatter that silence.

There is the expectancy —
there is the revelation — of the bud;
or to turn with a gesture of wearied tenderness
to a worn head, the hair greying.
In the nursery the children are asleep and
the consciousness of their sleeping fills
the house. The skies turn. Time burns.

Yes. God will humble
                    their silk skin
withdraw its flush
('the fever of life is over')

*   *   *   *   *

and leave that scrawny yellow.

242

from *Astapovo or what are to do*

for John Elton

3

Nausicaa's girls
           the whole giggling gaggle of them
burrowing their bottoms in the sand, kneeling,
making little wheelbarrows of themselves,
lisping the tenderest obscenities,
the happiest girls in Phaeacia, each
with a good hard fuck for the wanderer.
Odysseus, alas! must discriminate.
Like all wanderers he knows it is the Princess or nothing.

Pound opined
         it was 'difficult to discriminate in America',
food, clothing, looks, honey & wine/being
OFFICIALLY HOMOGENEOUS.
                     On the golden Californian coast
I count one hundred-&-twenty Phaeacians
undergoing long-range acts of copulation
with the sun. I could contentedly masturbate
myself into each of those male/female bodies—
REVERSING HOMER.
              The Homeric past shines on the shore,
destructible as life.

We all wish Odysseus had stayed longer
       the climate was clement—
snow does not lie long in Phaeacia.
       Homer liked that bit too:
the wanderer rehearses all that has happened,
       the minstrel's eyes glint through the mask.
The past shines in our knowing it.
       The past lives only in our knowledge of it.
Who but the poet can be our mediator?
On main lands
       snow empties

243

awkward things
        of awkwardnesses.
Snow makes void.
        And the Falcon hangs blindly in the void.
Among hollows that edge water
        smaller birds—
the pollen-gatherers
        —hop
happily
    the crocus & the daffodil between.
Flower-filled hollows that edge water
repel attentions of mindless snow.

Order is a convention of the blind.
When you feel like an octopus put your tentacles away.
When you feel like relating   : discriminate
When you feel like domesticating   : discriminate
When you feel like DOMINATING   : discriminate

6

for Antonio Crea

Violence swaddles all (love-) acts before & after

When Swinburne paid
        his weekly visits
to St. John's Wood,
        why should he associate
those unsubtly rouged ladies
        or their ostrich feathers,
with mushroom plumes?
        He thought (possibly)
of 'pagan' disciplines.

The first Olympic runner ran so fast he left no footprint on the sands.
SEX INSPECTION FOR FEMALE KOREAN WEIGHT-LIFTER
BRITISH PING-PONG TEAM SPURN SEX CHARGE.
Internationally organised displays of national rancour.

244

Were the Divine Afterbirth
                  to be recovered,

cased in glass
couched on wax flowers,
                who knows?
some sort of solution
might (were the dream 'true')
rise on the meditative eye.

As lust ebbed, he retained the pale halo of red,
inconsequential as a meteor's aftermath. One day
he was bending over a perambulator on a London pavement
when its owner projected herself, screaming, from a public house,
blew from the maritally gap-toothed mouth her warning fumes,
& admonished the poet thus:
                  "Taike yer faice aht've me baiby's pram
yew narsty owld man".
              A policeman led the fallen angel away.

La nave arrivò nel porto di Ostenda . . .
appena giunto in camera sua, Lord Byron
si precipitò come un fulmine sulla cameriera.
               (FIRST ACT ON LEAVING ENGLAND)

17

for Basil Bunting

POETRY TO GO
that's what
    Villon bought
at the hot dog
    stand
           the sleek hot dogs not so hot
           blotched thighs round a worn twat

Death. Margot
    sans linen

kept one wolf warm
    when the pack ran
through the streets
    outside her kitchen
in the cold season,
    I
Francis Villon
    clerk, poet
who lived by
    the short dagger
hung
    mid-stomach
between shanks.
    No engine cranks
the restless tongue
    the nicked lip.
Montfaucon
    temporal exit
from the death pit.
    The last jack-off
free
    on the city
gibbet,
    the turnip topped
galvanic in death
    the jack rabbit.

LEE HARWOOD

Animal days

Part 1.
"The polo season would start early in April
so there was no time to be wasted."

the night growing darker   the black plains
& below   the bright lights of the town

"knights on horses"?   "gentle ladies"?   "towers in the forest"?

it was as though your eyes filled with glass tears
crying some strange

there were peacocks on the high balconies
& a golden light   in fact a "heavenly rod"
came down from the heart of a clear blue sky
you see

Part 2.
"You're right, even though you won't accept it."

. . . with all the rifles brought back to safety
even the glimmer of polished metal

Buzzards, kestrels & hawks
circling high above the valley

the dust of the road   dazzling
with the white gate shut   do you understand
the garden so enclosed, & too green?

Part 3.
food is so very good

it is very black these days

the malevolence on the winter island

& what approaches in the darkness

beyond all knowledge   "the endurance"
surviving the fear

"but we're all so afraid"

& the children?

the indian chiefs
what are the wounds, anyway, & their cost?

In the morning everything is white
low clouds trail across the upper pastures
& the valley is thick with mist

"sometimes their cannoes only hollowed-out tree trunks"

Part 4.
standing in the shadows or maybe in the distance
he   Like a long arcade or cloister
It was far from the grim scenes of the north
In his red tunic

The morning spent loading cord-wood onto a trailer

five young foxes in the bean-field waiting for the wood-pigeons

in the beech woods up on the ridge—the bark
still green & wet, the "sticks" just felled.

It's reduced to a violent struggle
with heavy machinery, & boredom

the castle crumbling sedately   "damn fool!"
the gilding already flaking off

Cutting it up into "blocks" on the saw-bench
The forest floor all torn up with bulldozer tracks
the soil a bright red   exposed below
the white shale backbone of the ridge

248

the sun sinking lower
the whole forest dripping moisture & green

the old railway station

Part 5.
holding a young rabbit in my hands
walking across the stubble in the late afternoon

soft fur   shocking like the heart-beat

the dark river   & angry knights milling
in the courtyard

setting it free in a hawthorn thicket
safe from the dogs

at night the land so bare   "rustles"

"They have no tradition of keeping their colonies neat."
"I care for that woman" the song began

Part 6.
squandered in a matter called "the heat of the moment"
not knowing what

". . . . at dusk the sound of church bells from the valley floor,
an owl flying low over a passing tractor."

white with rain

The corrugated-iron roof of the mission discoloured
with rust   the deep green of the jungle
in the humid gourge

Like oppressors   striking fear into people
with threats of pillage — "no quarter"

Inside the walls where
"No!"
too heavy   on evenings like this

in the courtyard
"the battlements"

The Blue Mosque

a poem to Gus

1

The blue mosque had one tower higher than all the others
and it was from this that the muezzin called the faithful
to prayer and thoughts of God:
"There is no god but the God."

The city which contained the mosque
is unnamed, as it is unmarked on the map.
The school atlas was equally useless, and history was more
of an amusement than most would admit.

If you will accept this story for what it is,
then you may well be amused or even pleased;
the actual reality is of no importance.

The facts and words—even whole lines—
could so easily be seen as matters of pure style.
Even the cheapest trinkets can mean more,
in the end, than any heavy act of conscious gratitude.

The towers, I believe, are called "minarets"—but this
accuracy is completely lost as it progresses.
All there really is is a deep concern for "charm"
and the "pleasant surprise".

2

Despite appearances and the first reflex reaction to this—
there could be more love in this acceptance
of the ludicrous and obvious
than in the many books with titles like
"Morals" or "Morality" or "Truth" or "Logic" or. . . . . . .
and so on down the book shelves.

3

And now that the expedition was safe—
surely it was time for all the merchants
to thank their saviour and God?

—quarrels broke out almost immediately
over this order and precedence.
With the wilderness safe behind the city walls
it was not really unusual to see how quickly
memories and resolutions burst like soap bubbles,
and already few of them could even remember
the blackness of the storm clouds and,
least of all, their own helplessness and terror.

It was only a matter of days ago—
there was no question of it all being part of
some ancient riddle or alchemist's anagram.
It was all *too* simple, and that was why . . . .
books of authority and accepted formulas
were so violently seized.
The obvious and simple were like two men who
stood open-handed at the doors of the mosque.
It became essential for the merchants
to ignore them, if they were ever to continue as they were.

No one wanted the blood stains
on their own saddle cloth—yet . . . . .
The expedient had to be insisted on in private.
And the tanned hands' very openness—
that revealed pale tender palms
capable of so much love and gentleness
—was an unbearable threat.

4
The dull red neon in the bar windows and the "other things"
were left behind as they walked up Avenue B
to the brighter lights—there was no real malice
in this, nor in most actions in that city,
or any other town nearer or farther from home—
though "home" unfortunately is meaningless.

Is so much repetition always necessary?

When put bluntly again the question was
finally answered by "the man".

251

He said. "When faced with basic but *deep* emotions,
like (obvious, and so "extreme") love or fear, the common reaction
among this social and age group is to—
ONE: regard the experienc*ers* with hostility;
and TWO: urgently seek explanations (i.e. refuge)
for (i.e. from) the experience in the "copious realms"
of established reactions and common prejudice or
ignorance."
This was all pretty obvious. . . .

5
The muezzin, I'm sure, knew this,
and did not he proclaim the greatness of God
over the rooftops and the whole city every day
from his minaret in the blue mosque?
And, surely, when in the quiet of his study,
he knew that "the greatness of God" embraced
far more than the power of one individual?
Rather couldn't it be the power of this very openness,
whether in hands or love? The doors of the mosque.

There were so many books and already his head
began to ache. "Such is the life of a muezzin,"
he said, and laughed.

The sound of a fountain splashing in the courtyard
soothed him. This whole scene though
is only taken from another book—but
do the circumstances and scenery matter?
The mosque, the muezzin, even the expedition
that was claimed to be safe—
there can be no difference to their final reality
whether they exist only in the imagination
or in the physical world. It's only a matter
of the story holding people with its style
and lists of events, either curious or tender.

6
This preoccupation with words can only be boring
for the onlooker—painters arguing over the different

252

brands of paint—useless parallels.
What have any of these words to do with
praising a good man or a love?
No matter how exotic the decorations
and materials—the words always fail.
It's all been said before—and this
very questioning now heard only too often.
Even the clichés seem to contain less conceit
than the poem, and now the poem about the poem,
and the poem about the poem about the . . . .
and so on and on deeper into the cheap gaming house.

What has this to do or say with any weight
of the two men with open hands at the mosque
who will be murdered by the merchants' assassins?
or the good man that still knows how to love?
or the loved one whose kiss alone is beyond words?

The whole poem book must be left behind
(while I go to help the two men
and thank the good man), and then let it
be forgotten now we've become men and women.
And surely it's obvious to the simplest of men,
as it is for the muezzin to cry "There is no god but the God,",
that I should now leave writing this poem
when it is so late at night,
and go lie with my love.
It is late, but such blindness
could not go on forever, thank God.

Plato was right though

for Ed Dorn

1
The empty house—the empty country—the empty sky.
Reverse it to A—B—C.

A: The large house

filled with many people—servants and guests—
it is now a country mansion.
It is white and has extensive grounds and woods.
There are many people.
They hunt and shoot. They laugh and talk.
In the evenings they play games.
It is all like a picture-book
that teaches vocabulary to foreigners—
each different object in the picture is numbered,
and below are the list of words that correspond
to the many numbers. So—12 is table;
5: vase; 16: father. . . . . . and so on.

B: The full country.
The map blocked out with the red of cities
—that's the agreed colour in the atlas key.
This continues into the 3rd dimension with
"concrete and neon" parodying themselves.
Countries, armies, "The People" struggling with
"The People". The borders on the map look
so pretty, with dotted lines in bright coloured inks
—all yellows and reds—dot dot dot—and in practice
nothing more glorious than a stretch of
ill-kept road with a line of battered poplars
one side and strands of barbed wire on the other.
The bad spy story continues. . . . . The plot is very obvious
and stupid, even if it *is* all true.
No one could look at this and take it seriously.
And it wasn't just that the generals and borders
were ridiculous, but that the whole situation,
—including the very existence of the cities—
was wholly laughable.
The atlas became the one truly funny book,
and it did not escape our notice that what was portrayed
should be regarded in the same light,
To be totally "negative" in believing the
countries as they were (and the cities) were
painfully absurd and grotesque seemed
perhaps the saner and more realistic.
It was a very pompous speech. . . . . . .

C: The sky was crowded with airplanes of all colours—
a totally unreal picture with dozens of
happy red, blue, orange and green
airplanes filling the sky in a mechanical
rainbow. Each plane painted entirely in its
colour with no other markings, flies through a series
of aerobatic stunts, diving climbing,
rolling over and over, and "looping the loop".
This is happening in a clear blue summer sky—
there has been no trace of a cloud all day.

2

All the previous locations are now impossible.
There is only this confusion in which no one
knows exactly what is going on.
The planes or the hesitating crowd on the lawns,
the house party going its usual way,—
but this only in a vacuum.
Outside is total darkness
dominated by the sure knowledge of Death
that takes on an almost human persona
and vibrates like the engines of an ocean liner at night
that can be felt many miles away and yet never seen.
(Black, as you know, is the negation of colour
and strictly it is not even a colour,
while White is all colours.)
And white is the love and only light that can be seen
to really exist besides the blackness.
The White is the only sure and real force
in an otherwise brutal chaos, and the only
home when all else has been lost.
(This new "simplicity" was, in fact, a blessing
and advantage never before possessed, and that now
made the struggle easier and brought a sure relief
in the victory that before was confined to day-dreams.)
A lone parachutist drifting down through the blue. . . .
And even if he *is* shot dead in his harness
by the border guards, who really cares?
He has the same chances as anyone else.

"When you're facing death or junk, you're always on your own,
and that's exactly how it is," he said. It became daily
more obvious that such clichéd truisms were only too true.

It is not a question of doubts or a lack of faith
in the forces of Good . . . but from this black and white
landscape, what is it that will finally be launched?
There is an obvious and reasonable impatience
at the slowness of the expedition to set out and,
at least, attempt an exploration. . . . an examination
of what had happened in the past and what
could come out of the Interior afterwards.

3
The fact that there should be this co-existence
of opposites . . . A desert, a barren plain, or,
to reduce this to its basic elements, a complete emptiness and darkness,
—faced by a crowded world of absurd objects
and events, and a tangled "confusion"; and this portrayed
quite clearly in a desperate heaping-up of words
and pictures. The brightly coloured airplanes flying low
and at great speed over the countryside and approaching the towns
brought a wave of "cold fear" upon all who saw them,
that the jollity of the planes' appearance at first denied.

It was this fact, above all, that was finally realised—
and no matter how painful the realisation, it had to be accepted
that what had gone on too long was due entirely
to a mental laziness that could live with this "co-existence".
There was no expedition to be expected or any news
of it to be eagerly awaited. If anything
was to be found or gained it would only come through
a "personal action".
                    "All the necessary equipment was there.
I had only to dress and begin.
And it was not a matter of fierce lions from the story-book,
or navigating my sampan through a wild and thundering gorge
only to have to fight 300 Chinese rebels the other side
single-handed with only a revolver and my walking stick.
The fun of these jaunts was a thing of the past.

What it meant now was to live like anyone else
—getting up in the morning, washing, eating meals, ..."

The convalescence, though once necessary,
was now over. All the wounds had healed and
the neat white scars could only be mementos.
This left no real excuses or causes for further delay.
"And the one simple and basic fact that love
had become a supreme power that radiated from me
was now the key to everything. And no matter how much
time would be needed, the struggle to deal with this
and other pressures was there and only waited to be
used. Like the quiet in the ship's engine-room,
this inactivity seemed wrong."

For some reason the word "LOVE" does not suggest
a strength, or grace, only a mild ineffectuality.
Yet beyond the romantic charades and the gaudy neon letters
outside the theatre—when the Real, and
the True essence is gained (or found), it's only this
love that creates a joy and happiness able to finally
dismiss a cruel haunting by Death, and meet the "world".
And what the words and poems attempt degenerates into this—
a clumsy manifesto in which the words used
appear emptier than ever before and the atmosphere
more that of an intense but bad Sunday School.
————————————————PLATO was right to banish
poets from the Republic. Once they try to go beyond the
colours and shapes, they only ever fail, miserably—
some more gracefully than others.

257

JOHN DANIEL

My wife who is American

My wife, who is American,
will, when she is over-charged for ice-cream,
speculate on the Inferiority of English ices,
the Mendacity of shop-assistants (whom she calls clerks)
the Hypocrisy of our traditional decorum,
the Squalor of tea-shops, the Apathy that we call
Restraint, the Clogged and Bestial European Soul
lying like a Spent Dog on the shores of the Great Seas
that divide us.

        And I,
seeing this mountainous wave
on which the ice-cream and she come riding
like a tiny surf-board down to the creaming brink,
nod my head and say
                yes.

Watch

Formerly *the individual work of a Nuremberg artificer*
THE WATCH
has been transformed
into *the social product*
of an immense number of detail labourers,
           such as

    mainspring makers
    dial makers
    spiral spring makers

jewelled hole makers
ruby lever makers
hand makers
case makers
screw makers
gilders

with numerous sub-divisions

such as

wheel makers (brass and steel separate)
pin makers
movement makers
acheveur de pignon
(fixes the wheels on the axles,
polishes the facets etc.)
pivot makers
planteur de finissage
(puts the wheels and springs in the works)
finisseur de barillet
(cuts teeth in the wheels
makes the holes of the right size etc.)
escapement makers,
cylinder makers for
cylinder escapements
escapement wheel makers
balance wheel makers
raquette makers
(apparatus for regulating the watch)
the *planteur d'echappement*
(escapement maker proper)

then the

repasseur de barillet
(finishes the box for the spring etc.)
steel polishers

screw polishers
figure painters

dial enamellers
(melt the enamel on the copper)
fabricant de pendants
(makes the ring by which the case is hung)
finisseur de charnière
(puts the brass hinge in the cover etc.)
faiseur de secret
puts in the springs that open the case)
graveur
ciseleur
polisseur de boîte etc. etc.

and last of all
    the *repasseur*

who fits together the whole watch
and hands it over in a going state.

found in *Capital* by Karl Marx

Auto icon

My body I give
        to my dear friend
        Doctor Southwood Smith

        to be disposed of

in manner hereinafter mentioned

And I direct that . . .
he will take my body under his charge
and take the requisite and appropriate measures

        for the disposal
        and preservation

of the several parts of my bodily frame

260

in the manner expressed in the paper
annexed to this my will
and at the top of which
> I have written

AUTO ICON

The skeleton he will cause to be put
> together

in such manner as that the whole figure
may be seated in a Chair
> usually occupied by me

> > when living,

> in the attitude in which I am sitting
> when engaged in thoughts
> in the course of the time
> employed in   writing.

I direct that the BODY thus prepared
shall be transferred to my
> executor

HE will cause the skeleton to be clad
in one of the suits of *black*
> occasionally
> worn
> by me.

The body so clothed (together with the Chair
> and the Staff in my later years
> borne by me)

he will take charge of
> AND
> for containing the whole apparatus

> he will cause to be prepared

an appropriate BOX or CASE
> and will cause to be engraved

in *conspicuous characters*

on a plate to be affixed thereon
(and also on the labels on the glass Cases
in which the preparation
of the Soft Parts of my Body
shall be contained)
              my Name
              at length

              with the letters
                ob.

              followed by the Day of My Decease.

If it should so happen
that my personal friends
                (and other disciples)
should be disposed to meet together
on some day or days of the year

              for the purpose of Commemorating
the Founder of the Greatest Happiness System
              of
              Morals
              and Legislation

my executor will (from time to time)
cause to be conveyed
              to the room in which They meet
              the said
              BOX or CASE
with the contents
there to be stationed in such Part of the Room
as to the Assembled Company

shall seem
              meet.

        Found in the will of Jeremy Bentham

Excerpts from a diary of a war (1)

left Folkestone 5 p.m.
6.9.17
arrived Boulogne 8 pm
6.9.17
St. Martins Camp Boulogne midnight
6.9.17
left Boulogne 3 pm arrived Etaples 7 pm
11.9.17
left St. Etats 4 am
13.9.17
arrived Poperinghe Belgium midnight
13.9.17
transferred to 237 Battery as reinforcements
in firing line Ypres front
14.9.17
4 casualties. First time in action.
Big push commenced 5.30 am
20.9.17
Ypres-Menin Tower Hamlets Ridge
Sunday
all day and night
and Monday
20/30.9.17
heavy bombardt. by enemy
4 of us on gun trail
3 knocked out left me unscratched
4·5 shell
3.4.5./10/17

Excerpts from a diary of a war (2)

Moved to forward position at Lovidina
and was heavily shelled

Piave 20/10/18 heaviest shelling either France
or Italy lasting from 9 pm 20/10 to
                4 am 22/10

263

H.E.
H.V.
& Gas Shells
& Bombs

Push started on Piave

first shot of bombardment
11.47 pm 26/10/18
Bombardment lasted until
8.30 am 27.10.18
Piave taken 7 am 27.10.18
Jerry retreating still
thousands of prisoners coming in
5 pm 29/10/18
Guns now out of range 6.45 pm
moved forward
bridge blown up
fell in Piave
21 drowned or killed by the shell
15 saved

Excerpts from a diary of a war (3)

21.10.17
left billet
(Assurance and Arrival forms)
for 9 days leave 21.10.17
6 pm wounded
taken to C.C.S.
then by ambulance train
to hospital at St Etats
arrived 5 am
23.10.17
*   *   *

too rough to cross
mines loose 25.10.17
started for Blighty midnight

26.10.17
Dover 10 o'clock
(Hurrah)
Charing X 3 o'clock
Richmond Military Hospital
27.10.17
inoculated 21.10.17
inoculated 28.10.17
operation 4.11.17
inoculated 11.11.17
inoculated 6.12.17
operation
inoculated 18.12.17
operation
operated upon 18.12.17
out of bed 20.4.18

found in my grandfather's diary

Of 91 men leaving
an underground station

Of 91 men leaving an Underground station,
41 wore hat and gloves
and carried an umbrella

61 wore hat and gloves,
and 68 wore gloves.

There were 7 who wore a hat
and carried an umbrella,
but wore no gloves,
and 21 who wore a hat
but no gloves.

Only 2 carried an umbrella
but wore neither
hat nor gloves,

although there were 50 men with umbrellas
altogether.
How many of these
wore gloves
but no hat?

found in *Sets and Logic* . .
by C.A.R. Bailey

Injury to insured

total loss
by physical severance
at or above
the wrist
or ankle
of ONE hand
or ONE foot £250

total and irrecoverable
loss of sight
on ONE eye £250

total loss
by physical severance
at or above the wrist
or ankle
of ONE hand
or ONE foot
together with
the total and irrecoverable
loss of sight
of ONE eye £500

total loss
by physical severance
at or above the wrist

266

or ankle
of BOTH hands
or BOTH feet
or of ONE hand
together with ONE foot £500

total and irrecoverable
loss of sight
of BOTH eyes £500

death £1,000

found in *North British and Mercantile Motor Car Insurance policy*

Phrases for everyday use by the British in India

Come here
Come near
Come in
Come with me
Go away
Go quickly
Go there
Go with him
Keep quiet
At once
Don't make noise
Wait
Sit down
Make haste
Don't be late
Take it
Take it away
Bring it here
Give it to me
Give it to him

Leave it alone
Get out of the way
Bring a ghari
On the right
On the left
Mind your business
All right
That will do
Show it to me
Whip him

found in *India Explained*
by Prof. Vaswani

JOHN MONTAGUE

Beginnings

For Anne Madden

Beginnings of a language,
first sign to escape from darkness,
scrawl on a cave wall:

the hunters do not move,
so close together their bodies
are the five fingers of the hand

which draws, their joint shape
the living image being drawn;
not the elongated animal of daylight—

splintered horns, eager to charge—
but a more frightening enemy; blood
dark strokes on an albino ground:

the circle shaped like a sound.

Sentence for Konarak

Extravagantly your stone gestures
encourage and ease our desires
till the clamour dies: it is not
that man is a bare forked animal,
but that sensuousness is betrayed
by sensuality (a smell of burning flesh);

though here face turns to face,

not ashamed (the word barely exists,
so calm the movement, limpid the smile
above your monstrous actions)
that we are rebuked to learn
how, in the proper atmosphere,

the stealthy five-fingered hand
is less thief than messenger,
as the god bends towards her
whose head already sways towards him,
pliant as a lily, while round them,
in a teeming richness, move

the ripe-thighed temple dancers
in a field of force, a coiling honeycomb
of forms, the golden wheel of love.

The country fiddler

My uncle played the fiddle—more elegantly the violin—
A favourite at barn and cross-roads dance,
He knew *The Sailor's Bonnet* and *The Fowling Piece.*

Bachelor head of a house full of sisters,
Runner of poor racehorses, spendthrift,
He left for the New World in an old disgrace.

He left his fiddle in the rafters
When he sailed, never played afterwards;
A rural art silenced in the discord of Brooklyn.

A heavily-built man, tranquil-eyed as an ox,
He ran a wild speakeasy, and died of it.
During the depression many dossed in his cellar.

I attended his funeral in the Church of the Redemption,
Then, unexpected successor, reversed time
To return where he had been born.

During my schooldays the fiddle rusted
(The bridge fell away, the catgut snapped)
Reduced to a plaything stinking of stale rosin.

The country people asked if I also had music
(All the family had had) but the fiddle was in pieces
And the rafters remade, before I discovered my craft.

Twenty years afterwards, I saw the church again,
And promised to remember my burly godfather
And his rural craft, after this fashion:

So succession passes, through strangest hands.

The road's end

May, and the air is light
On eye, on hand. As I take
The mountain road, my former step
Doubles mine, driving cattle
To the upland fields. Between
Shelving ditches of whitethorn
They sway their burdensome
Bodies, tempted at each turn
By hollows of sweet grass,
Pale clover, while memory,
A restive sally-switch, flicks
Across their backs.
              The well
Is still there, a half-way mark
Between two cottages, opposite
The gate into Danaghy's field,
But above the protective dry-
Stone rim, the plaiting thorns
Have not been bill-hooked back
And a thick *glaur* floats.

No need to rush to head off
The cattle from sinking soft
Muzzles into leaf smelling
Spring water.

From the farm
Nearby, I hear a yard tap gush
And a collie bark, to check
My presence. Our farmhands
Lived there, wife and children
In twin white-washed cells,
A zinc roof burning in summer.
Now there is a kitchen extension
With radio aerial, rough outhouses
For coal and tractor. A housewife
Smiles good-day as I step through
The fluff and dust of her walled
Farmyard, solicited by raw-necked
Stalking turkeys;

to where cart
Ruts shape the ridge of a valley,
One of many among the switch-
Back hills of what old chroniclers
Called the Star Bog. Uncurling
Fern, white scut of bogcotton,
Spars of bleached bog fir jutting
From heather, make a landscape
So light in wash it must be learnt
Day by day, in shifting detail.
'I like to look across', said
Barney Horisk, leaning on his *slean,*
'And think of all the people
'Who have bin.'

Like shards
Of a lost culture, the slopes
Are strewn with cabins, emptied
In my lifetime. Here the older
People sheltered, the Blind Nialls,
Big Ellen, who had been a Fair-
Day prostitute. The bushes cramp
To the evening wind as I reach

The road's end. Jamie MacCrystal
Lived in the final cottage,
A trim grove of mountain ash
Soughing protection round his walls
And bright painted gate. The thatch
Has slumped in, white dust of nettles
On the flags. Only the shed remains
In use for calves, although fuchsia
Bleeds by the wall, and someone
Has propped a yellow cartwheel
Against the door.

Hymn to the New Omagh Road

1. *Process*
As the bull-dozer bites into the tree-ringed hill fort
Its grapnel jaws lift the mouse, the flower,
With equal attention, and the plaited twigs
And clay of the bird's nest, shaken by the traffic,
Fall from a crevice under the bridge
Into the slow-flowing mud-choked stream
Below the quarry, where the mountain trout
Turns up its pale belly to die.

2. *Balance Sheet*

> *LOSS*

Item: The shearing away of an old barn
        criss-cross of beams where pigeons moan
        high small window where the swallow builds
        white-washed dry-stone walls

Item: The suppression of stone lined paths
        old potato-boiler full of crocuses
        overhanging lilac or laburnum
        sweet pea climbing the fence

273

Item: The filling-in of chance streams
uncovered wells, all unchannelled sources
of water that might weaken foundations
bubbling over the macadam.

Item: The disappearance of all signs
of wild life, wren's or robin's nest,
a rabbit nibbling a coltsfoot leaf,
a stray mouse or water-rat.

Item: The uprooting of wayside hedges
with their accomplices, devil's bit and dent de lion,
prim rose and dog rose, an unlawful
assembly of thistles.

Item: The removal of all hillocks
and humps, superstition styled fairy forts
and long barrows, now legally to be regarded
as obstacles masking a driver's view.

SO

THAT

GAIN

Item: 10 men from the district being for a period of time fully employed, their wives could buy groceries and clothes to send 30 children content to school for a few months, and raise local merchants' hearts by paying their bills.

Item: A man driving from Belfast to Londonderry can arrive a quarter of an hour earlier, a lorry load of goods ditto, thus making Ulster more competitive in the international market.

Item: A local travelling from the prefabricated suburbs of bypassed villages can manage an average speed of 50 rather than 40 miles p.h. on his way to see relatives in Omagh hospital or lunatic asylum.

Item: The dead of Carvaghey Graveyard (including my grand-
father) can have an unobstructed view—the trees having
been sheared away for a carpark—of the living passing at
great speed, sometimes quick enough to come straight in:

Let it be clear
That I do not grudge my grandfather
This long delayed pleasure!
I like the idea of him
Rising up from the rotting boards of the coffin
With his J.P.'s white beard
And penalizing drivers
For traveling faster
Than jaunting cars

3. *Glencull Waterside*

Clen chuil: the Glen of the Hazels

From the quarry behind the school
the crustacean claws of the excavator
rummage to withdraw a payload,
a giant's bite . .

'Tis pleasant for to take a stroll by Glencull Waterside
On a lovely evening in spring (in nature's early pride);
You pass by many a flowery bank and many a shady dell,
Like walking through enchanted land where fairies used to dwell.

Tuberous tentacles
of oak, hawthorn, buried pignut,
the topsoil of a living shape
of earth lifts like a scalp
to lay open

The trout are rising to the fly; the lambkins sport and play;
The pretty feathered warblers are singing by the way;
The blackbirds' and the thrushes' notes, by the echoes multiplied,
Do fill the vale with melody by Glencull waterside.

275

                    slipping sand,
          shale, compressed veins of rock,
          old foundations, a soft chaos
          to be swallowed wholesale,
          masticated, regurgitated
          by the mixer.

Give not to me the rugged scenes of which some love to write—
The beetling cliffs, o'erhanging crags and the eagle in full flight
But give to me the fertile fields (the farmer's joy and pride)
The homestead and the orchards fine by Glencull waterside.

                    Secret places,
          birds' nests, animal paths,
          ghosts of children hunkering
          down snail glistering slopes
          spin through iron cylinders to
          resume new life as a pliant stream
          of building material.

These scenes bring recollections back to comrades scattered wide
Who used with me to walk these banks in youthful manly pride;
They've left their boyhoods' happy homes and crossed o'er oceans wide
Now but in dreamland may they walk by Glencull waterside.

                    A brown stain
          seeps away from where the machine
          rocks and groans to itself, dis-
          colouring the grass, thickening
          the current of the trout stream
          which flows between broken banks
          —the Waterside a smear of mud—
          towards the reinforced bridge
                    of the new road.

4. *Envoi: The Search for Beauty*
          My sympathy goes out to the farmer
          who, mad drunk after a cattle mart,
          bought himself a concrete swan

for thirty bob, and lugged
it all the way home
to deposit it
(where the monkey
puzzle was meant to grow)
on his tiny landscaped lawn.

A chosen light

I

11 rue Daguerre
At night, sometimes, when I cannot sleep
I go to the *atelier* door
And smell the earth of the garden.

It exhales softly,
Especially now, approaching springtime,
When tendrils of green are plaited

Across the humus, desperately frail
In their passage against
The dark, unredeemed parcels of earth.

There is white light on the cobblestones
And in the apartment house opposite—
All four floors—silence.

In that stillness—soft but luminously exact,
A chosen light—I notice that
The tips of the lately grafted cherry-tree

Are a firm and lacquered black.

II

Salute, in passing

The voyagers we cannot follow
Are the most haunting. That face

Time has worn to a fastidious mask
Chides me, as one strict master
Steps through the Luxembourg.
Surrounded by children, lovers,
His thoughts are rigorous as trees
Reduced by winter. While the water
Parts for tiny white-rigged yachts
He plots an icy human mathematics—
Proving what content sighs when all
Is lost, what wit flares from nothingness:
His handsome hawk head is sacrificial
As he weathers to how man now is.

III

Radiometers in the rue Jacob

In the twin
Or triple crystalline spheres
The tiny fans of mica flash;
Snow fleeing on dark ground.

I imagine
One on an executive's desk
Whirling above the memoranda
Or by his mistress's bed

(next to the milk-white telephone)

A minute wind-
Mill casting its pale light
Over unhappiness, ceaselessly
Elaborating its signals

Not of help, but of neutral energy.

Beyond the Liss

For Robert Duncan

Sean the hunchback, sadly
Walking the road at evening
Hears an errant music,
Clear, strange, beautiful,

And thrusts his moon face
Over the wet hedge
To spy a ring of noble
Figures dancing, with—

A rose at the centre—
The lustrous princess.

Humbly he pleads to join,
Saying, 'pardon my ugliness,
Reward my patience,
Heavenly governess.'

Presto! like the frog prince
His hump grows feather
Light, his back splits,
And he steps forth, shining

Into the world of ideal
Movement where (stripped
Of stale selfishness,
Curdled envy) all

Act not as they are
But might wish to be—
Planets assumed in
A sidereal harmony—

Strawfoot Sean
Limber as any.

But slowly old habits
Reassert themselves, he
Quarrels with pure gift,
Declares the boredom

Of a perfect music,
And, with toadish nastiness,
Seeks first to insult,
Then rape, the elegant princess.

Presto! with a sound
Like a rusty tearing
He finds himself lifted
Again through the air

To land, sprawling,
Outside the hedge,
His satchel hump securely
Back on his back.

Sean the hunchback, sadly
Walking the road at evening.

HARRY GUEST

A twilight man

The black flakes on the quiet wind
  drift through the rib-cage:
Charred reductions of evidence—
  letters, dossiers,
Photographs. The bonfire
  crackles to silence.
Smell of dew supersedes
  the acridity
In the back of the heat.
  A wry peace now. Embers
Creep, write enigmatically, twist,
  fade. No messages.
Scraps' float, soon lost in the
  thicker air contours abandon.
A skeletal hand disturbs
  the site, prods, stains the
Bone. Faces, afternoons on
  sofas, decisions, success, now
Ash. The head tilts towards the
  stars of slower change
Whose light prickles the empty eye-
  sockets and, dropping into the black
Skull, vanishes, unretained.
  Water beads coldly on
Spine, jaw, poised knuckle,
  and the darkness settles
Substantiate since the last red
  point has gone leaving only
Meaningless wafers for the night to
  obliterate, disperse.

Matsushima

(The Pine Islands)

These islands   gathering images
dry slowly from the night
                    Words
comb the pine-trees free of snow
            Saffron limestone
lurching up from the sea-floor,
quivers dripping in the telescope,
            recedes into stillness

Cameras click and conversation
misses me. Before we move on
as tourists (there being
a choice of views from the peninsula)
            our awkward,
isolating minuet
mazes the snow.
                Death hitherto
was others'
            Metal doors eventually
slamming to on it, the
volubility's boxed up,
driven downhill, leaving
the light to merge into one wet slope
the black footprints
            recalled in prayer
or literature.
            (Now
nothing resembling
smashed windscreens, atomic fire

            (Shown the end, "the
shadow-line traversed": theoretic
security was, the armour,
merciful complacency,
wrenched from me and a shove in the back

had me stumbling in the seismic desert
. . . .hailstones   . . . .drifting
gases   . . . .chasms
)never
reaching the gate to see my wife
smiling in the shadow on the
window of our dark orange-tree
          comfort of books and music
laughter and whisky and bed

          These islands mount the sky

Surrounded by no-one I love,
          a tour a
          microcosm, the horizon
          deceptive,
transfixed as never before
on no future)

          "enisl'd"

                    my private mouth goes over
                    the dark memory of your body

A semi-colon of death
inside my glance
lends   the islands, my presence,
          that grey salt-beaten temple,
          untrodden snow, shift of conifers
          from colourlessness back to green,
          scud of gull across the sunlight,
               all these, the grace,
     a break in them like finality

                    Shops face the water. I buy
                    a wind-bell, some pottery,
                    a necklace
                    wanting that sailor
                    lounging in indigo
                    against the melting quay

uninterested stance, bulge
in the tight jeans

and not forgetting what I'm not thinking of
the poems cut in rock,
theories of Japanese wives,
the postcards and the ghastly dolls,
the Zen priests' caves

Credible an unborn breeze
in mid-Pacific then; green tea,
poured, steams near the paperbacks
and the vase of carnations; or
next year's neon
trickling into the cone of shadow
between her breasts

We separate
till lunch
fuses gossip and impressions
eroded
shape beyond shape
trapped in black plastic,
joining anonymous groups
to be ignored in albums

Fear in my chest, I'm dying quicker now
memories   illicit
sanctioned desires
crowd
The pamphlet shows
two views from each peninsula
and disbelief
as an acrid coil of mist
strangles the eyeball
remains

The islands   along the bay
horde distance
as growing light assembles

the scooped stone and contorted pine

            Fake, fake correlatives
     islands accrue
     nothing, solving
     sunrise and the flesh gains
     nothing,
     the fear, Ransome's fear,
     stays a lump of pain

the shutting-off of the pulse
my mother knew
    at her Christmas cards

breath halted
my father knew
    'phoning from the darkness

the   gasp, the
squeezed lung, the
heart's irregularity, night
rammed down your throat
I shall know

my wife,
my daughter,

you, you

engulfed, dropped, enearthed
    Indifferent, grown hard and ill,
This place we're emptying jostles me

from the tour, what,
emblem, we visited,
my spattered eyes, the gone past,
to, glimpsed, the notes

    fragments, which, slopes
bar of shadow   only half-

remembered   a boat
cancelled by islands
      maybe
              blurred
tree-trunks from the car-window

desultory, haunted

     are left with, littered,
a complex of terror,
cravings and souvenirs

Montage

I swing round the corner, still alone.
There's no one now at the saluting-base,
and the pavements here in the centre
are all deserted.
          I wrote once
"Very drunk I raped you and the rain outside
fell on to roses."
           The morning lies empty
to another sky, half the street indigo,
half dusty yellow. After so long.

The lamp made your skin glow, at last
naked underneath my kisses. Our year started.

The regime's altered, that I know. A breeze
takes the gulls across the blue gap
between the gutted block of the Royal Hotel
and the bomb-scarred Post Office over which
a new flag strains its colours.

           In my arms
you were always elsewhere: an absent mouth
soured my embrace. Enigma
of your possession. Once, a tarnished exile

in a borrowed room over a café,
I lay with you on the rumpled bed,
and talked about Axel Heyst, the paperback
tossed on the one table by the cheap wine,
the tooth-mug stained a hard, irregular maroon,
and the cigarette-packets in an alien script.

Months of preparation, briefing, prayers even.
For this. The patient advance by night,
over cold ploughed fields, through the uninterested
villages. Gained confidence. Pre-dawn
in the rain: watches fixed for the attack.
Vengeance on a capital which had for so long
refused to recognize an opposition,
let alone the third party. One green flare;
quick penetration; clubbing
the indifferent sentries; concrete pyramids
across the road; contact with saboteurs;
brief fighting in the squares and the usual
anticlimax. Shirt-sleeved with a bottle
by the shattered fountain. Garlands
assorting oddly with the dirty khaki.
You miles away.

       Some bunting
blows across my path, its rustle and the wind
surround the echo as I tread
the locale of victory, unarmed. There's
the overturned streetcar we used as cover,
the piles of rubble where a ministry was.
Pitted walls here and there still flap
with bygone posters. "CAUSE FOR ALARM"
"TERRORISTS" "23rd" "WANTED" "FORMATION"

When, satisfied, I got off that first time,
pulled up my trousers in the quiet, you'd
already re-arranged the past, contrived
to crown the moment with your privacy.
(So long ago now—noise of the rain—heavy
sense of the summer flowers through

the tang of liquor, perplexed desire, smell
of our rough nakedness and your bruised lips.)
Nowhere to stay, no legal papers yet,
I had to leave you for the tricky streets
at dawn, the danger, no address.
I'd done what I could in service of myself
though you could always champion me
up over roses, violence, still later
the dog's bark in the clogged yard, trickle all night
from the rusty cistern.
                                I can remember
divers codes, the grimy lantern in the farmhouse,
Colonel Hand's eye-patch, the dash for the railway-yards.

You'd skein the triumph out of me and even to-day
it stirs uneasily at my temples. . . . The odd
moonlight over the curfewed town,
your boredom with my body, our ambitions
altering in subversive pamphlets with their
conflicting rumours of achievement.
And then you yielded to me, all straining gone soft,
you pupils huge, liquid.
                               Reaching the far end of the street
I glance back at the desolation, at
the torn streamers of victory, the empty stands—
frameworks for a memory of cheering.
I move on, turn the other corner.
They are all there as I had expected,
wearing different uniforms, waiting for me,
rifles levelled.

(

NATHANIEL TARN

Last of the chiefs

I speak from ignorance.
Who once learned much, but speaks from ignorance now.
Who trembled once with the load of such knowledge,
trembled and cried and gritted his teeth and gripped
with his fists the ends of the arms of his throne.

Who once distilled this island in his green intestines
like the whale distils her dung gone dry called ambergris—
a perfume for faraway races

who wrecked us.

Only here and there, like lightning before the rain's whips,
like a trench along the deep, a thought much as I had:

in the belly of the whale there is room for such an island.

I laugh. I come now. I clear space. My name, my very being
is that: I clear space. I pass over them with my thongs, laughing,
that have died fighting the island-bellied whale, not prevailed,
turned at last their steels against themselves, lie in spasms,
their cheek and chest muscles like rock. I pass over them,
smoke them, whip them, revive them, send them out again.

Wise wind singer with a forked tail like white lightning
and your black pin eye. Paradise tern on her tail-long hair.

I am thankful. I accept. I take your offerings of pork lard
and the myriad flowers of the scissored palm leaf. I take.
I accept. But above all I thank you for the breasts in heaven
of my daughters of the island which is Nukahiva of the Marquesas

that you know as Herman Melville's green garden, his Pacific.

Some say he beautified this green back yard.
I speak from ignorance. I remember little.

Projections for an eagle escaped in this City, March 1965

AND HOW I BARE YOU ON EAGLE'S WINGS

Towards the poem
as towards
any winter initiative,
fatigue cubes effort.
To be evil is nothing but to be tired,
selling short takes little more than to be weary,
those born to stumble claim no redress.
> Wrong done to them
> is wrong in General.

SO THE STRUCK EAGLE STRETCHED UPON THE PLAN

To have swept upwards
past startled hands, past
frightened fingers, past bars, past
the idea of liberty even,
to have swept up
out of his iron Egypt, this winter day
was this coincidence?
> *By acting now on the external world*
> *and changing it,*
> *he at the selfsame time*
> *changes his nature.*

OFFICIOUS HASTE DID LET TOO SOON THE SACRED
EAGLE FLY

In the prison
of the underworld,
in Sheol (Tropicana),
their spectrum of colours
spreads the radiance of Egypt
for the golden bull
and his spangled heifer.

290

In the 19th century,
from Bogota, Columbia,
millions of hummers p.a.
One London firm alone:
400,000 corpses
plucked for adornment.

FOR WHERESOEVER THE CARCASE IS THERE WILL
THE EAGLES BE GATHERED TOGETHER

Though the people do not even flock to their king.
It is enough that the king rules again
wingtip to wingtip spanning the upper air
and clouding the nether air with his shadow.
All those these walls enthrall, while more
than mathematic gloom envelops all around,
peer up from city windows and compute
the king's position in the famished skies.

The gates of Sheol
open on corridors
which open onto light
in this our world. But that illusion,
quantum of darkness in the rush of light,
bars hummers from the knowledge of their freedom.
Egypt is weariness of heart. Specifications of
              319 Apodiformes Trochilidae:
              flight muscles forming
              some 25% of body weight,
              unique wingbone to shoulder swiveljoint
              permits wingplane adjustment to the air.
              55 wingbeats per second in hoverflight,
              75 w.p.s. in level flight. Courtship:
              (O as for U-loop love-buzz) 200 w.p.s.

SKYWARD IN AIR A SUDDEN MUFFLED SOUND THE
DALLIANCE OF THE EAGLES

While the king has not learned his trade.
Who shall, from the holarctic rim, in legions,

as in the days of Aquila Chrysaëtos, hoist in Rome,
bate bearing crowns and sceptres in their pinions,
lightning in talons, the blizzard in their tails,
flutter'd your Volscians in Corioli,
and teach to kill? and teach to wind
the kingdom out on ever widening orbits?

The list of his Majesty's subjects
in his provinces of latter-day Egypt:
Cuban Bee, Calypte Helenae, 2½ in., Isle of Pines.
Frilled Coquette, Lophornis Magnifica, 2¾ in., Brazil.
Adorable Coquette, Paphosia Adorabilis, 3 in., Costa Rica.
Popelaire's Thornbill, Popelairia Popelairii, 4½ in., Ecuador.
Violet Sabrewing, Sampylopterus Hemileucurus, 5 in., Mexico-Panama.
Collared Inca, Coeligena Torquata, 5½ in., Colombia-Peru.
Sappho Comet, Sappho Sparganura, 7 in., Bolivia.
Greentailed Sylph, Aglaiocercus Kingi, 7½ in., Andes.
Crimson Topaz, Topaza Pella, 7½ in., Guianas.
Streamertail, Trochilus Polytmus, 9½ in., Island of Jamaica.
             And others as per itemized list attached.

Here in Sheol
by skeletal willows,
by ghostly streams,
their exiled harps are hung.
They doze in hibernation by the hour.
Their king has gone out of bondage from Egypt,
Babylon, Spain, New Spain and all the Russias.
             Ring'd with the azure world, he stands.
             And the best of merry luck to him.

THAT WITH HIS SHARPE LOK PERSETH THE SONNE

While the king has not learned his trade.
He addresses, fratres, the flannelled crowd, Romani,
the keepers and dogs, populares, he addresses,
the city truants, workers, the photographers, of the world,
the journalists, unite, he addresses, the Sunday idle,
every valley, scorning the ladders, shall be exalted,

or baited lures, and every mountain shall be laid low,
the other dainty captives brought to tempt him,
he addresses, comfort ye, his tormentors, comfort ye,
dropping away, my people, with one flap of his leathers.

Towards Sheol
as towards
a fear to find, within the body's watch,
the jewelled bone responsibility,
they are content, in cages wide as breath,
wide as breath only, to spring the adequate
and whip their whirring wings from sip to song.
        Crests, fans, tufts, wires, pendants and
        pantaloons, shields, gorgets, whiskers
        and iridescent plumage. Nature
        plus History will shortly be as one.

THE WRENS MAKE PREY WHERE EAGLES DARE NOT
PERCH

Beyond these walls, this stone circumference,
lie his enthusiasms, snow-pure, untampered with,
ready to leap-frog time. Which, born in slavery,
he has not learned to scan. Here where the earth is glue
and feeds but stubble he dreams an Israel,
the rocks and crags on which he builds his nest,
the hearth of cedars where he plants his banners,
the dove-grey prey so hot of blood, the sun
crazing the day, the soothing moon,
the taloned stars: Sheol in splinters.

The hummer never walks or climbs. Feet are
for perching only. Metabolism rate
being so high, migrations of
500 miles would call
for subcutaneous fuel loads
adding 50% to body weight
before the Exodus.

Lab. tests have proved
such feats impossible.
Yet hummers could

back in their days of Nature,
before the massacres and slaughters
(tears of the Indies),
perform it nonetheless twice every year.

THAT IS THE HUM-BIRD NOT MUCH EXCEEDING
A BEETLE

Wherefore the king, as all such stories end, will learn
his trade. His shadow magnifies the swelling land,
stooping to prey grown fat on idleness.
He has gone to Pharaoh, who said No. He has decided Yes.
He has worked out that frontiers concern subjects
who may rot in their colours and emblems if they will.
He will shift continents, change poles, night into day, day, night.
Freeze deserts, make of the sands his snows.

Fire the snows, renew himself in ice.
Quit his armies if need be and resign after Canaan.

Though the city change coin into weapons, and ingots
to instruments of war, his lungs will flower, his heart
bear fruit. Mounting up with wings as a storm cloud, unafraid.
That the seas may not run dry, nor the rivers falter.

Burying his right wing in orchards and vineyards
against the whirlwind bred on Sinai,
honey lapped from a lion gut, milk from the mouths of lambs,
men lie with beaks and talons, marrow for talismans,

where they shall not fear, naked bone, but for him in his air,
in this crucible's fire, a throne, a torch of spices—
in the fan of his wings now, his resurrected voice,
the assent of these palms, in this wind, peace,

nor shall there be slaves here any more. Peace. Selah. Poem. Amen.

from *A Nowhere for Vallejo*

I.

> "Tal la tierra oirá en tu silenciar,
> cómo nos van cobrando todos
> el alquiler del mundo donde nos dejas
> y el valor de aquel pan inacabable."
>   TRILCE

And they went down into the king-city
Tahuantinsuyu   four-quarters   limbs of man
                              to find the skull
happening there   first thing   on the poet's name
who'd become such a hero to his country
                 though he had left it
they'd finally put up a statue in the square
                 fronting the church of famine

and he walked up to the monument
                 and kissed the poet's name
with his hand

In "La Langouste Selon Désir"
he heard the wind going through her tears
the bird feeds its young in the myth
opened its breast   blood flowing out
                 flapped lazily over city and harbour
catch of fish   dying children

Bird-glider over the city
wall-wings / oven-beak
falls on the statue of the caesar-poet
                 bread on the sea
Where they buy and sell a country
                 we were talking about the dead with the rich
eating their platos criollos
                 in "The House of the Thirty Coins"
talking with the satellite vendors
                 with which the country we don't know
listens to the one we do

In a city full of movement
with the woman he loves
crying for the caesar-poet to come back
          and eat them alive one by one
the friends   the enemies
                    eat them all
in words born and dead at this table

and then a constant
     quiet
murmur about gold

he hears the wind going through her tears
her tears   the queen-city
married a king with her hair in his eyes
above the grave of the caesar-poet

he feeds the children crying in her tears

II.

> "Es el tiempo este anuncio de gran zapateria
> es el tiempo, que marcha descalzo
> de la muerte   hacia   la muerte."
> *POEMAS HUMANOS*

Call of green things to his hand
          no longer pulls
underworld gold
          pales for his lack of envy

The things of poverty
          he sees as clear
as mountain teeth
          about to bite the sky
as the backbone of mountains
          about to puncture the sky's belly

The city is grey with white hands
          the city
                    the city

is grey with white   and green   hands
        beckons the forests
cold mountain's reaches

They say the same mists will come down
        but be drunk by the Sun
they say there will be a Sun up there
        but it will be cold

Old man in a brown hat
        drip at his nose
passing
        the eyes / of a door through mountains
one way
        with no thought of return

Frozen to gold
        demonetized gold
to be dug up at dawn
        changed into mountains
glass-enclosed
        changed into mountains

Wind on the sands   cat-god   mouse
        mouse on cat   cat on mouse
lovers lying side by side in the mountains
                he is about to enter

Her oyster is the Moon's
        around it   a city
prayer in his hands
        calls to the caesar-poet

                venture out there

And where are you
        macho
in all this sleep
        rotting about our bodies

Taken a bus twice only   these fifteen years

VIII.

"En el muro de pie, pienso en las leyes
que la dicha y la angustia van trocando:"
LOS HERALDOS NEGROS

Borders slide backwards   forwards
weak kings   lose a strong king's conquests
          Sun-image on the mountain lakes
empire provider   whether cold or hot
          reigns from the start of time

His train   a messenger
agonizes between the mountains

          at loss for a breath of air
through eye of rock
          into the mountain's skull
forward   then back   forward   then back
          forward again
locates a stream of air
          hardly dares breathe it

At four thousand five hundred   climbing
          passes out of earth's hold
out of its grasp and keep
          spine   transparent now
     snake-vertebrae
          in a royal necklace
     eyes crystallized
          gone beyond darkness
     on the edge of light
          lungs failing
     sucking like bellows
          sight improving
all the time
          until at last he comes
a riveder la luce delle stelle

298

And he has seen
            gigantes / monstruos
teeth   prison-bars
            gargantas   famine
dueños de los montes
            the archangelical
Michel et toute sa compagnie
                  du temps de sa jeunesse
in his day of youth

Where Justice goes   puffs along tracks
            with her dimmed eyes
breasts   flanks of mountains
            purse-bellied after many children
and cleft of earthquake

Sun astride mountains   mail of gold

XIV.

                  "Cállate. Nadie sabe que estas en mí,
                  toda entera. Cállate. No respires."
                                    TRILCE

On the train to the ruins
as the mountains grew taller and taller
            until no one believed them
wrapped in himself   he cried behind his glasses
            his eyes two white moths
and she watched him   from behind her book
            grieving for him
                  never moved forward

Had lain three days   face to the floor
            how sick she must have been
                  of weeping men

and I speak for her   he thought
            since she has no mouth
            sleeps under dust   with all my dead

Coming back from the ruins
meaning of height made clear
they touched each other's hands
as each marvel appeared
breasts of a Moon survivor
hard nipples   bitter ink
nestled in her white shirt
brushing his cheek as they moved

A preacher at the back of the train
        was telling young men how to live
        whose eyes already knew

Gringas   in nearby seats
        a bitter tale of dollars
        things they had failed to buy

Eyes of puma   fox   llama
rushes lying down in the fire
        eyes of deer in evening sunshine
eyes of adobe huacos
        eyes in which corn has brewed
eyes of charcoal cinders
        eyes of alpaca wool in mist
        under the smoke of his hurt

We shall arrive by night   he thought
we shall arrive in the city by night
        the city we've not seen for some time
no one will know we've come
        we'll go about our dowry
our marvelous marriage-bed
        a little later yet
        be heard of elsewhere

XVI.

        "No es grato morir, senor, si en la vida nada se
            deja y si en la muerte nada es posible, sino sobre
            lo que pudo dejarse en la vida."

300

"Y la gallina pone su infinito, uno por uno;
Sale la tierra hermosa de las humeantes sílabas,"

POEMAS HUMANOS

And he passed   around midnight
      from the living land into the living land
      from the one shore to the same shore
      from the mountain to the mountain
saying   do you believe
      saying   do you believe
as she laughed him happy

the nail-heads reached his palms
      how long a time it was
      he saw some heaven   and much more hell
      passed to the selfsame shore
saying   do you believe
      the other shore is there
has no description

while she fussed among children and hens
      fussed among shadows and flowers
      in a garden they'd made of Peru
      with Vallejo's mother's roses
saying   do you believe
      the poet's lost his crown
and brought the breakfast round

at each end of the house   in the sun's long arms
      windows brood streets
      their curving iron bars
      swans' necks and harps
saying   do you believe
      we have inheritance
we've taken to this earth

white sheets washed in the lakes   blue sheets in rivers
      pillowslip on the wind

                    mattress in fire
                    this is the bed of life   beyond description
saying   do you believe
                    the only shore worth knowing
there is no other

and come she said come   into this living room
                    the center of the house
                    the locket of my arms
                    I'll make such brews   as peace is made on
saying   do you believe
                    this angry zeal   this searing love
is our geography

and he took his life   this life   into his hands
                    and made to use it
                    and he saw the laughter brimming in her eyes
                    feared not to lose it
saying   do you believe
                    after all the loves in my life
you are the one

all poems have dissolved into a song   and we survive
                    this poem goes that way
                    cannot go wrong
                    peak climbed   sea swum
saying   do you believe
                    what a crime against the country of our life
nearly committed

and rose again   around noon   with joyful rising
                    setting the world to work
                    along their daily rounds
                    and taught the ass to bray   and dog to bark
saying   do you believe
                    this is a destiny
the sun is in the sky   and needs no moving

from *The Beautiful Contradictions*

ELEVEN

When Caesar decided to measure the world   as told in Hereford

a Cesare Augusto orbis terrarum metiri cepit   belted by Mors
Nicodoxus east   Polyclitus south   Theodotus north and west

there went out a decree from Caesar that the universe should be taxed
veici beu fiz mon piz dedeinz la quele chare preistes
e les mameleites dont leit de virgin queistes

while they from occidental pars   unknown among these maps
entered the womb of the old globe   along the hot equator
past Gades Herculis into the middle sea   there to survey
where they could find twelve labours   for to recruit the world

In the steps of the ancient stars   swilling the mermaid's milk
took Baleares first   Etna and Sandaliotes
harrowed the hells from Lipari   the cheapest way to do it
hugged bulls to death in Crete   decapitated Rhodes
stormed the white-windmilled Delos   sacked Chypre for wine

then sailed the Nile south-east   past Joseph's granaries
seized for themselves his seven years   stored in the pyramids
spun salamander's wool   plucked out mandragora
suckled the sphynx full-dry   smothered the spinster phoenix
tempted Saint Anthony under the burning mountain
sank out of human ken   to reach the outer Nile

enrolled the Agriophagi   their panther snacks   their king
the cheetah-swift Monocoli   the pouting tribes
the mouthless people who suck their food through reeds
Himantopodes creeping on all fours   the dwarfish Psylli
the Blemmyae with sunken eyes and mouths   the Troglodytes
guzzling in caves and ignorant of speech   the ethnocentric ones
the Garamantes' mare who fetched the gold of auts

rose out of Carthage to harry Rome once more
shattered each scallop shell in golden Compostela
silenced the university of Paris   stopped Flanders looms
sank Britain in its own miasmata   anchored the Hebrides
(took rest at Carnau   place of singing birds
where I was staying   out of Hereford)
denied the Germans thrice   published the news in Prague
skewered a choir of Essedones   shared out their parents' limbs

tarried among the Hyperborei   who knew no sickness
taught these to look about them   at other people's problems
before they took the high jump to join the seven sleepers
gave emerald-guarding griffin some recent news of Wales
and smote on his behalf the one-eyed Carimaspi
enlisted the Albani   grey-pupilled   for the watch
and the bat-like Phanesii who sleep wrapped in their ears
crested por fin king Alexander's walls   in which he had imprisoned
the yellow Gog and Magog   the nightmares of his world

sat cuckoo-like among the pelicans drinking their father's blood
lulled by the sybil voice of a crimson manticore
lived on the scent of apples among the bronzed Gangines
tried Amazons for paramours and found them wanting
lay in the shade of Sciopodes   under umbrella feet
inspected one small infantry warred on by cranes
tickled the crocodile between Chenab and Jhalum
propped up an elephant   his turret like a city
who swam them to Ceylon to prove his gratitude
covered by avalerion   the fabled eagle pair

as last they circle Palestine   the navel of the world
landing on Sinai from the two-fingered sea
kiss Abraham's cheek as he leans out of Ur
weep with the wife of Lot   melt down her salt
walk the chameleon up Babylon's towers
flit with the cinnamolgus among cinnamon trees
ducking the fire-shit of angry bonnacon
take tea at Ararat with lord and lady Noah
accept a flower wand from web-foot tigolopes
the lynx's carbuncle against the royal pox
and bask at Troy   in fallen Helen's sheets

Now from corona mundi   Caesar in judgment sits
and in the hunter's mirror loses his cubs again
down from the buried rivers   under paradise
and from Saint Michael's eyes as he shuts down the east
a rain of spears fixes the stigmata
into the carcase on hillock Calvarie
The dry tree withers   the dry tree waxes green
as the western lords survey Jerusalem
the twelve winds blow from the encompassed earth
the twelve apostles sing in the abundance of waters
as they lie in the Jordan surrounded with light
Jerusalem   the heart of heaven   shimmers among the waves

their losses have been few as yet   they are greenly remembered
Javier Heraud   poet   shot in Maldonado   Peru

Arbelio Ramirez   historian   in Montevideo
Camillo Torres   priest   in Chucuri   Colombia
Danilo Rosalez Arguello   doctor   in Matagalpa sierra
Jorge Vasquez Viana   poet   in the Bolivian sierra
Camillo Cienfuegos   doctor   drowned at sea   Cuba
Ramón Soto Rojas   professor   drowned in sky   Venezuela
Otto René Castillo   poet   burned alive   Guatemala
Ernesto Guevara   "prince"   deposed near Higueras
and other names that poetry cannot fit into last lines
they died as Jerusalem lay in the waters about us
ready to bud this year   their resurrected mother

FIFTEEN

The elders at the zenith of their power look down the sky
from the decline of the mountain   the ocean slide
the homeward slope   an uninhabited moon
in the path of the westering sun   their hair shining
theirs is forgetfulness   intermittent recognition
remembrances of youth greatly outnumbering recent events
they look down with patience mostly

they range the empty desert   they are few and far between
they go back into the dream companionless
they sit for hours on end throwing their shadows on time
their blood spurts into the earth they worship

305

they urinate into dishes to mix their paints
their saliva and snot goes into gum for a few tools
with which they keep the earth in movement

If I had not waited for all the bricks to be baked in the kilns
for the measurements of the house to be laid out on plans
if I had not thought of improvements time after time
not given way to desire for larger establishments
with more impressive gardens   a greater variety of flowers
if I had not insisted day in day out on the need for construction above all
if I had recognized the imperfection of created things

and made no more than a living room with table   chair   pen
paper in the table drawers   variable weather on the panes
I would have salvaged much of the life I have slept away
for no matter how long the years at our disposal
how often do we feel for any lasting moment
that we are inhabited by the exact voice of what we need to say
not riding alongside   but upon our voice

You have probably known also the desire to be free of these bones
this envelope of skin   this skin sail full of wind
you have probably wanted to fill your beds with as many lovers as could
be heard

above the din of individual love
you have been the curators of your own properties
filled your house with goods that will not talk back
tried to collect the uncollectable world

and yet I am not so sure that this desire to encompass all is vanity
it may be the only effort most of us are allowed to make at wisdom
for if rightly understood the balance of this universe is perfect
there is not a hairbreadth of distinction between our good and our evil
though there be room enough to die when feet tread dreams
I accept the imperfection of man   the impurity of action now
allow it all to come at me in its almost unbearable complexity

let it be my task   my pride   to ride it out like breakers
let me be at its mercy like a swimmer in water   a bird on the wind
that my arms   my wings   might twist and turn in the weathers

let me trust that the sum of our imperfections is the body of justice
whose mould squats in the empty desert awaiting our return
let us lay our single flowers   coffin them down together
let their fruit be ground again   let there be new seed

Among all who cut the knot in the name of sanity   of progress
among the ever more busy hives   the ever proliferating systems
without which this planet cannot take its place in the concourse of planets
who then   charged with the task of preserving language
in this babel of dialects where none has the desire to legislate any more
but only blindly and efficiently to follow the conventions of his task
shall discriminate   select   unite the corpus of law   if not the poet

being acknowledged at last as maker among makers   master of dialectic
rhyming the fields and cities   scanning the roads
apportioning the harvests   liberating the days
motor of energies   guide of hands   bed of rest
setting his songs to music   his music to the spheres
he has time in the earth his body   he has time to spare
for the most beautiful revolution of all

being acknowledged at last   master of dialectic
when this is going to be a unity of which you have no conception as yet
the earth will have gone over the horizon for good into the stars
the one to one love of men and women be an indulgence of the past
we shall be half fish   a quarter bird   something of animals in love
though keeping the root of man   reclassify the angels among the planets
remember our past lives   set out our futures in their frames

there shall be no separation any more between parents and offspring
the leap-frog generations   the interminable execution of fathers
the suffering of mothers donating sons in war
the anguish of younger brothers unprepared to take their elders' places
the giving away of brides to the holocaust
the offer of children to fire in the streets
the milking of human seed to perpetuate the races

The prophet finds it impossible to live for he who predicts in time
robs himself of his own present and what shall I make of my life
who have brought it to this point in time   to this place

where shall I meet with my existence   where encounter it
among what bones can we come to terms with each other   my death and I
shall I be standing at the door after all those years still ignorant
of how I got there in the first place   still unready to go in

with what voice shall I describe the ceremony of passing out of this
                                                              incarnation
looking down upon myself in peace a fourscore year man
the great worm may writhe in his hole in the centre of the stage
the hero who passed me earlier and transfixed me with his spear
may fight body to body with it   overcome it to birdsong
with the seductive smile   the very smile I had around his age
before going to find his bride on the burning mountain

where do I tell you the secrets a lifetime has stored for you
where can I speak to you face to face if not here
as I prepare to sing out the praises of created things
completely forgetting what cannot be said on their behalf
The rooms of my life grow wide
in all their corners there is room to breathe   there are windows
my house is built upon the labyrinths   the mazes of the worm

I have known the worm too in my time   the worm is not alien to me
I have had the worm in my guts for most of my life
there is no distinction to be made between species of worm
the worm has paraded up and down in me twisting his cocky head
in my childhood science was ignorant   tests always negative
in my maturity society too careless   I writhed daily of the worm
I am a corridor through which the worms pass and take their ease

the worm does not wait for my death to go in and come out of me
he finds his solace in my bed   he makes his breeding ground
he promenades in and out of the bodies of my wife and children
passing from one person to another at a touch of the fingers
almost it seems he passes at the glance of an eye
the worm multiples in my house as I have less and less years to keep
this is how he lives off me   I do no more than house him

yet I welcome his passage and the beautiful contradictions of his work
the lichen of excrement he leaves in me that excrete him in due time

308

as a denominator of the flights that we all take through one another
the most material sign of certain processes   some of which are of spirit
All of a sudden life is very beautiful
there is an everbloom in the center of my existence
I want life to go on for ever

among the blossoms of this floribunda which has forgotten seasons
each of whose individual flowers sucks the paps of justice one by one
as they hang from the bosom of the sky
there is a fruit for each one of you I encounter on my path
and one for each one that I do not encounter
we shall all meet one day on a long lawn   at the age of eighty
and talk over tea or drinks why we did not love each other more

There is a lady in blue with red hair going through a garden in Seurat
she is surrounded with a light of green and blue
she carries a parasol that says everything about the uses of paint
she has collected us together   herded our offerings
she shepherds our lights along in dabs of colour
she goes to meet her lover with our souls in her skirts
I think she may be the bride of God going back to her husband

we are her sons here looking up the sky along our white beards
we have waited a long time for her to go back to him
it is strange that we are so much older than she appears to be
as we see her walking with her free hand tucking her gown
towards the husband that has never been painted in any picture
through the rows of multicoloured flowers we can no longer number
we can think of no questions for her anymore   nothing we wish her to ask

TOM RAWORTH

North Africa breakdown

it was my desert army.   no fuss.   no incidents.
you just have to be patient with it.   take your time.
a child leaving a dirty black car (with running boards)
wearing a thick too large overcoat: grainy picture.
each night round the orange dial of the wireless.

or innocence.   oh renaissance.
a dutch island where horses pull to launch the lifeboat.
we are specifically ordered that there shall be no fast cars.
where can we go when we retire?

it was their deduction we were afraid of
so shall we try just once more?
nothing is too drastic when it comes to your son, eleanor.

and nothing works in this damn country.
no, it's not a bit like home.

Hot day at the races

in the bramble bush shelley slowly eats a lark's heart
we've had quite a bit of rain since you were here last
raw silk goes on soft ground (result of looking in the form book)
two foggy dell seven to two three ran
crouched, the blood drips on his knees
and horses pass

shelley knows where the rails end
did i tell you about the blinkered runners?

shelley is waiting with a crossbow for his rival, the jockey
all day he's watched the races from his bush
now, with eight and a half furlongs to go
raw silk at least four lengths back disputing third place
he takes aim

and horses pass

his rival, the jockey, soars in the air
and falls.   the lark's beak neatly pierces his eye

Here in Polynia

horses move sideways to start
this is the burden of my poem
the west

to start
as the white horse has hooves so have i

the room is divided by the windows
her melody ran before me into the arroyo
hair, in a band, what became of her letters
inscribed in the cyrillic alphabet she had forgotten

now it is night, the night that is around each city
and only the horses stir   his body is an anchor between the boulders

the west   ah see how my penny has on it a chicken

in the mementoes of my mind the decimal system has some uses
nothing can be as it used to be
the old times are going, ada

he is training the circling white horse to ride without hearing

You were wearing blue

the explosions are nearer this evening
the last train leaves for the south
at six   tomorrow
the announcements will be in a different language

i chew the end of a match
the tips of my finger and thumb are sticky

i will wait at the station and you
will send a note, i
will read it
           it will be raining

           our shadows in the electric light

when i was eight they taught me *real*
writing
         to join up the letters

listen you said i
preferred to look
           at the sea.   everything stops there at strange angles

only the boats spoil it
making you focus further

Sliding two mirrors

sliding two mirrors together to
make a puzzle of his face

oh she said moving across the room
19 years after the liberation i arrive there   soldier
carrying a guitar   a
         ring

you gave me   twisted
where it caught and broke your
        finger.   smell

of must from the drawer with the japanese soldier's hat
        a yellow star it also
travelled   diamonds
on the backs of german prisoners singing at christmas

and jeremiah clarke
who wrote the trumpet voluntary and later
shot himself through the head
in the precincts of st. pauls cathedral   for love

in some way cheated
like monica vitti with black hair

There are lime trees in leaf
on the promenade

(for ed & helene)

the blossom blows
            across the step
no moon.   night, the curtain moves

we had come back from seeing one friend in the week
they celebrated the twentieth anniversary of victory. fireworks
parades.   and all across the town the signs the french
people are not your allies mr. johnson   who were
then, the old photographs.   garlanded the tanks with
flowers now
choke-cherry
         a poison   we came
separately home

the children were there

covered with pink blossoms like burned men   taking
the things they laughed
                              at the strange coins, tickets.   ran
around the house pointing up at the plane then
the only noise

there can be no dedication   all things in their way
are   the actual scars   tension.   the feeling
of isolation.   love
for me in one way is waiting for it to end

what to do? the woman, they said
lived on a boat   swans
built their nests behind the lockgates   the eggs
when the gates were opened
smashed.   each time in pairs the swans
would hunt out ducklings, and whilst one
held off the mother, would drown them
beating them under the water with their wings

we heard the phone ringing in the empty house then went to bed
later that morning we spoke for the first time

the sun just through the trees but still dark in the room
she with the hem of her dressing gown torn sitting at my desk
i looked at the things and touched them
                              waiting to hear the voices

we had come back from seeing one friend in the week
they celebrated the twentieth anniversary of victory.   now
speaking to them for the first time i thought of him
from that same country living in another place.   his tongue
he said, felt heavy now whenever he spoke english

there would not   perhaps   be time

saturday may 15th.   the sun higher   covered
with a faint sweat i read sun tzu
the art of war   'anger
may in time change to gladness.   vexation

314

may be succeeded by content,
                              but a kingdom
that once has been destroyed
can never come again into being; nor can the dead
ever be brought back to life.   hence the enlightened ruler
is heedful, and the good general full of caution'   i read
the wind blowing the blossoms in that week
two thousand four hundred and sixty five years after

Not under holly or green boughs

(*for david & nicole*)

the voices move.   they are walking.   it is time
it is time.   they are moving, walking
talking
          some thing faintly sweet
          the lemon drops
                    dialogue

a pause they
speak in   place
          this is hans in front of
them and in the background they are held and
also in the movies

this is the banner.   music.   the whiskey
in the sunlight enters the water like gelatin   the gravel
white.   flags are frayed.   as she smiles the skin
tightens along her nose

                    a record we save for certain days

in spain the garotte   twenty years
the woman said drawing the number large with her finger
a tightening screw, the lines got less   he
would keep them in a drawer in this new room
with the old stool
          years ago

a forecast of a present war.   this
is our job

                    gipsy on the packet moves through the smoke

the place was empty the stairs
had marks of old carpet the
aircraft's trail dispersed into cloud
he entered the car at the lights and gave me an apple

we passed the arch at seven
already in the sunlight the flame was invisible   a place
you can get a drink at any time.   here
the garden is thick with weeds.   dandelions
buttercups.   yellow.   we tilt back our heads
they have stopped.   they are looking

Six days

monday

i was alone then looking at the picture of a child with the
          same birthday
a key turned in another lock there was a noise through the
          window
the cigarette made noises like a cheap firework
in the ruins of so much love in this room i must leave something
the morning was sunny it is easier to die on such a day a
          blister under your foot and easier still to mention it
a need to explain this and a french dictionary i worried how to
          carry the bottle in my case with only a cork
sweat dripped from my nose in the picture a man wrote in a
          room behind a peacock there were two clocks in the
          room and two watches twenty nine bottles four
          of them my own
i wanted to share everything and keep myself it would not work

on the door a drawing of a lion in this room on the mirror in
        soap it said *write*
the plane was always level and the moon dipped

i had cleaned the room all my taste had gone the whiskey
        tasted like milk chocolate
i had bought all the books for my friends my shoulder still
        ached from the case i would be carrying more back
a leaf i had found and given to her all green with four brown
        eyes
five years ago i had stood on those steps the next month she
        was wearing a white dress the car was late i combed
        my hair in a window in the tube it was still summer i
was and still am addicted to self-pity

a handkerchief to my face and the blood dried i would have
        left it
the shelter smelled of earth there was a shovel inside to dig
        yourself out nine paving stones in the path
a tall brown girl in jeans who came up the steps of the bridge
        something about rhythm the line and breathing
motions

tuesday

the whiskey began to taste like whiskey the cigarettes still made
        noises
i had not noticed that beside the peacock was a quieter bird in
        front of it a dish and thru the window a countryside
day of daniel there had been noise and i fitted a lock to my door
a long while ago i read silone 'i came home,' he said, when
        he was able to continue
'and told my parents the doctor had advised me to return to
        my native climate.'

so wrote to you this letter
my jacket was wet from the window it was all grey except for
        one green tree by the pantheon
there was a sound of water in the streets the americans wore
        white trousers and red shirts

i counted my money it was tuesday i ate salt because i was
        still sweating
then the rain stopped and it was all white the tree vanished
        there were red tiles

he was five and he said to me why are you not nice look i gave
        you that calendar
i bought him a toy french car every year he looked after them
        and never lost the tires
i was aware of having a family the policemen all had mustaches
bought oranges and chocolate, bread, wine and coca-cola
soda à base d'extraits végétaux
i could not write anything without repeatedly using i someday
i would get over it
my teeth ached from politeness it felt like october '62

they take up the cobbles and re-lay them in the same pattern
they wear blue jackets and blue trousers and blue caps
the stones are grey underneath is sand
they do this every year and wash the public buildings

let me tell you about the needles i said
isn't it the truth? you find them everywhere.   even in bay city.

wednesday

today it is warm and the americans wear blue nylon raincoats
it is with a 'c' she said shall i wait outside a skin formed on
        the soup
there were brown leaves already it was only july
and between the grey stones drifted green buds dead fish
        in the river

i have no love and therefore i have liberty it said on the wall
        and underneath with my key i scratched 'lincoln'
pas lincoln she said bien sûr i answered an elastic band floated by
there are statues of all the queens of france she said there was
        cream on her nose

my throat is sore do not go down those alleys at night there
        are thieves and murderers

this cinema is the biggest in europe maurice thorez est mort
enregistrez un disque a way to send letters

when we left ravensbruck she said we could not stop laughing
        and joking for half an hour

thursday

in the musée national d'art moderne there are three modigliani
        paintings two sculptures a copy of matisse's book
        'jazz' five statues by germaine richier a plaster con-
        struction to walk inside statues by arp a restaurant
        and a reconstruction of brancusi's studio
it was half past three the girl in the american express looked
        sad and shook her head
everyone was kissing it was like a commercial for paris
on a newstand i read in the guardian about the strike they said
        at the british council library mr ball has left?
in les lettres nouvelles june 1960 i read requien spontané pour
        l'indien d'amérique with a footnote saying little
        richard—jazzman célèbre
from a corner of his studio the stairs went up to nowhere
there was a blowlamp and an axe a pile of wood
i looked at myself in brancusi's mirror and it was round

friday

they were painting the outside of david's house white
30 rue madame i would not have recognized it
posters say tous à la mutualité avec pierre poujade
pigeon shit runs into apollinaire's left eye

the light through her sunglasses makes her eye look bruised
other pigeons coo a sound of water splashing men shovel the
        leaves as the yacht is thrown it moves
a blue balloon the carts stand there are cigarette ends in the
        gravel
wearing a black dress with green spots gold sandals an indian
        girl walks through the gardens reading a music
        manuscript

on the steps at night five spaniards singing *la bamba*
long r's and a noise like a cricket
she moves another chair to rest her feet

one spot of nail polish on her stocking little song you have
                been pushing behind my eyes all day

saturday

a letter came i felt very strange at gloucester road she said
                after you went and i had kisses from four people
i wanted to be there people move into church a door slams
                the car moves

i could not say i tried
i said i
could not   people have hair on the backs of their hands
what did we eat we ate sausage a stew
of onions tomatoes and courgettes below in the square they
                played boules
six men and a fair brown woman in a black dress

emptiness a taste of brass the holes in my head filled with
                warm sand
a scar beneath her left eye yellow bruises inside her elbows
in the *marais* we bought sweet cakes in the heat without shirts
                there were still tattooed numbers
birds walk inside the dry pool the flowers are dark and even
on the wooden floor the cup broke quickly calvados a faint
                smell of apples

looking at the etruscan statues in the louvre there is a green
                patina on my hands my expression has taken its
                final shape
everything becomes modern inside these cases there is nothing
                without touching

children crawl under the glass   things are reflected several times

GAVIN BANTOCK

Bard

Heroes screamed from my fingertips.

Steel organ pipes of many statures and multiple array,
and I was master of stops and keyboards,
welder of dirges and anthems.

But music is only mathematics
falling into water
majestically.

Note of the harp is none other than
the discipline of the wind
and petal of bluebell.

And sound is a long journey.

Blame

If any man sits up suddenly in the dark at night,
struck by the turmoil churning on the surface of this world—
the battle of atoms in a flaring match,
the battle of dandelions and pedigree cornflowers,
the battle of chafing rocks at the sea's edge,
the battle of antlers, of bison shoulder to shoulder,
the battle of child furies in the playground,
the battle of men eye to eye across the polished tables
or the battle-field itself and the advancing myth of war—

Let him not blame any man:
the disparity of things is not of his making.

Let him examine the tinder-box and the flint,
or walk from the garden suddenly into the wild steppes.
Let him stand by the shore and consider the rain and other cliffs,
or understand that the earthworm thrives in every land.
Let him caress the head of the half-caste boy,
or walk in the shoes of one of the three leaders of the world.
And let him witness both ends of the brief ballad of machine-guns.
Let him not blame any man:
the disparity of things is not of his making.

Let him stand by me here in this temperate land and hear
the fanaticism of the howling poles and the drumming equator.
Let him scan the widening rift and the constant
drift of the landmass east and west of Atlantic.
Let him marvel at the scar left by the snatched moon,
and the circle of fire ringing the greatest ocean.
Let Atlas teach him of the unjust lie of the land and sea,
and let him blame the wayward history of the stars.

Let him lie down again in the dark in his warm bed and dream that
the disparity of things is not of his making; let him
blame not any man.

from *Person*

I

Is this pain, when my heart
longs to be elsewhere?

Is this   this   pain, when I look into empty
rooms where dust is outside
the sunbeams?

Is it, when the streets do not answer, pain?
Or in the night, when my eyes see the dark, pain?

Bare bulbs hang in rooms
smelling of the damp
and his bed is single.

Is this pain?

It is not, no, it is not,
for he loves saying so. But saying cannot
soothe every corner of the mind
nor slacken the steel in every nerve

II
I can speak but cannot
modulate accent to the subtlety of occasion.

Sometimes when my throat is sore
I know I've shouted many hours
thinking I was murmuring.

Sometimes I've roared my secrets
out to my friends and enemies alike;
and when I had to speak in the auditorium,
I mumbled one long inaudible monotone
or whispered like sea heard from the cornfields,
thinking I was eloquent.

And no undulation of gentle sympathy now
comes to me in the drawing room;
no murmur, as I hold hands by the stream,
can bend my mind from this affliction
whistling and buzzing across my skull's acoustics,
as if strips of cat-gut twanged from one
ear-drum to the other all day, or a room was
full of zithers with slack strings.

You don't know, when the sound of drowning
comes on the dry land, what that means.

They hate me for my quiet, uncouth utterance,
and I would rather walk with my true love

where people never come, but us,
and I would rather lie down in a green glade
with my ear to the grass
and look into her eyes and know
hers, looking into mine.

But they will
will they
never understand
through the rough-cut gully of my speech,
and they will never
understand that I am, crossing my heart,
gentle, here.

Japan

Turquoise and scarlet
brushed on white paper. Always
one mountain painted.

Waterfalls maroon
Nature, and water-colours
reign; and the wood-cut.

Art is not making:
reflections in these waters
exceed their makers.

Islands float over
fire under moving waters where
steam and mist converge.

Water is sacred.
Nudity is not profane.
Pebbles are temples.

Cherry blossom fades.
Lanterns are stone and paper.
Autumn's no coda.

Nod of greeting though
brief is friendly. Celts would be
friends in Hokkaido.

Man is master here:
patience in long lines. Woman
opens eyes; fans whirr.

Millions of white shirts
miraculously controlled:
seething refinement.

Industry governs:
Buddha observes shipyards clang
for Hirohito.

Immobile faces
shield heirlooms of Samurai,
teeth sharp as razors.

Strength of Karate
is decision, discipline,
strict hierarchy.

Noh: is flute, tapped drum,
bird-shiver; catastrophe—
one finger bending.

Hiroshima is
myth. Crimson torii stands
in Miyajima.

from *Christ*

Rolleth the seventh wave.

Jesus said, I am not the only man.
... As I sit here in this dark room,
I know there are men moving,

cities thundering and alive,
engines on parallel rails,
automobiles on the great highways,
liners on the sea roads,
and planes in the humming air;
voices and machines, a sound which does not end,
which I do not hear,
which I am not part of,
as I sit here in this dark room . . .

Jesus said, There are other things and other men.

(Rome.)

There are other men

There is another shore to land at.

And when the seven thunders had uttered their voices,
I was about to write:
and I heard a voice from heaven saying unto me,
Seal up those things which the seven thunders uttered,
and write them not.

from *Ichor*

I opened my eyes at the foot of a grey mountain,
and felt I had moved a boulder out of my skull.

I looked at my hands. They were cut, and my hands were bleeding.
And my hands were running with mucus.

As though I had lain three days at the foot of the mountain.
And my head was a recurrent heart-beat.

My right leg was bent between knee and ankle.
There was no pain.

I craved for a cup of cold water
and some white bread, and some butter and cheese.

My mind was clear: there was no salt,
and there was no blood in my brain to clog the thought.

Only the slow-moving mucus of my torn hands
and the awareness of cranium.

It was daytime when I opened my eyes and another time
it was night when I opened my eyes.

And the mountain hadn't changed, and there was
pain in my right leg.

Once it was raining, and at other times it was silent,
and a bird stood on two feet on a nearby boulder
which I had lifted out of my head.

There was this roaring for many hours
there was this roaring inside my ears
there was a bird's beak and a near eye
and a claw that moved once and a sudden clatter of wings
and a great rising shadow and a whirring of wings
and a long silence
there was a bird's beak and there was a bird's eye
and a claw and a whole bird standing by my head
and a pain in my black dry hand
and a fresh appearance of bood and Ichor.

Ichor! I shouted and all the mountain shouted
Ichor! And I was in terrible pain and a great
flock of birds rose from the dead rocks
and I dragged myself to a dead rock
and I raised myself so as to look over the dead rock
and I saw a valley of dead rocks
and the remains of a tank with rusted rivets
and a pile of rusted bayonets and barbed wire and white sand
and a trickle of screes behind me
then a long silence and a paralysis of my eyes.

327

And my brain registered
                    terror
and my eyes registered
                    terror
in the loneliness of the terrain
and my ears registered
                    terror
in the silence of the terrain
and my nose and tongue registered
                    terror
in the smell and taste of dried blood
and my hands registered
                    terror
in the pain of the bitten flesh
and my brain registered
                    terror
for the mountain hadn't changed
and my brain registered
                    terror
in my brain.

And the terror halted and turned into numb fear
and the fear turned like the head of a moron
slow like a huge head with a bulging brow
and the fear became hatred
and my hatred found a voice
and screamed.

from *Hiroshima*

There were many of us at that time
labouring up a white hill made
it seemed, of moon splinters.
and a cross stood on the hill's top,
but some of us were too weary to go on . . .

I opened my knapsack of books
and settled down to read
in spite of the noise of breathing everywhere.

And my book was the story of the Black Death.

42 million dead in 15 years:
two thirds of Europe.
                         No matter whose foot
stamped on that patch of earth, or whose hand
extinguished so many fires at random:

It was wonderfully done.

It came from the East, but no matter,
all things come from the East
which emulate the sun.

So rose in brilliant emulation
fresh longing for life and eager cities built

the Renaissance

in the dense dead continent:
a sudden concentration on lost cults,
old mines re-worked, and new gold, new diamonds
picked out, cut, polished and lain
bright in huge temples and museums
designed to recognize the salvation of the race
risen out of the pain and the horror of the
Black Death.

Yet not a universal purge.

Nor was the Flood a universal purge.
Nor was the Whip in Zion a universal purge.
Nor was the Black Death.

I know that there will never be a universal purge
until the galaxies collapse upon themselves
in the billion-blinding future.

Never a star-wide purge in our time:
only impermanent cleansing of the world's bullion:
a land here, another land, and then . . .

If only some pristine flame-thrower would throw
flame over the little brown towns down there,
and set up after everywhere an aluminum city, and yet

somehow leave the green fields,
the mountains and the lambs.

If only the sea were green all down to the sea's bed,
and no dreadnoughts, tins, and wrecks
clutter the marine forests, however much the sharks
need dark dens to hide in.

Then down there our city could begin, and down there
our grass be green, and our bodies immunised
against the grey pollution of the air,
and the rusty edges which make the blood flow
no more graze us.

Melt the North Pole and the South, someone,
is the cry.   Flood the lands:
and let the only Ark be that of men pacific.

Out of this maelstrom
how to choose sound occupants is the entire agony
before we ourselves crack the shins of Atlas . . .

Hiroshima
warned of the latest affliction
to scorch the ill plains and the green sea.

And   Christ
shall lead a wonderful destruction
as he led the Deluge
walking in the green rain   and walking on
the waters left there thereafter
and walking under the Dove
and in the Temple   and in the Black Death
and in the sun which shone there thereafter
and in the red-cross Crusades.

And in Einstein's mind
undermining war's cause and the reason for it

And in Hiroshima

and now

coming soon hereafter   here
after Hiroshima came.

And Christ shall lead this wonderful destruction.

For it shall come—
this utter blitz of the leading cities:
for minds have
delegated power to engines fallible as minds . . .
and they shall see the Son of Man
coming in the clouds with great power.

And great glory in the cloud above each city.

And the earth shall be cleansed somewhere
and the scourge
scour the land deepest yet, spreading invisible
insidious murder in the man's blood,
visibly struck down vomiting
hair falling out
and blotches on the skin
and slow decline
rising from the fall-out in the wind
and great glory.

60 thousand dead in Hiroshima
in the flash of it.

And 60 thousands more
dying in the homeless weeks when Geiger forbade return.

And altogether 2 million less to bread-win.

Human hand in Nagasaki
bedded in the melted glass of green bottles:
our new amber.

I have stood in Hiroshima's pristine tomb,
seen specimens of human skin
torn by a boy in body-blitz
from his red, raw limbs.

And faeces on the Clinic steps,
no different from the living and the dead.

And they put flour on their wounds,
and the flour dried, and the flesh:
and no way to rip off the fast pain.

I am utterly out of dream:
this was Japan in 1945
when I was six.

And Hiroshima is my God,
and I love my God, and ask my God

Come
and burn up the cities, Lord.
Come now
while the city's air burns up
and communities sigh.
Come
there's no way out of the city—
burn up the dried up streets.

I fear not,
my city, I fear not.
Surely the way to prepare the way is
surely
to fear not.

Christ comes:
accept the holocaust of millions.

Christ is this entire war

come to cleanse and salve and create
air after   and song in the air   that is
clean and saved and creative as the sea-wind.

For the rain will wash the stones
and fishermen shall float out there always
where there's sea for fishes
and men pacific living on the green shores.

And bread enough for the hungry and no hunger

until

Again the land no more
can breathe in the city air,
till cities creep down into the quiet bays
and to the sheltered coves.

I would choose to take my end as children
take their end.

As Toshio Nakamura
boy of ten:

"The day before the bomb I went for a swim.

In the morning I was eating peanuts.

I saw a light.

I was knocked to little sister's sleeping place.

When we were saved I could only see as far as the tram.

My mother and I started to pack our things.

The neighbours were walking round burned and bleeding.

Hataya-san told me to run away with her.

I said I wanted to wait for my mother.

We went to the park.

A whirlwind came.

At night a gas tank burned.
I saw the reflection in the river."

Seeing their reflection in the river,
cities hurt me.
         How much more
may cities hurt me, when I see their ashes
join the wind.

Then some of us will have to join the caravan
guiding the treasures of the race across the desert
until a land's found
rain-washed enough
and ready for the blue sky,
when Geiger's silent.

Every mirage shall project the ruin on the sky
in the first years after.
         And we shall meet dumb
emigrants racing across the desert from the distant
dust.

There shall be fear in their eyes:
they found the sea   salt:
it will be tears in their eyes.

And those who came back from the moon
wept tears of white dust, when Khrushchev
said
  Our spacemen
scoured all the wide expanses of the sky and found
no trace   of God   anywhere there.

But
listen
now
for I may not be there later

There are islands somewhere
and fishermen singing there
I hear them
cry welcome over the still waters

There
I think
I will think of pebbles   of green
ponds on the sea-shore
and sea-urchins

Fishermen there
shall fish from long boats

Now say this
for later you may not be there

I shall think of the silent floating
and I shall think of dolphins

Sit
with me by the sea-shore watching
and watch
the stillness   of the fishing boats

Then
you shall see
the miracle of the sound

sun rising   and the sun
shining down

And our single ditty shall be heard

"Save
the sunshine
in the green ring of our lifetime

Take
a pebble in your hand
shining with the sun-in-the-water
upon the smooth stone

And gaze
there
filled with swan-mute wonder

And gaze
there
at the night sky

No further urge the mind
out of the green ring
for this present time"

Einstein told me

What does a fish know of the sea
he swims in?

                              *

Thought is a drop of flesh in the skull

I give you thought
of the city

And a city
to think in
as finish
echoes in the wind now
as Christ
beckons   and comes
singing in the crimson clouds.

335

Acknowledgments

DAVID JONES. Three sections from *In Parenthesis*. Reprinted by permission of Chilmark Press and Faber & Faber Ltd. "Angle-Land" and "Redriff" from *The Anathemata*. Reprinted by permission of Chilmark Press and Faber & Faber Ltd. "The Wall" first appeared in *Poetry* LXXXVII, No. 2 (November 1955) and, more recently, in the David Jones Special Issue of *Agenda* (Spring-Summer 1967). Reprinted by permission of the author.

HUGH MACDIARMID. "Second Hymn to Lenin" from *Collected Poems* © 1948, 1962 Christopher Murray Grieve. Reprinted by permission of The MacMillan Company. "Esplumeoir" and "Diamond Body" from *A Lap of Honour*, © 1969 Christopher Murray Grieve. Reprinted by permission of The Swallow Press. "The World is Fast Bound in the Snares of Varuna" from *In Memoriam James Joyce* and "O Wha's the Bride". Reprinted by permission of the author.

BASIL BUNTING. "Vestiges," "What the Chairman Told Tom," two sections from *Brigflatts,* and "Chomei at Toyama" from *Collected Poems,* © 1968 Basil Bunting. Reprinted by permission of Fulcrum Press.

CHARLES TOMLINSON. "Observation of Facts" from *The Necklace*. Reprinted by permission of Oxford University Press. "Up at La Serra" from *A Peopled Landscape*. Reprinted by permission of Oxford University Press. "A Death in the Desert," "Las Trampas U.S.A.," "Mr. Brodsky," and "Idyll" from *American Scenes and Other Poems*. Reprinted by permission of Oxford University Press. "Paring the Apple" from *Seeing is Believing*. Reprinted by permission of Astor-Honor, Inc.

TED HUGHES. "October Dawn" from *The Hawk in the Rain,* © 1957 Ted Hughes. Reprinted by permission of Harper & Row, Publishers, Inc. "Pike" and "Thrushes" from *Lupercal*. Reprinted by permission of Harper & Row, Publishers, Inc. and Faber & Faber Ltd. "Ghost Crabs," "Out," "Pibroch," and "Wodwo" from *Wodwo,* © 1967 Ted Hughes. Reprinted by permission of Harper & Row, Publishers, Inc. and Faber & Faber Ltd.

CHRISTOPHER MIDDLETON. "The Thousand Things," "China Shop Vigil," and "Five Psalms of Common Man" from *Torse 3* © 1962 Christopher Middleton. Reprinted by permission of Harcourt, Brace and Jovanivich, Inc. "January, 1919," "Disturbing the Tarantula," "Poem Written After Contemplating the Adverb 'Primarily'," "Young Woman in Apathy," and "Octobers" from *Nonsequences,* © 1961, 1962, 1963, 1964, 1965 Christopher Middleton. Reprinted by permission of W. W. Norton & Company, Inc. "Found Poem With Grafts" and "The Historian" from *Our Flowers and Nice Bones,* © 1969 Christopher Middleton. Reprinted by permission of Fulcrum Press. "Jindrichuv Hradec" printed by permission of the author.

GEORGE MACBETH. "Drop" and "Early Warning" from *The Broken Places.* Reprinted by permission of Scorpion Press. "The Twelve Hotels" from *The Colour of Blood,* © 1965, 1966, 1967 George MacBeth. Reprinted by permission of Atheneum Publishers. "Against the Sun" from *"The Night of Stones,"* © 1968 George MacBeth. Reprinted by permission of Atheneum Publishers. "At Hünegg" is printed by permission of the author.

IAN HAMILTON FINLAY. "Ring of Waves," "Green Waters," "Line Boats," "Le Circus," "Sea-Poppy 1," "Sea-Poppy 2," "Marine," "Poem/Print No. 11 (with John Furnival)," "Sundial in Landscape," "Sundial in Detail," "Stem and Stern," "The Land's Shadows," "Wave/ave," "Signpost Poem," "Son/wind/wood," and "KY" printed by permission of the author. Print/poem photographs, © Ronald Gunn.

GAEL TURNBULL. "Twenty Words Twenty Days" from from *A Trampoline,* © 1968 Gael Turnbull. Reprinted by permission of the author and Cape Goliard Press. *A Trampoline* is distributed in America by Grossman Publishers, Inc.

ROY FISHER. "City" from *Collected Poems,* © 1969 Roy Fisher. Reprinted by permission of Fulcrum Press.

CHRISTOPHER LOGUE. Two sections from *Patrocleia.* Reprinted by permission of Scorpion Press. From *Pax* © 1967 Christopher Logue. Reprinted by permission of the author.

MATTHEW MEAD. "The Barbarians," "Identities I, IV, VII" and "To Redistort a Weltanschauung" from *Identities and Other Poems,* © 1967 Matthew Mead. Reprinted by permission of Rapp & Whiting Ltd. "The Administration of Things I, II, VI, VIII" from *The Administration of Things,* © 1970 Matthew Mead. Reprinted by permission of Anvil Press Poetry.

D. M. THOMAS. "Elegy for an Android" from *Penguin Modern Poets 11.* Reprinted by permission of Penguin Books Ltd. "O My America" (first published in *New Measure)* and "Labyrinth" (first published in *New Worlds S.F.)* printed by permission of the author.

ANSELM HOLLO. "& how it goes" from *The Man in the Treetop Hat,* © 1968 Anselm Hollo. Reprinted by permission of the author and Turret Books. "instances," "buffalo—isle of wight power cable," "the charge," "bouzouki music," "your friend," "on the occasion of becoming an echo," and "he she because how" from *The Coherences,* © 1966, 1967, and 1968 Anselm Hollo. Reprinted by permission of the author and Trigram Press Ltd. "bison flower days" (first published in *New Measure)* is printed by permission of the author.

KEN SMITH. "Facts" and "The Street" from *The Pity,* © 1967 Ken Smith. Reprinted by permission of the author and Cape Goliard Press. "The Amana Colonies" (first published by *Shenandoah)*, "Persistent Narrative" (first published by *The New Statesman* and *Poetry Northwest)*, "After a Journey" (with acknowledgment to B.B.C. 3), "The Stone Poems" (No. II first published by *Poesie Vivante)*, "Beyond Breath," "Old Mill, Newton St. Cyres," "Inventory/Itinerary," printed by permission of the author.

PETER WHIGHAM. "Catullus: 2, 8, 12, 42" from *Catullus and the Traditions of Ancient Poetry.* Reprinted by permission of The Regents of the University of California. "Love Poems of the VIth Dalai Lama: 1, 5, 8, 11, 16, 23, 26, 30" and three sections from "The Ingathering of Love" from *The Blue Winged*

337

Bee, © 1969, 1970 Peter Whigham. Reprinted by permission of Anvil Press Poetry. Three sections from *Astapovo or What We Are To Do,* © 1970 Peter Whigham. Reprinted by permission of Anvil Press Poetry. "The Orchard Is Not Cut Down" from *Clear Lake Comes from Enjoyment* printed by permission of the author.

LEE HARWOOD. "The Blue Mosque" and "Plato Was Right Though" from *The White Room,* © 1968 Lee Harwood. Reprinted by permission of Fulcrum Press. "Animal Days" (first published in *Tzarad)* reprinted by permission of the author.

JOHN DANIEL. "My Wife Who is American," "Watch," "Excerpts from a Diary of War," (all first published in *Poetry: Introduction I),* "Auto Icon," "Of 91 Men Leaving an Underground," "Injury to Insured," and "Phrases for Everyday Use by the British in India" printed by permission of the author.

JOHN MONTAGUE. "Beginnings," "Sentence for Konarak," "The Country Fiddler," "The Road's End," "A Chosen Light," and "Beyond the Liss" from *A Chosen Light,* © 1969 John Montague. Reprinted by permission of The Swallow Press. "Hymn to the New Omagh Road" (first published in *Agenda)* printed by permission of the author.

HARRY GUEST. "A Twilight Man," "Matsushima," and "Montage," from *Arrangements,* © 1968, 1970 Harry Guest. Reprinted by permission of Anvil Press Poetry.

NATHANIEL TARN. "The Last of the Chiefs" from *Old Savage/Young City,* © 1964 Nathaniel Tarn. Reprinted by permission of the author, Cape Goliard Press, and Random House Inc. "Projections for an Eagle Escaped in this City, March 1965" from *Where Babylon Ends,* © 1967 Nathaniel Tarn. Reprinted by permission of the author and Cape Goliard Press. *Where Babylon Ends* is distributed in America by Grossman Publishers Inc. Sections 11 and 15 of *The Beautiful Contradictions,* © 1969 Nathaniel Tarn. Reprinted by permission of Random House, Inc. and Cape Goliard Press. Sections I, II, VIII, XIV and XVI from *A Nowhere for Vallejo* printed by permission of the author.

TOM RAWORTH. "You Were Wearing Blue," "Sliding Two Mirrors," "There Are Lime Trees in Leaf on the Promenade," "Not Under Holly or Green Boughs," and "Six Days" from *The Relation Ship,* © 1966, 1969 Tom Raworth. Reprinted by permission of the author and Cape Goliard Press. *The Relation Ship* is distributed in America by Grossman Publishers, Inc. "North Africa Breakdown," "Hot Day at the Races," and "Here in Polynia," from *The Big Green Day,* © 1968 Trigram Press Limited. Reprinted by permission of Trigram Press Ltd.

GAVIN BANTOCK. Section R from *Christ.* Reprinted by permission of Donald Parsons & Co. Ltd. "Bard," "Blame," "Japan," and two sections from "Person" from *A New Thing Breathing,* © 1969, 1970 Gavin Bantock. Reprinted by permission of Anvil Press Poetry. Two sections from "Ichor" (first published in *The Poetry Review*) and the conclusion of "Hiroshima" (first published in *New Measure)* reprinted by permission of the author.

PETER JAY, Introduction, © 1971. Printed by permission of the author.

338

Errata:
    Stanza break following line 16, p. 34
    Stanza break following line 11 of Coda, p. 41
    Stanza break following line 19, p 42.
    Lines 7-12, p. 72 should be
    spaced as couplets.